THE JOY OF
PICKLING

ALSO BY LINDA ZIEDRICH

The Joy of Jams, Jellies, and Other Sweet Preserves

THE JOY OF
PICKLING

REVISED EDITION

250 Flavor-Packed Recipes
for Vegetables and More from Garden or Market

LINDA ZIEDRICH

FOREWORD BY CHUCK WILLIAMS

The Harvard Common Press
Boston, Massachusetts

The Harvard Common Press
535 Albany Street
Boston, Massachusetts 02118
www.harvardcommonpress.com

Printed in the United States of America
Printed on acid-free paper

Library of Congress Cataloging-in-Publication Data
   Ziedrich, Linda.
   The joy of pickling : 250 flavor-packed recipes for vegetables and more from garden or
   market /
   Linda Ziedrich. — Rev. ed.
      p.   cm.
   ISBN 978-1-55832-375-9 (pbk.)—ISBN 978-1-55832-374-2 (hardcover)
      1. Canning and preserving.   2. Vegetables—Preservation.   I. Title.
   TX601.Z52 2009
   641.4'2—dc22   2008036446

Special bulk-order discounts are available on this and other Harvard Common Press books.
Companies and organizations may purchase books for premiums or resale, or may arrange a
custom edition, by contacting the Marketing Director at the address above.

Interior design by Ralph Fowler / rlf design
Cover design by Night & Day Design

10 9

CONTENTS

"My chutneys and kasaundies are, after all, connected to my nocturnal scribblings——by day amongst the pickle-vats, by night within these sheets, I spend my time at the great work of preserving. Memory, as well as fruit, is being saved from the corruption of the clocks."

—*Salman Rushdie*, Midnight's Children

FOREWORD

When I think of pickles, I immediately think of my grandmother's kitchen; when I was a child, pickle making was a yearly project. There were almost always pickles on the table, and the pickles were made when the cucumbers, onions, tomatoes, carrots, lemons, and other vegetables and fruits were ripening.

If you like eating pickles, I am sure that you will enjoy making them. In fact, you will be surprised how simple they are to make. There are many special times during the year that an assortment of pickles can be especially enjoyed: during the summer, when entertaining outdoors around the barbecue; in the fall and winter, while entertaining for the holidays; in the spring, when celebrating Easter and other seasonal occasions. An assortment of pickles will always be welcomed and enjoyed by your guests.

But homemade pickles aren't just for entertaining or special occasions. There are pickles that can be enjoyed almost every day: vegetable pickles with lunch, ethnic pickles with an international dinner, even pickles with breakfast (perhaps the pickled oranges or figs in these pages) if you are preparing a leisurely meal for a weekend. You will be surprised how many vegetables and fruits can be easily made into pickles.

Read the "Pickler's Primer," the first chapter of the book, to get you started! You will love the pickles that you make.

—Chuck Williams
Founder, Williams-Sonoma, Inc.

PREFACE

Never a big pickle eater myself, I became inspired to write this book after my son Ben, then about seven years old, developed a taste for cucumber pickles. I hesitated to buy the ones in the grocery store, which were dyed and preserved with scary-sounding chemicals as well as the usual salt and vinegar. I'd occasionally made pickles from farm-grown cucumbers, but truly fresh ones were very hard to find. Although I kept a large vegetable garden, I had never grown my own cucumbers. So I planted some. Soon I was pickling homegrown cukes, and our abundant pears, plums, peppers, and beans as well.

I didn't get really interested in pickles, though, until I started making the fermented kind. My husband and I are both endlessly intrigued by the way invisible little creatures transform raw plant materials into wonderfully nourishing and tasty foods; this must be part of the reason he makes beer and wine and I make about ten pounds of bread every week. We relished the complex flavors of my home-brined pickles, each batch a little different from the one before. I was amazed, too, to discover that cucumbers aren't the only foods suitable for brine-pickling; many other vegetables, and even some fruits, are enhanced by this magical metamorphosis.

Not all of my experiments were entirely successful, though, for I had little guidance in learning the art of pickling. General preserving books gave scant attention to pickles of any sort, and the one book then in print that was wholly devoted to pickles concentrated on cucumbers. I wanted a more comprehensive book, on pickling all sorts of produce and in all sorts of ways—by brining, with vinegar, and through unusual methods such as Japanese miso and rice-bran pickling. My dream book started taking shape in my head, coincidentally, about the time my first cookbook was published; I knew I'd soon have time for another project. If I needed a good pickling book, I figured, other people would probably find one helpful, too. I decided to write it for us.

I began to study pickling by searching through old, out-of-print books and, especially, ethnic cookbooks. In many parts of the world pickling is still a commonplace household art, and travelers and nostalgic emigrants have taken pains to record what they know of it. By comparing their accounts and trying their techniques, I began to piece together the puzzles of pickling methods used halfway around the world. Some of the recipes here are my renditions of traditional pickles; others are unique inventions, but even these are based on methods that have stood the test of time.

In Chapter 1 and in the text that introduces each chapter, I explain how each pickling method works. Throughout the book, also, I try to provide a sense of the range of possible variations for each traditional pickle. This approach, I hope, will allow you to vary the recipes to suit your tastes without worrying that your pickle may turn out bad-tasting or even unsafe to eat. (Before you get too creative, however, be sure to read Chapter 1.)

Friends and relatives helped me along the way. Ann Kaiser, Eleanor Thompson, Michael Kim, Barbara Waterhouse, Jocelyn Wagner, Tom and Ann Orwick, Leslie Darland, Dolores Ziedrich, and Roxanne McMillen gave me favorite pickle recipes. Muslehuddin and Rafia Ansari, Irina Sheykova, Vladic Kasperchik, and Mei Ow Waterhouse told me about the pickles their families make in their respective homelands. Sally White and Celestia Nelson lent me precious old cookbooks, and Shawn White brought me a big box of quinces to pickle. Ann and Rick Kaiser, Cheryl Ziedrich, Paul Smith, Matthew Cover, Mary Parkinson of the *Albany* (Oregon) *Democrat-Herald*, and, especially, Robert, Ben, Rebecca, and Sam Waterhouse all served as tasters. I thank them all.

Food preservation specialists also gave me invaluable support. Judy Burridge, Linn County home economist for Oregon State University Extension, was my teacher in an excellent Master Food Preservers' course. Nellie Oehler, Lane County home economist for Oregon State University Extension, and Kenneth Hall, Ph.D., professor emeritus of food science at the University of Connecticut, provided their expert review of the manuscript. I'm most grateful for their help.

Finally, I thank the staff of The Harvard Common Press, especially Bruce Shaw, Dan Rosenberg, Christine Alaimo, and Laura Christman, for their resolute faith in the book and in me.

NOTE TO THE SECOND EDITION

Ten years after the original publication of *The Joy of Pickling*, I have reviewed all of the recipes and made small changes throughout the book, usually with the goal of greater clarity. I have also added twenty-five new recipes, including eight for relishes, because of their great popularity, and several for quick pickles, which appeal especially to hurried cooks and those lacking in space and equipment. New to this edition, also, are many bits of historical, nutritional, and miscellaneous information about pickling that I couldn't resist sharing with readers.

I thank Valerie Cimino and Karen Wise for their gracious and thoughtful editing of this second edition, and all the staff of The Harvard Common Press for their devoted attention to the production and marketing of the book. I also thank all the readers of the first edition who took the time to write or call me to share their pickling recipes, stories, questions, and suggestions.

Please feel free to contact me in care of The Harvard Common Press, 535 Albany Street, Boston, Massachusetts 02118, or by going to my website, www.lindaziedrich.com.

1

PICKLER'S PRIMER

Read This First!

I N CORVALLIS, OREGON, Chinese scientists arriving for a two-week stay open suitcases full of pickles and dry noodles. In Hyderabad, India, pickle heaven for many, a Japanese businessman travels with a heavy bag of pickles from home. In Knoxville, Tennessee, a Yugoslav friend takes offense when I turn down one of her brined cucumber pickles until she tells me they are home-made, as essential to her transplanted life as slivovitz is to her husband's. Big kosher dills at the county fair, little dishes of fire on a Korean table, Middle Eastern turnips dyed scarlet with beet juice, intensely sour cornichons with French pâté—pickles come in a great variety of forms and flavors, sometimes mystifying or repellent to strangers. But people everywhere are passionate about the pickles of home, pickles that somehow represent satisfaction and safety.

In an age when fresh produce is flown around the world, so that few must survive the winter on preserved foods, pickles still retain their power of enticement. Salt and vinegar not only preserve foods, after all, but they sharpen flavors, and salt firms the texture of watery vegetables. The brine of fermenting pickles is as wonderfully aromatic as baking bread; in eastern Europe and elsewhere, pickle brine is a drink, a soup stock, and a skin conditioner. Pickle brine can purify vegetables of microorganisms that might make us sick. Besides preserving nutrients, fermentation can actually increase them. For those of us who raise our own food, pickling with salt brine or vinegar is still an excellent way to provide for our families through the seasons. And, since pickles travel well, they can serve as familiar, safe sustenance on short or long journeys.

Pickling is an international art with many schools, but the basic methods have been with us a long time. As early as 1000 B.C. in the Middle East, people were preserving crabapples, pears, plums, onions, and walnuts in vinegar and spices. Caesar's soldiers ate vinegar pickles, as did Cleopatra, who believed they made her more beautiful. The Romans taught people throughout western Europe how to make vinegar pickles, and western Europeans brought this skill to America.

The practice of making pickles by fermentation—souring through the action of microorganisms—evolved further east. Laborers constructing the Great Wall of China in the third century B.C. were given mixed fermented pickles as part of their food rations. Later, the Tartars spread a taste for fermented pickles throughout eastern Europe, where brined cabbage and other fermented vegetables are still daily fare. Germany, on the culinary divide between east and west, still favors brined and vinegar pickles about equally.

In southern lands, such as India, pickles fermented in the usual ways generally didn't catch on, since vegetables tend to spoil when brined at high temperatures. Indian pickles make use of some or all of various natural preservatives: not only vinegar or citrus juice (in minimal amounts) and salt, but also sunshine, for its antiseptic as well as evaporative properties; spices; oil, to help the seasonings adhere to the fruits and vegetables and to seal out air; and sugar.

In the Far East, where vinegar was made from rice wine instead of grape wine or hard cider, vinegar pickles came to share popularity with fermented pickles. Pickle preferences vary greatly from one Asian region to the next, however. Koreans, who may eat more pickles than any other people in the world, ferment most of theirs, although their famous pickled garlic is preserved with vinegar and soy sauce. The Japanese salt vegetables, too, but usually eat them before fermentation gets under way. They also pickle vegetables by immersing them in salty fermented foods—miso, fermented rice bran, and soy sauce.

In the United States and England, new sorts of pickles grew popular as imperialism supplied cheap cane sugar and trade with Asia brought new culinary ideas. Fruits were put up with vinegar, sugar, and spices, in a sort of cross between a preserve and a pickle. Chutneys, ketchups, and chowchows, all relishes with Asian roots, were transformed into ever more sugary concoctions.

In the meantime, brined pickles were also becoming part of American cuisine. German immigrants began teaching other Americans to make sauerkraut even before 1700. Later, in the late 1800s and early

1900s, immigrants from eastern Europe shared their taste for fermented cucumbers.

Before pickle jars could be hermetically sealed, fresh pickles were made with undiluted vinegar, and many pickles were further preserved with sugar and long cooking. Oil was often added to the top of the pickle jar to keep air out. Fermented cucumber pickles were made with a very strong brine, stored in the cellar, and then soaked for days in fresh water before they became edible. Sauerkraut was stored in cool cellars or outdoors to slow fermentation through the winter.

After home canning came into fashion, a new sort of pickle arose. Stored in vacuum-sealed jars, vegetables could keep for a long time in a dilute vinegar solution, even if salt and sugar were omitted entirely. Home canning reached a peak during World War II, when the U.S. government commandeered 40 percent of commercial pickle output for the armed forces. Extension agents promoted food preservation along with Victory Gardens, even going so far as to divert steel from the munitions industry to pressure-canner production. "Novice canners using shoddy wartime equipment also produced a record number of disasters," writes Harvey Levenstein (*Paradox of Plenty*, 1993). "Innumerable stoves were ruined, kitchens were splattered, and victims were hospitalized with severe burns, cuts, and botulism." If U.S. Department of Agriculture (USDA) guidelines today seem to be based on the assumption that the typical home canner won't follow half of them, this history should explain the government's conservatism. Actually, even after their boiling-water baths, USDA-style pickles generally taste much fresher than their nineteenth-century predecessors.

PICKLING PRINCIPLES

There are two basic kinds of pickles: those preserved with vinegar (or, occasionally, lemon or lime juice or citric acid) and those preserved with salt. Vinegar pickles, also called fresh pickles because they aren't fermented, usually contain salt as well. Likewise, fermented pickles, which are always made with salt, sometimes include vinegar.

Although salt is not an essential ingredient in canned fresh pickles, a pickle is hardly a pickle without salt. By drawing off excess liquid from vegetables and fruits, salt firms their texture and concentrates their flavors. Salt also balances the flavor of the finished pickle, though the right flavor balance is a matter for each pickler to decide.

Most pickles made with salt are fermented. Others, like Japanese pressed pickles, are only briefly salt-cured and therefore won't keep long, especially if they're not refrigerated. Fermented pickles keep longer for the same reason vinegar pickles do: They are acidic.

Fermented pickles fall into two categories: dry-salted and brined. Sauerkraut is a dry-salted pickle; when mixed with salt, shredded cabbage makes its own brine, even before the cabbage is pressed or weighted. The brine protects the cabbage from air. Other pickles are made with a premixed brine: The salt is dissolved in enough water to cover the vegetables. In both dry-salted and brined pickles, salt helps control the fermentation process.

In general terms, fermentation is a controlled decomposition of food, involving yeasts, molds, or bacteria in an aerobic or anaerobic process. Whereas bread, beer, and wine making involve yeast fermentation, brine pickling involves fermentation by bacteria (although yeasts are usually present, too). The bacteria break apart sugars to create acid—mainly lactic acid—which for some weeks or months preserves the food in its partially decomposed form. This process is mainly anaerobic: The microorganisms that initiate it produce carbon dioxide, which replaces the oxygen in the pickling crock.

Vegetables crowded into a crock together will ferment with or without salt. Without the proper salt concentration, however, enzymes may soften the vegetables, and the wrong microorganisms may predominate, causing off-flavors or even putrefaction. Even without these problems, fermentation without salt is likely to progress too quickly, so that the vegetables never get sour enough to keep well for very long, and the seasonings haven't enough time to work their magic. The right amount of salt fosters the right progression of bacterial activity that produces firm, delicious pickles.

Just as vinegar pickles usually contain salt, fermented pickle brines often include some vinegar, partially for its flavor and partially to discourage the growth of the wrong microorganisms before fermentation gets under way. Too much vinegar, however, stops fermentation completely.

SALTS

Throughout this book, I call for "pickling salt." This is simply fine, pure granulated salt. In supermarkets, it's sold in four-pound boxes as "canning and pickling salt." In natural foods stores, it's labeled "sea salt." Since the use of the term *sea salt* is unregulated, however, you may see it on supermarket bins that actually contain table salt. Table salt often contains iodide, a nutrient, and dextrose, a stabilizer, and it always contains chemicals that prevent caking, such as calcium silicate, sodium silicoaluminate, tricalcium phosphate, magnesium carbonate, silicon dioxide, and yellow prussiate of soda. You can identify table salt by stirring a little into a glass of water; it won't dissolve completely, but will form a whitish haze and sediment. The white stuff can't make you sick, but it can ruin the appearance of your pickles.

Beware of any sea salt that isn't white. Green, gray, black, pink, and red salts contain impurities that could adversely affect the pickling process.

Kosher salt is often used for pickling. Because its flakes are larger, and therefore less densely packed, than the crystals of pickling salt, you

CUCUMBER VARIETIES FOR PICKLING

AMERICAN: These traditional knobby cucumbers come in many varieties—some more disease-resistant than others; some thicker, others thinner; some with black spines, some with white. But American cucumbers of all varieties look and taste more or less alike. Although they make good gherkins at 1 to 2 inches, they're typically pickled at 3 to 5 inches long. You can leave them whole, slice them crosswise for bread-and-butters or lengthwise for tongue pickles, or cut them into spears. When they grow longer than 5 inches, though, they become very wet and seedy in the middle. Seed the big ones before cutting them into chunks for pickles. You can get seeds of these cucumbers from any seed catalog or garden center.

CORNICHONS: These European cucumbers are also called gherkins (from *gurken*, Dutch for "cucumbers"). Seed catalogs say that these European cucumbers must be harvested at 1 to 2 inches long, but I find they make excellent pickles at up to 6 inches long. Even longer cornichons can be sliced for bread-and-butters, since these cucumbers tend to be skinny, with small seed cavities and tiny seeds. The tiny prickles come off easily with a light rubbing and are mostly absent on larger cornichons. The skins are thin, which means you should begin processing cornichons within a day of picking them; this is probably why they aren't grown commercially in the United States. But if I could grow only one cucumber variety in my garden, this would be it. Cornichon seeds are available from some mail-order seed companies.

ASIAN PICKLING CUCUMBERS: Not all Asian cucumbers are good for pickling, but one year my Mennonite neighbors grabbed up all my extra China Hybrid cucumbers for making bread-and-butters and chunk pickles. China Hybrids are knobby, over a foot long at pickling size, and suitable for trellising, though I let mine spread over the ground. Orient Express is a smooth variety that's also good for pickling. China Hybrid and Orient Express cucumber seeds are available from many mail-order seed companies.

WEST INDIAN GHERKINS: Also called bur cucumbers, these are small, prickly fruits that grow on watermelon-like plants. They are very good for Sweet Gherkin Pickles (page 230), provided you pick them just before they reach full size, when they become tough and seedy.

need a greater volume of kosher salt—about one and a half to two times as much, depending on the brand—if you're substituting it for pickling salt. A disadvantage of kosher salt is that it is slow to dissolve. To make a brine with kosher salt, you have to heat the water and salt together. This is why many pickling recipes call for heating a brine and then cooling it before pouring it over vegetables. If your water is clean and your salt fine, the heating step is unnecessary.

VINEGARS

Throughout this book, I assume you will use vinegar that is approximately 4 to 6 percent acetic acid, or 40 to 60 grain. Commercial vinegars made in the United States are all standardized within this range. Among these vinegars, you have several types from which to choose:

DISTILLED WHITE VINEGAR is fermented from a solution of pure alcohol and diluted to 5 percent acidity. Although this vinegar has a harsh, uninteresting flavor, in the United States it is probably used more in pickling than any other vinegar. This is because distilled vinegar doesn't darken pickled foods, and, more important, it's cheap. I generally use it only in pickles that are very sweet or contain other strong flavors to balance the vinegar. Distilled vinegar is most useful, I think, in cleaning windows and floors.

CIDER VINEGAR is fermented aerobically from hard cider, which is apple juice that has already undergone an anaerobic fermentation. This vinegar has a golden color and a mellow flavor, although the quality will vary somewhat depending on how the vinegar was made. The traditional pickling medium of early Americans and their English ancestors, cider vinegar can be used whenever you're unconcerned about the fruit or vegetable darkening a bit. Cider vinegar is sold in supermarkets in gallon jugs as well as smaller containers. Generally, it is standardized to 5 percent acidity.

APPLE CIDER-FLAVORED VINEGAR is now common in supermarkets, some of which sell only this fake cider vinegar. Distilled white vinegar with flavorings and colorings added, it is priced a little cheaper than real cider vinegar. I can't say this stuff tastes bad, because I haven't tried it, but I hope you don't succumb to the marketing ploy.

WINE VINEGAR is the traditional pickling medium of France, Italy, Spain, and other countries where wine grapes are grown in great quantity. Wine vinegar is used full strength for *cornichons à cru* and similar fresh pickles preserved without sugar or pasteurization. Like cider vinegars, wine vinegars vary in quality, but all tend to be sweeter and mellower than any distilled vinegar. Unfortunately, supermarkets generally sell wine vinegar only in small, expensive bottles, but you may be able to find an economical gallon jug in a Middle Eastern grocery or a restaurant-supply store.

White wine vinegar isn't the only wine vinegar suitable for pickling. Splash a little red wine vinegar into a crock of brined pickles; the color won't be noticeable, and you may like the subtle effect of this full-flavored vinegar on the taste (a little vinegar may also prevent the growth of "bad" microorganisms before the "good" ones get going). In beet and prune pickles, red wine vinegar enhances both color and flavor. French cooks like red wine vinegar so much that they often pickle cornichons in it, despite its graying effect.

For its special flavor, you can even use dark, sweet balsamic vinegar in some pickles. Balsamic vinegar is usually standardized at 6 percent acid, whereas other commercial wine vinegars are usually 5 percent acid (although my favorite brand of white wine vinegar, from Italy, is labeled as 7 percent acid).

RICE VINEGAR is the traditional vinegar of the Far East. Very mild in flavor, it comes in two varieties, brown and white, made from unpolished and polished rice, respectively. White rice vinegar is sold in supermarkets in small, rather expensive bottles, often with added sugar and salt. Some Asian groceries, however, carry more economically priced gallon jugs, without additives. Brown rice vinegar is available in natural foods stores and Korean markets. Rice vinegars are usually standardized at 4.3 percent acid.

MALT VINEGAR, fermented from sprouted barley, is the sharp but pleasant brown vinegar used in English pub–style onions. It became popular in Britain as a cheap by-product of the brewing industry. In the 1990s, Spinnakers Brewpub in Victoria, British Columbia, began producing high-quality malt vinegar aged in oak barrels. Today malt vinegar is sold in small bottles in some supermarkets. It is typically diluted to 5 percent acid.

You may find other kinds of vinegar, such as pineapple or coconut, in ethnic groceries. Feel free to experiment with these and the vinegars described here provided you check their acidity. For recipes in this book in which the pickles are to be either canned or stored at room temperature without canning, use vinegar that is at least 5 percent acid. Within this limit, there is no danger in changing the type of vinegar in a recipe.

Beware, though, of reducing the proportion of vinegar to water in a recipe for pickles to be either canned or stored at room temperature without canning. This would lessen the acidity of the pickle, perhaps making it unsafe to eat. Although salt and sugar may combine with vinegar to inhibit microbial growth, fresh pickles generally should contain at least one part 5 percent vinegar for each part water. (Follow this rule of thumb in judging whether Great-Grandma's old pickle recipe is safe to use. She may have used less vinegar because her vinegar was more concentrated.)

Take care also not to boil pickling liquid for a long time, since acetic acid evaporates faster than water does. Boil pickling liquid only as long as the recipe calls for. Then, if you're not ready to use the liquid immediately, remove the pan from the heat and cover it.

If you dispense your own vinegar in a natural foods store, be aware that the vinegar may not be pasteurized. Unpasteurized vinegar will develop a "mother," a slimy, whitish mass that appears at the top of the vinegar and eventually sinks to the bottom. To halt the biological activity in unpasteurized vinegar, bring it to a boil before using it.

WATER

If your water tastes good and doesn't make you sick, it's probably suitable for pickling. If, however, it contains large quantities of minerals or chlorine, you may need to either purify your water or buy distilled or deionized water for pickling.

Hard water may cloud and discolor pickling liquid. If your water stains your toilet and sink with iron deposits, you definitely have a problem. Boil the water and then let it sit for 24 hours before using it for pickling. Skim off the scum and ladle off water from the top of the container, leaving any sediment undisturbed.

Be aware, too, that most public water supplies in the United States are treated with chlorine. If your shower often smells like the public

WHAT'S YOUR PICKLE'S pH?

Pickles, both fresh and fermented, are preserved primarily by their acidity, which can be measured according to pH. Pure water has a neutral pH, about 7.0. More acidic substances have lower pHs; more alkaline substances have higher pHs. To prevent the germination of *Clostridium botulinum* spores, food that is to be stored in airtight containers must be acidified to pH 4.6 or lower. Pickles are normally acidified within a range of 2.6 to 4.0.

If you're not sure you have followed a pickling recipe correctly—if, say, you have added only half of the vinegar or used apple cider instead of apple cider vinegar—you can test the pH of one jar after the acid in the liquid has equilibrated with the vegetables or fruit— that is, after the acidity has become consistent throughout the ingredients of the jar. This takes about three weeks.

To test the pH of fresh or fermented pickles before they're stored, suggests Kenneth Hall, professor emeritus of food science at the University of Connecticut, puree the contents of one jar in a blender. For both fresh and fermented pickles, the pH should be no higher than 4.0. Some people use litmus paper from the drugstore for testing pH, but I recommend the more accurate pH meters available from merchants who specialize in scientific instruments. These meters are also useful in testing the pH of homemade vinegar.

swimming pool (when you haven't just cleaned the shower with a chlorinated product), your water may contain enough chlorine to delay the fermentation of brined pickles. Boiling the water for at least 2 minutes will vaporize the chlorine. Let the water cool overnight before combining it with the vegetables.

AROMATICS

Spices are sold in every supermarket, but some traditional pickling spices, such as juniper berries and mace (the dried aromatic skin of the nutmeg seed), are usually missing from the shelves and may even be hard to find in natural foods stores or gourmet shops. You can leave out the juniper berries and substitute slivers of nutmeg for the mace, or you can buy hard-to-find spices from a mail-order catalog or Internet source.

Spices used in pickling may be whole, crushed, or ground. Although whole spices look attractive in pickle jars, they are often used only during brining or heating, then removed and discarded. Otherwise, the spices might darken the pickle over time, and their flavors might become overwhelming. For these reasons, whole spices are often tied in a spice bag or piece of cheesecloth, which can easily be removed before the pickles are put into jars. You can make spice bags from unbleached muslin or buy some from Internet sources. Unless you're using very small seeds, such as celery seeds, a scrap of good cheesecloth tied securely around the spices works just as well.

When I call for crushed spices, I mean that you should smash them with the side of a knife blade or pound them briefly in a mortar. The purpose is to crack them so they'll release their flavors faster, without grinding them to dust. This technique is very useful in making quick pickles.

Ground spices are used only when there is no concern about their clouding the pickling liquid—in thick relishes, for example, or Indian pickles. Since ground spices go stale rather quickly, especially if they're exposed to heat or sunlight, I recommend buying whole spices and grinding them yourself as you need them, in a spice grinder, coffee grinder, or mortar.

Although some people prefer to select just a few flavorings for each batch of pickles, others like the indefinable spiciness imbued by a blend of many aromatics. Commercial pickling spice mixtures vary, but they typically include a dozen or more flavorings. Whether you use a commercial blend or make your own (see the recipe on the opposite page), be careful when measuring from the mixture, since little seeds such as dill and mustard will tend to fall to the bottom, and big ones such as allspice will tend to rise to the top.

DILL is one spice—and herb—that you should try to grow yourself. The seeds look prettiest when they are still attached to the heads—compound umbels, each like a bouquet of little umbrellas—and they taste mild and fresh before they dry out. The feathery leaves are milder still. Especially in rural areas, some stores occasionally sell uprooted dill plants, but these are often old and shriveled, and they may be unavailable when you want them. To guarantee a supply of fresh dill throughout the cucumber harvest, plant some before the last spring frost date, and plant more every few weeks until midsummer.

If you have no fresh dill handy when it's time to make pickles, you can substitute dried dill seeds for the fresh umbels. Dill umbels differ greatly in size; as a rule of thumb, though, one teaspoon of dried dill seeds will substitute for one dill umbel.

MUSTARD SEEDS come in two types: yellow or white (*Sinapis alba*) and black or brown (*Brassica nigra*). American and European picklers have traditionally used yellow mustard seeds; Indians generally favor the more pungent but less bitter black mustard seeds, which they sometimes grind. You can easily grind mustard seeds with a spice grinder or coffee grinder.

PEPPERS not only star in numerous pickling recipes, but they play compelling minor roles in many others. I often call for small dried hot peppers, the Japanese (japonés, *hontaka*) type that are sold in both Mexican and Asian markets or chiles de árbol, which are hotter and also strikingly elongated. To extract the heat from a dried pepper faster, break it in half, slit it lengthwise, or crumble it. Hot pep-

MIXED PICKLING SPICES

You can buy mixed pickling spices at any supermarket, but you may prefer to mix your own to suit your tastes. Here's an example:

One 4-inch cinnamon stick, broken into small pieces

6 Mediterranean bay leaves, torn into small pieces

6 small dried hot peppers, such as japonés or de árbol, cut into small pieces

1 tablespoon whole black peppercorns

1 tablespoon whole yellow mustard seeds

1 teaspoon whole fennel seeds

2 teaspoons whole allspice berries

1 teaspoon whole cloves

2 teaspoons whole coriander seeds

½ teaspoon blade (unground) mace

1 tablespoon dill seeds

Combine all of the ingredients in a small jar. Mix thoroughly before measuring. If the spices are fresh to start and you keep the jar tightly capped in a cool, dark place, the mixture should keep well for at least 1 year. **Makes about ½ cup**

per flakes—peppers crumbled with their seeds—decorate a pickle with bright red speckles. But be careful; pepper flakes can pack more heat than you might expect.

Some pickles require ground dried hot pepper. In most cases I call for cayenne, since "cayenne" is the term usually used on containers of ground hot pepper in supermarket spice sections. Typically, these powders are very hot. You can instead use a less incendiary sort. The ground dried pepper sold in Korean markets, I've found, is generally much milder, and this is the pepper I prefer for kimchi. Mexican markets and even Mexican sections of supermarkets stock pepper powders that are comparable to the Korean kind.

SPICY UMBRELLAS

The umbelliferous—that is, umbrella-shaped—seed heads of cumin, fennel, celery, and anise as well as dill make pretty and tasty additions to pickle jars.

If you grow hot peppers in your garden, you may prefer to use them fresh in your pickles. You can slit, halve, or slice jalapeños, serranos, de árbols, or other small hot peppers before adding them to your pickles. Be careful, though, because they may be much hotter than dried peppers.

You may have learned to ignore the frequent warnings in cookbooks to wear rubber gloves when handling hot peppers. Some people get rashes from working with peppers, but most of us can chop a chile or two with impunity. Don't think you can dispense with gloves, though, if you're making a gallon of salsa or slicing two quarts of jalapeños. If you use your bare hands, they may burn for a day or two (or longer—a friend of mine put ice packs on her hands for three days after pickling sliced jalapeños). The burning sensation may not bother you much—unless you touch your eyes. If you wear contact lenses, avoid handling them for at least eight hours after chopping even a few hot peppers.

FRESH GINGER is almost universally available in supermarkets, so I use it liberally. When I call for a "thin slice" of ginger, I mean one about the thickness and diameter of a quarter. If the section you're cutting is wider or narrower, adjust the amount accordingly. In the store, look for plump gingerroots without a trace of mold.

HORSERADISH is a perennial plant in the mustard family grown for its pungent-tasting root. Pieces of the root are only very occasionally sold in supermarkets, so if you like horseradish it makes sense to grow your own. (Many mail-order seed companies sell small root pieces for planting.) For pickling, wash and scrape or peel the root, and slice, chop, or grate it. You can store horseradish in the freezer, scraped clean and wrapped in airtight plastic or foil. I recommend against buying commercially prepared horseradish, which is typically laden with adulterants. If you can't get fresh horseradish, or find you don't like it, you can leave it out of any pickle recipe.

GARLIC, to some people, is what makes a kosher pickle kosher, but since garlic is now so widely used in pickling and American cooking generally, we should probably leave kosher to its older, religious meaning. Anyway, make sure your garlic is fresh; it shouldn't be shriveled or sprouting or have brown spots. Leave it whole or slice or chop it. Smaller pieces will spread their flavor faster, but garlic never wastes much time in making its presence known.

Pickled garlic occasionally turns blue or green. This color change has no effect on the flavor or safety of the pickle (see page 163).

FIRMING AGENTS

LIME used in pickling is calcium oxide, also called slaked lime or builder's lime. The calcium in pickling lime is absorbed into the tissue of a vegetable or fruit, where it combines with pectin to form calcium pectate. This makes the pickles—usually cucumber, melon, or green tomato—firm and crisp. Southerners, especially, have long loved lime pickles. In the 1970s and 1980s, when natural foods were in, pickling lime was out, at least among recipe writers. But commercial food processors never stopped using lime, for much more than pickling. They add lime to canned tomatoes, potatoes, green beans, peas, and many other foods.

Provided it is food-grade (don't buy it at a lumberyard), lime is a harmless food additive, but it can raise the pH of a pickle just as it can that of your soil. So, after vegetables and fruits are soaked in a mixture of about 1 cup pickling lime to 1 gallon water for 12 to 24 hours, they should be soaked three times in fresh water for an hour at a time and rinsed well after each soaking. Even when you follow this rule, the pH of your pickle may be slightly increased, so use lime only in recipes that call for it.

If you can't find pickling lime in a supermarket, you can order it from Internet sources.

ALUM, an aluminum compound that is used medicinally to induce vomiting and check bleeding, was a popular pickle ingredient in the 1950s and 1960s. Like lime, alum makes pickles crisp and crunchy. Its use went out of favor, however, when people began to worry about the health effects of aluminum in the diet. Since only a very little alum is needed to make pickles crisp, and since pickles play only a small part in the American diet, adding alum to your pickles probably won't hurt anyone. The astringent taste of alum is detectable, though, even when only a minimal amount is used. Many people like this taste. As my husband (with a grimace) described my alum-firmed fresh dills, "They taste like store-bought."

Alum is sometimes sold in spice sections of supermarkets; you can also buy it at a pharmacy. I suggest using no more than ⅛ teaspoon per quart.

HORSERADISH is not only a traditional pickle flavoring; it's also said to be a firming agent. From my limited trials, I suspect that horseradish may help prevent the softening of fermenting pickles by inhibiting yeast growth. The fresh pickles I made with horseradish, however, were noticeably softer than those I made with alum, grape leaves, and sour cherry leaves. Unfortunately, it seems that no scientist has done a proper study of horseradish in pickling. So I suggest using abundant amounts of grated or chopped horseradish with fermenting cucumbers to see what happens (let me know!), but none at all with fresh pickles unless you happen to like the mustardy flavor.

LEAVES of various kinds are also used as firming agents. Grape leaves are most popular, and they do seem to have a slight firming effect on both fermented and fresh cucumber pickles; they are also supposed to make pickles greener. Leaves of the scuppernong grape, native to the southeastern United States, have been shown especially effective in firming pickles. Russian picklers like to use a variety of leaves, sometimes all at once. They recommend oak leaves and sour cherry leaves for their tannin (which is, like alum, astringent). One Polish author claims that peach leaves work as well as sour cherry leaves. Although I neglected to include oak leaves in my fresh-pickle study, I found that leaves of sour cherry, *Prunus cerasus*, firm pickles at least as well as *Vitus vinifera* grape leaves do, although not as well as alum does. (But don't use the toxic leaves of *P. serotina*, the wild black cherry of eastern North America.) Put a few washed leaves, if you like, into each jar of fresh pickles. If you're fermenting pickles in a crock, scatter or layer the leaves with the other ingredients, or put handfuls of leaves at the bottom and top of the crock.

WEIGHING PRODUCE

You can use a food-grade plastic bucket in place of a pickle crock, mayonnaise jars in place of canning jars, a knife in place of a kraut board. But I hope you won't try to do a lot of pickling or other preserving without a kitchen scale. Fruits and vegetables of a given kind—whether cucumbers, cabbages, or corn ears—tend to come in various sizes, so measuring them by either number or volume usually just isn't accurate enough. I therefore often call for produce by weight. If you buy your fruits and vegetables, of course, you can weigh them at the market before you bring them home. But having your own scale will make your preserving much easier—and perhaps even more successful.

BOWLS AND POTS

Because salt and vinegar react with most metals—sometimes with toxic results—the recipes in this book frequently call for *nonreactive* bowls, pots, and pans. Bowls used in pickling can be stainless steel, glass, ceramic, or food-grade plastic; pots and pans can be stainless steel, heatproof glass, or hard-anodized aluminum. Aluminum, copper, or tin pans or bowls are not safe to use unless they are lined with stainless steel (although people used to use copper to brighten the green color of cucumber pickles). Even enameled metal containers can be risky to use, since fine cracks and chips in the enamel could allow the metal to react with the acid in the pickling brine. Plastic can be toxic, too, if it's not intended for culinary use.

CANNING YOUR PICKLES

Many pickles can be vacuum-sealed in mason jars—that is, "canned"—for longer keeping outside of the refrigerator. This includes cucumbers fermented in a medium-to-strong brine, sauerkraut, most of the fresh pickles in Chapter 3, and almost all of the relishes in Chapter 9. (Canning is unnecessary for pantry storage of *cornichons à cru* and similar, very sour pickles.) Whenever a pickle is suitable for canning, I call for mason jars, in specific sizes, and two-piece caps, although you can dispense with these things if you'd rather store your pickles in the refrigerator.

If you've never canned food yourself or watched family members do it, the whole idea may intimidate you. Canning, after all, involves special equipment and a lot of heat and steam. Mason jars and lids, and the techniques for using them, have changed over time, as have the governmental guidelines that are meant to ensure that home-canned food is safe to eat. For these reasons, instructions from cookbooks, Mom, the neighbor, the canning-jar company, and the extension agent may conflict. Even recently published cookbooks may include outdated guidelines. But canning your pickles is a sensible thing to do if you're making a lot and don't have multiple refrigerators, or if you'd like to give some jars to friends or relatives. When you understand the canning process, it is generally simple, quick, and safe.

Canning is a way of preserving food by sealing it hot in airtight containers, or by heating the containers after they're filled with food. Heat raises the vapor pressure of the liquid inside the canning jar, or mason jar. As the vapor pressure rises, air is forced out of the jar. As the jar and its contents cool, a vacuum forms as the vapor pressure drops, and the softened adhesive on the rim of the lid creates an airtight seal.

Although a vacuum seal prevents oxidation and the growth of microorganisms such as mold, the anaerobic environment in the jar can enable growth of the scariest food-borne pathogen, *Clostridium botulinum*, if the food is low in acid and the jar is heated too briefly or at too low a temperature. This is why you must carefully follow established guidelines in canning such non-acidic foods as beets or beans without vinegar.

But canning pickles is inherently much less risky. *C. botulinum* can't grow in high-acid foods; it needs a pH of over 4.6 to reproduce. (Nor need you worry about the notorious *Escherichia coli* O157:H7 bacteria that infect the intestinal tracts of warm-blooded animals. *E. coli* bacteria are killed by cooking, and all of the pickled meats in this book are thoroughly cooked.)

The equipment required for canning pickles demands much less expense and attention than that required for canning low-acid vegetables. In other words, you don't need a pressure canner to put up pickles. Not only is a pressure canner expensive to buy, but its gasket must be replaced and its gauge checked regularly. Steaming and rattling like some sort of bomb on the stove, it can also be frightening to operate, even for someone who has been using one for years.

I do, however, recommend boiling-water processing or low-temperature pasteurization for many of the pickles in this book. These heat treatments have two important advantages: They tend to produce a very tight vacuum seal, and they kill molds, yeasts, and bacteria that can grow in lower-acid pickles, particularly if the jars aren't well sealed. They help you avoid ever having to throw out pickles that have gone bad.

Many people hesitate to subject their pickles to a lot of heat for fear it will ruin the texture of the pickled foods. A boiling-water bath can definitely soften cucumbers and some other vegetables. For this reason a scientist at the University of California developed the low-temperature pasteurization method for home picklers. By this method you don't boil your jars; you just immerse them in 180° to 185°F water for 30 minutes. The recipe instructions indicate when this method can be used.

If your mother or grandmother always canned pickles without a boiling-water or hot-water bath, you may wonder if you can safely do the same. In many cases, you can. By the now-maligned "open-kettle" method, you boil first the jars, then the food you'll fill them with (the kettle isn't necessarily open during these processes, but the jars are). This method is in some ways more trouble than water-bath canning, however, since the jars, lids, and what's going into the jars must all be very hot to ensure that the jars will seal. The jars, moreover, can't just be clean, as for water-bath canning, they must be sterilized, which means you've still got to boil a kettle of water. And if your lids fail to seal, you may end up having to give your jars a water bath after all. The open-kettle method is dangerous with low-acid foods because of the risk of contamination between the time the jar is removed from hot water and the time it's sealed. For all these reasons, the USDA no longer recommends the open-kettle method. But many home preservers still use it for pickles and fruit preserves, especially when they're making small batches or want to ensure that their pickles stay firm. Generally the method works fine, but occasionally pickles at the top of a jar get softer and discolored or even moldy, or a lid comes loose after the jar has been put away in the pantry. Forgoing a water bath works best with sweet pickles, those preserved with a lot of sugar as well as vinegar.

Because the processing instructions are abbreviated in the recipes, please read the following sections carefully for a thorough explanation of water-bath processing, low-temperature pasteurization, and the open-kettle method.

Basic equipment for canning includes mason jars, which come in half-cup (4-ounce), half-pint (8-ounce), one-and-a-half-cup (12-ounce), pint (16-ounce), quart (32-ounce), and half-gallon (64-ounce) sizes. Pint and quart mason jars are available in two mouth sizes: regular and wide.

Mason jars can be used over and over for years; some of mine are older than I am. Before each use, though, you should check the glass for cracks and the rims for nicks. Even a tiny nick could prevent a good seal.

In place of mason jars you can use other glass jars, such as ones that held commercial mayonnaise, provided that the mouths fit the two-piece mason jar caps. If you use such jars, though, expect more failed seals and occasional jar breakage, since these jars have narrower rims and are less tempered. Some people use mayonnaise jars for pickles and jams and reserve their mason jars for pressure canning, which puts more stress on the glass.

New mason jars come with two-piece caps. The flat lids are meant for one-time use only. When you reuse the jars, you can also reuse the metal rings if they're not too rusty, but you must replace the flat lids. (You can use old lids—and jars with nicks in the rim—for storing dry foods. To avoid damaging the lid the first time you open a jar, push it up gently with the blade of a table knife.)

You may prefer to use European canning jars, with glass lids and separate rubber gaskets. Many home economists frown on these because you can't check the seal by pressing on the lid. I see no danger in canning pickles in these jars, though, provided you use fresh rubber gaskets, follow the manufacturer's instructions, and make sure the jars are approximately the same size as those called for in the recipes. If the jars are larger, you may need to increase processing times slightly.

Boiling-water processing and low-temperature pasteurization require a large kettle with a rack at the bottom to protect the jars from overheating and breaking. Most cooks use an inexpensive enameled metal kettle made for the purpose, with a jar rack that you can raise or lower while the kettle is full of water. Many of these kettles, though, aren't quite tall enough for quart jars, and the racks quickly get rusty.

In fact, you can use any large kettle for boiling-water processing. Internet sources sell stainless-steel racks that won't rust and may fit well into your stainless-steel stockpot. I use my pressure canner for boiling-water processing, without screwing on the lid all the way. Made entirely of aluminum and tall enough for quarts, it works very well for me, although because the rack has no handles I have to remove the jars one at a time.

Many people use steam canners instead of boiling-water canners. Steam canners save water, energy, and time, and they don't boil over. But neither the USDA nor anyone else has determined minimum processing times for foods canned with steam. The steamers tend to have cold spots, and the food in the jars generally doesn't get as hot as it would in a boiling-water bath. For these reasons I can't recommend steam canners.

Very helpful tools for canning include a jar lifter, a special kind of tongs for lifting hot jars safely; a stainless-steel or plastic canning funnel, which just fits into the mouth of a canning jar; a magnet on a stick, for lifting lids out of hot water; and a narrow plastic spatula, disposable plastic knife, or Japanese (pointed) wooden or plastic chopstick, for releasing air bubbles in a filled jar. Canning tools are available from many department stores and supermarkets as well as farm-supply stores and Internet sources.

BOILING-WATER PROCESSING

To process jars in a boiling-water bath, you first fill the canner about halfway with water and begin heating it. Heat some more water in a tea kettle, in case the water in the canner doesn't cover the jars adequately. Have ready clean, preferably hot jars; I wash mine in the dishwasher and leave them there until I'm ready to use them. (If the jars are going to be processed for less than 10 minutes, though, you should immerse them in boiling water for 10 minutes before filling them.) Immerse the lids in hot water in a small bowl.

Fill each jar with cold vegetables or fruit, and pour hot liquid over them (this is the "raw pack" method), or fill the jar with pickles and liquid that have been heated together (the "hot pack" method). For some pickles, such as sauerkraut, you can pack both the vegetables and the liquid cold (you might call this the "cold pack" method). Don't overpack the jars with pickles; their contents should be at least 35 percent liquid to maintain the proper acidity. Leave the specified headspace— that is, the unfilled space at the top of the jar. Headspace of ¼ to ½ inch allows for the expansion of food as the jars are heated and the formation of a vacuum as the jars cool.

After filling the jar, release air bubbles by inserting a narrow plastic spatula or similar tool between the pickles and the inner surface of the jar. Move the tool up and down while slowly turning the jar. Add more liquid if the level drops in this process, and then wipe the rim with a clean, damp cloth or paper towel. Remove the lid from the hot water, using a magnet stick if you have one handy (I usually angle the edge of a lid out of the water with my spatula or chopstick and then pick up the lid between two fingers, touching only the rim). Place the lid gasket-down on the jar. Screw on the metal ring firmly, but not as tight as pos-

VOLUME EQUIVALENTS

3 teaspoons = 1 tablespoon

16 tablespoons = 1 cup

2 cups = 1 pint

2 pints = 1 quart

4 quarts = 1 gallon

2 gallons = 1 peck

4 pecks = 1 bushel

sible. Overtightening the ring could cause the lid to buckle or the jar to break, or could prevent air from venting during processing, so the pickle wouldn't keep as long.

When the water in the canner is hot—about 140°F if you've raw-packed the jars or about 180°F if you've hot-packed them—load them into the canner. (If you drop cool jars into boiling water, they may break.) Add as much hot water as you need to cover the jars by at least 1 inch. Bring the water to a boil over high heat and reduce the heat. Gently boil the jars, with the canner lid on, for the specified length of time.

If you're canning at an elevation of over 1,000 feet, you should process your jars longer than the recipes specify. The higher your elevation, the lower the temperature at which water boils. When the boiling temperature is lower, the boiling time must be increased. The USDA publishes elaborate charts for figuring out processing times according to altitude, but I find these confusing. Generally, 5 minutes' time is added for each higher altitude range, although occasionally you can skip a range before you must add 5 minutes. Since this 5 minutes' difference is trivial, I offer simpler guidelines in the chart on page 27.

When the boiling time is up, remove the jars promptly. Lift them straight out of the water (if you tilt the jars so the water on top runs off, sloshing liquid might break the vacuum seal or keep it from forming). Set the hot jars at least 1 inch apart on a rack, towel, or hot pad (if you set them directly on a tile or stone counter, they would probably crack). Leave the jars undisturbed until they're completely cool. As they cool, you may hear a "ping" as each vacuum seal forms, pulling the center of the metal lid downward.

When the jars are cool, test that the lids have sealed well by pressing in the center with a finger. If the center stays down, the seal is good. If the center pops up, store the jar in the refrigerator, or reprocess the jar after making sure the rim is clean and free of nicks and adding a new lid. A second processing should be done within 24 hours of the first, for the same amount of time.

If you like, you can remove the metal rings from the cooled jars. Most experienced preservers wash their rings after using them, dry them well, and store them in a dry place. This way the rings can be used over and over, although they probably won't last as long as the jars do. If left on the jars instead, rings usually rust faster.

LOW-TEMPERATURE PASTEURIZATION

This method has proven effective for many kinds of pickles, but it is perhaps most valuable with fresh and fermented cucumber pickles, which tend to soften at high temperatures. By the low-temperature pasteurization method, you pack the vegetables and liquid into hot jars, seal the jars with hot lids, and place the jars in a canner filled halfway with water heated to 120° to 140°F. Add hot water to cover the jars by at least 1 inch and heat the water to 180° to 185°F. Hold that temperature for 30 minutes. (You may notice that the water starts to whisper at about 165°F; it whispers louder at 180°F. Still, you should use an accurate thermometer to ascertain the temperature. You can calibrate your thermometer by immersing its tip or bulb in boiling water. If your altitude is near sea level, water boils at 212°F.) Check the temperature often and make only small adjustments in the heat level, because if the water gets hotter than 185°F the cucumbers may soften.

OPEN-KETTLE METHOD

This method requires that you sterilize your mason jars and heat the lids thoroughly. Boil the jars in a kettle full of water for 10 minutes. Put the

ALTITUDE ADJUSTMENTS FOR BOILING-WATER PROCESSING

If your altitude (in feet) is—	Increase processing time by—
1,001–3,000	5 minutes
3,001–6,000	10 minutes
Over 6,000	15 minutes

lids into a pan or dish, pour boiling water over them, and let them sit for several minutes so the sealing compound softens. Don't boil the lids, and don't leave them in water so long that it becomes cool.

Drain the jars very well and then fill them immediately with very hot pickles or relish. Leave the specified headspace, release the air bubbles, wipe the rims completely clean, and add the hot lids. Screw the rings on securely. If a lid hasn't sealed within 12 hours, store the jar in the refrigerator or process it in a boiling-water bath for the specified length of time.

STORING PICKLES

If you're not canning your pickles, you can store them in any sort of glass jar. Do be sure, though, that the lids to your jars are nonreactive. Mason jar lids, even if they're used, fit this definition when their undersides aren't nicked or scratched. The metal rings and outer edges of the rims can rust, however, and the rust can spread to the inside of the jars. This is particularly likely to happen in pickles made with full-strength vinegar, such as *cornichons à cru*, especially if you fill the jar to the rim with vinegar (the best way to ensure that the vegetables stay immersed). Rusting can occur even with refrigerator pickles if the jars are placed, or fall, onto their sides, or if they're stored for a long time.

1. Fill the canner about halfway with water.

2. Heat the water to about 140°F for food packed cold, or about 180°F for food packed hot.

3. Lower the jars into the canner, all together on the canner rack or individually with a jar lifter. Add boiling water, if needed, so the water level is about 1 inch above the jar tops.

4. Bring the water to a vigorous boil and begin timing the processing. Put the lid on the canner and lower the heat to maintain a gentle boil.

5. When the processing time is up, remove the jars with a jar lifter. Set them to cool on a rack, towel, or hot pad.

For all non-canned pickles, therefore, I like to use all-plastic lids. In both regular and wide-mouth sizes, they are available in many supermarkets, department stores, and farm-supply stores. When I can't find a plastic lid in the cupboard, I reuse a two-piece cap in good condition, but I line it with two layers of plastic wrap.

Pickle brine is not an embalming fluid; don't expect pickles left in a shed for several years to be fit to eat. Although canned pickles and cornichon-type pickles often keep well for over a year, you should try to use them within six months. Pickled cucumbers, especially, are likely to soften with longer storage. Lower-acid pickles designed for refrigerator storage will stay firm and appealing for a shorter period, about two months. (Some pickles should be eaten immediately, or within a week or two, but the recipes will alert you to this.) If, however, your pickling liquid contains at least one part vinegar for each part water, the pickles should keep in the refrigerator for much longer—perhaps a year or more if the jar is tightly closed with a nonreactive cap and the liquid completely covers the vegetables or fruit. Pickles fermented in a medium-strength brine and refrigerated in their original containers will keep well for as long as six months, if any scum or mold is promptly removed. When I've strained and boiled the brine and refrigerated fermented pickles in clean jars, I've had them keep well for over a year. Generally, though, after the first several weeks pickles don't get better with age, so enjoy them while they're still young. Throw out any pickles that have become furry, slimy, or foul-tasting, no matter how they have been stored.

Fermented pickles are usually cured at room temperature or thereabouts, and so are Middle Eastern vinegar pickles. After their curing, though, all pickles that needn't be refrigerated should be stored in a cool, dry, dark place. Although I refer throughout the book to "pantry storage," if your pantry is a cupboard near the kitchen stove or open shelves in front of a window, this is not the best place to store your pickles. A dry cellar is ideal; second best is an unheated room where the pickles are protected from light.

CAPS THAT WILL NEVER RUST

All-plastic mason jar caps are useful even if you can your pickles. If all the pickles in a jar aren't eaten at once, you can replace the metal lid with a plastic cap for refrigerator storage. Plastic caps are much handier than separate lids and rings, which tend to lose each other in the kitchen and rust if refrigerated for too long. When you give canned pickles as gifts, you can fit a plastic cap over the flat metal lid, so that after the lid is removed the plastic cap can replace it.

2

FERMENTED PICKLES

FRESH VEGETABLES, SALT, WATER, and some spices or fresh herbs are all you need to make fermented pickles. You don't really need a recipe, not any more than you need one for baking bread, provided you keep in mind the right proportion of salt to water. You don't have to limit yourself to cucumbers, either; other vegetables, such as cauliflower, snap beans, peppers, zucchini, peas, tomatoes, carrots, and Brussels sprouts, are also very good brined. Among the world's pickles, brined cabbage—whether it's called sauerkraut, kimchi, or something else—is probably even more popular than brined cucumbers (see Chapter 4 for pickled cabbage recipes). You can even brine some fruits, as Russians do, though the methods are a little different for these. Most fun of all, I think, is mixing vegetables, and this may be the most practical kind of pickling for you if your garden is small.

Although brining is slower than vinegar pickling, the process is remarkably simple and trouble-free. You just put your fresh, clean, unwaxed vegetables and aromatics into a clean crock or jar. Then you mix up a brine, stirring pure salt into water until the water first clouds and then clears again. You pour the brine over the vegetables to cover them well, and then weight them so they stay immersed. Within three days, usually, fermentation will have begun. If you're using a clear jar, you'll see tiny bubbles rising inside. A yeasty scum may begin forming on top; you'll want to skim off most of this every day. The room will fill with an irresistible aroma, and if you taste the brine you'll find it quite tart. (You'll understand why some people prefer the brine to the pickles, and use it as a soup stock, a hangover remedy, or just a refreshing drink. For many women in eastern Europe, it is also a cosmetic.) Within a week or two, or four or six, fermentation will have slowed, and your pickles will be deliciously sour. If they are cucumber pickles, they will be olive-green throughout. They will be ready to eat.

If you're making kimchi or another Asian pickle, the fermentation

VEGETABLES AND FRUITS SUITABLE FOR BRINING

Apples

Asparagus

Broccoli

Brussels sprouts

Cabbage

Carrots (up to ½ inch thick)

Cauliflower

Cucumbers

Garlic

Lemons and limes

Onions

Peas in their edible pods

Peppers, green or ripe, hot or not

Shallots

Snap beans

Tomatoes (half-ripe)

Watermelon

Zucchini

time may be only a few days. In this case, the brine gets sour, but the vegetables don't completely ferment. These pickles are pleasantly sour but still fresh-tasting.

As you start experimenting with brine pickling, you'll want to keep several considerations in mind:

CONTAINERS. The cucumber pickle recipes are designed to suit containers of various sizes, from 1 quart to 3 gallons or larger. I don't recommend searching antique stores for an undamaged stoneware crock. You can get a brand-new one, U.S.-made and identical to the old ones, for much less money, from Internet sources if not from a local merchant. These crocks come in sizes as small as 1 gallon, and so are suitable even for a household of one or two. For a higher price, you can order a Gärtopf, a German crock with a water-lock rim and stoneware weights made to fit inside (page 36).

Remember, though, that stoneware crocks are heavy. If you want to make a big batch of pickles and you're not very strong, you might want to use a food-grade plastic bucket. These are available from restaurant-supply stores and sometimes from restaurants. (*Don't* use a laundry-soap container or plastic garbage can.)

To ferment smaller batches of pickles, I like to use glass jars, ranging in size from one gallon to as small as one quart. (Two-quart mason jars, which were out of production for a year or two, are now available again in farm-supply and other stores.) Glass jars are usually narrower at the top than in the middle, but a water-filled food-grade plastic bag can take the place of plate, weight, and cloth cover.

A cooking pot might do as a pickle crock, too, but only if its inner surface is stainless steel. Other metals react with the salt and acid in pickle brine.

BRINE STRENGTH. This term refers to the weight of salt as a percentage of the weight of the solution. Brine strength is important because it affects the sourness of the pickles, the speed of the fermentation process, and how long the pickle will keep. Because pickling salt is of uniform density, you can easily translate between brine strength, salt weight, and salt volume for a given amount of water by using the charts on pages 38 and 39. In the recipes, I make life easier by specifying volume measurements only.

Until salt producers began using vacuum evaporators in the 1920s, pickle makers couldn't rely on volume measurements, because there was no guarantee that the density of one year's salt matched that of the preceding year. Without kitchen scales, old-time picklers couldn't weigh their salt, either. So their recipes often called for "enough salt to float an egg." This meant a 10 percent brine, which resulted in very salty pickles that would keep all winter in the cellar, but would have to be soaked in fresh water for days before they became edible (after which they might be pickled anew in vinegar and sugar). Upon experimenting with pickles made in a 10 percent brine, I decided they were too awful to turn into a recipe for this book. You can make them if you want, though, by simply using about 1½ cups salt for each gallon of water.

Conversely, if you don't like salty pickles at all, you can make your pickles with a brine of only about 3½ percent salt, using ½ cup salt for each gallon of water. If you're fermenting cucumbers, you can call these pickles half-sours. They will be ready to eat within a week. They won't be suitable for canning, though, since they may not be sour enough to prevent the growth of harmful microorganisms.

If you want fully sour pickles that aren't overly salty, use a 5 percent brine; at room temperature the fermentation will last two to four weeks. Full-sours are suitable for canning.

If you like salty pickles and want a slower fermentation—of six to eight weeks, say—use a 7 to 8 percent brine. With stronger brines, though, lactic-acid fermentation happens more slowly, so more yeast and gas develop, and cucumber pickles often become "bloaters"—hollow, floating pickles. Mold is more likely to develop, too.

These are my own rules of thumb for brine strength: If I'm not canning the pickles, I use 10 tablespoons salt per gallon of water or 2½ tablespoons salt per quart. If I'm canning the pickles, I use ¾ cup salt per gallon of water or 3 tablespoons salt per quart.

PICKLE CROCKS WITH BUILT-IN FERMENTATION LOCKS

Irene Kuo (*The Key to Chinese Cooking*, 1977) describes the beautiful and ingenious pickle crocks once made in Kwangsi province. About 3 feet high and 1 foot in diameter, the vase-like porcelain urns each had a deep cup around the neck into which water was poured. "When the cover, shaped like a deep rice bowl, was placed over this cup its rim was submerged in about 2 inches of water, thereby preventing air from seeping in but allowing the gas of fermentation to escape through the water as the brine aged."

A similar pickle jar, the Gärtopf ("fermentation pot"), is today made in Germany by a company named Harsch and available in the United States from various Internet vendors. This stoneware pot is available in several sizes—10, 15, 30, and 50 liters—and comes with two half-round weights that fit together inside the pot. I now use a 10-liter Gärtopf to make most of my sauerkraut and fermented pickles.

FERMENTATION TEMPERATURE. You don't need a cold cellar to ferment vegetables, although a cellar is useful for storing finished pickles. Traditionally, pickles are fermented in an out-of-the-way corner of the kitchen. Except when indicated in the recipes, temperatures anywhere between 55° and 80°F are acceptable. The lower the temperature, though, the slower the fermentation; at 55° to 60°F, fermentation in a 5 percent brine may take five to six weeks. Generally, a temperature of 70° to 75°F is preferable, especially in the beginning, as fermentation gets under way. Temperatures of more than 80°F might encourage the growth of microorganisms that could make the pickles soft. If you have very hot summers, you may prefer a stoneware crock to a plastic bucket, and a ceramic tile, stone, or cement counter or floor to a wood or linoleum surface (which might be damaged, anyway, by dripping brine or condensation).

WEIGHTS. The vegetables in your crock or jar must be fully submerged in the brine, or they'll eventually get soft and off-flavored. One protruding pickle, in fact, could spoil the whole batch. Since you may be skimming off some of the brine with the yeast scum, you'll want to add plenty of brine at the beginning of the process. To keep the vegetables submerged, you might pack larger ones on top of smaller ones. Then add an inverted pie plate or dinner plate just a little smaller than the opening of the crock, and weight it with tightly capped mason jars filled with water (two quart jars distribute the weight better than one half-gallon jar, which might crush the vegetables). Some people use well-scrubbed rocks instead of water-filled jars; other heavy objects may work as well if you enclose them in a leak-free, food-grade plastic bag.

Or you can omit the plate, and just use a brine bag—a leak-free, heavyweight, food-grade plastic bag placed directly in the crock or jar, filled with extra brine, and well sealed. I use zipper-top freezer bags, always fresh out of the box. If you're afraid your bag might leak, use two, one inside the other. You needn't worry much, though, since leaking brine won't hurt the pickles (unsalted water,

BRINE STRENGTH, BY THE GALLON

Pickling salt added to 1 gallon water at 68°F

Salt volume (in cups)	Salt weight (in ounces)	Brine concentration (percentage salt, by weight of solution)
⅓	3.10	2.28
½	4.65	3.37
⅔	6.20	4.45
¾	6.98	4.98
1	9.30	6.53

of course, would weaken the brine). Pickling with a brine bag is particularly undemanding, since, provided the bag completely covers the surface, no scum will develop. Sometimes I use three gallon-size bags in my large crocks; if I set the bags in carefully, they work as well as one large bag.

You can avoid dealing with either scum or a brine bag by investing in a special crock with a water-lock rim (page 36).

YEASTS AND MOLDS. Unless a water lock or brine bag seals out all air, yeasts and molds can grow on the surface of a pickle brine. Usually indicated by white, foamy scum, yeasts are particularly common with fermenting cucumbers. Especially in eastern Europe, yeasts are often considered desirable for their effect on a pickle's flavor. But the growth of yeasts must be checked by regular skimming, or they may gradually cause softening, darkening, and off-flavors in the pickled food.

Molds appear less often, usually when fermentation is slowed by low temperatures, a high salt content, or both. Looking like tiny eyeballs floating on the brine, molds are harmless if they are promptly removed. Once fermentation gets under way, they are

BRINE STRENGTH, BY THE QUART

Pickling salt added to 1 quart water at 68°F

Salt volume	Salt weight (in ounces)	Brine concentration (percentage salt, by weight of solution)
1½ tablespoons	0.88	2.57
2 tablespoons	1.15	3.35
2½ tablespoons	1.46	4.19
3 tablespoons	1.73	4.94
¼ cup	2.34	6.46

Source: Robert Waterhouse, personal communication, 2008

unlikely to develop, provided the vegetables are well covered by brine. If they appear on the wall of the crock, wipe them off with a paper towel. You can limit the growth of molds by scalding your crocks before and after using them. A clean towel or cloth covering the crock during fermentation helps to keep out mold spores as well as dust and bigger pests.

When I use one of my old-fashioned crocks with a plate and weights, I skim the pickle brine daily with a wide, shallow spoon. I don't try to remove all the yeast scum, since it tends to break up and float away. I get rid of much of it, though, by rinsing off the brine bag or the plate and canning jars before replacing them. You might instead lay a clean piece of muslin or two or more layers of cheesecloth on top of the pickles (under a weighted plate), and lift off the cloth every day or two. Boil the cloth and reuse it, or replace it with a new one.

LEAVES. Grape leaves, sour cherry (*Prunus cerasus*) leaves, and oak leaves are used to help keep pickles firm. (Don't use the toxic leaves of *P. serotina*, the wild black cherry of eastern North America.)

Russian cooks also use black currant leaves in pickling, for their subtle, smoky flavor and aseptic qualities; horseradish leaves, as well as horseradish roots, are said to have aseptic qualities, too.

You can scatter or layer leaves with other flavorings throughout your pickle crock, or even wrap each cucumber in a leaf. But most often people put handfuls of leaves at the bottom and top of the crock, where the leaves serve additional purposes. At the bottom of the crock, the leaves lift the vegetables out of the sediment that

GROWING AND HARVESTING CUCUMBERS

You can start cucumbers in the ground, after the soil has warmed, or indoors a little earlier. Either way, you may want to stagger your plantings to fool the cucumber beetles, if these disease-spreading, 1/4-inch-long striped or spotted insects infest your garden.

I like to plant my cucumbers in hills—that is, clusters of two or three plants each—rather than in rows, which tend to spread until there is no place left to walk. I never trellis my plants, since I have more garden space than carpentry skill, but long varieties may grow straighter if the vines can climb.

Water your cucumber plants regularly to avoid bitter or hollow fruits, but don't keep the soil soaked.

Harvest cucumbers at least every other day. Even with this schedule, you'll find overgrown fruits, since young cucumbers are very adept at hiding. The big ones can be seeded for salads or "sunshine" pickles (page 93). Harvest your cucumbers just before watering, not after. Cleaning mud from between tiny spines is aggravating work; besides, if you're fermenting your cucumbers you don't want to end up scrubbing off all the good bacteria. Mulching with straw will keep your cucumbers cleaner.

Pick your cucumbers with a little bit of stem attached, if possible; this may be easiest to do with a small knife. Leaving a bit of stem helps to keep them from shriveling, and many people think the stem makes an attractive little handle for a pickle. Brush off any remaining blossoms as you pick, because they can cause softening.

If you can't process your cucumbers immediately, keep them in a cool place. If the only cool place is the refrigerator, put the cucumbers in lightweight plastic bags in a salad drawer to help keep them from drying out.

settles there and could perhaps cause softening. At the top of the crock, the leaves cushion the vegetables against the pressure of the plate and weight above, protect them from exposure to the air, and also collect the yeasty scum so that it doesn't settle on the vegetables. Cabbage and other vegetable leaves can be used for these purposes. One recipe I found calls for daily replacement of the leaves on top of the crock. If fresh leaves are always handy, this is both more effective and easier than skimming the pickle brine every day. You can instead rinse and reuse the same leaves.

STORAGE. Fermented pickles may keep well for a few months in a cool cellar, but they are best stored in the refrigerator. You can leave them in their original containers, or, for longer storage, you can boil, skim, and cool the brine, rinse the vegetables, and refrigerate them in the cooled brine, perhaps with some fresh seasonings such as dill and garlic.

As indicated in the recipes, some fermented pickles are suitable for canning. Canned pickles will keep for over a year in a cool, dark, dry place but are best eaten within six months or so. See Chapter 1 for basic canning instructions.

HALF-SOURS, BY THE QUART

MAKES 1 QUART

ALF-SOURS AREN'T PICKLES taken prematurely from their brine; rather, they're cured quickly in a low-salt brine, which hastens the fermentation so the pickles never get very sour, no matter how long they remain in the brine. John Thorne (*The Dill Crock*, 1984) describes half-sours as "cucumbers still, not pickles—little cucumbers who [have] died and gone to heaven."

¼ teaspoon whole black peppercorns, crushed

¼ teaspoon whole coriander seeds, crushed

1 Mediterranean bay leaf

1 garlic clove, chopped

1 quart (about 1 pound) 3- to 5-inch pickling cucumbers, blossom ends removed

1 dill head

1 small fresh hot pepper, such as japonés or de árbol, slit lengthwise

1½ tablespoons pickling salt

3 cups water

1 Put the peppercorns, coriander, bay, and garlic into a clean quart jar. Pack the jar with the cucumbers, adding the dill head and hot pepper. Dissolve the salt in the water, and pour the brine over the cucumbers, leaving 1½ inches headspace. Push a quart-size freezer bag into the jar, pour some or all of the remaining brine into the bag, and seal the bag. Keep the jar at about room temperature, with a dish underneath if the seeping brine might do some damage otherwise.

2 Within 3 days you should see tiny bubbles rising in the jar; they tell you that fermentation has begun. If scum forms on top of the brine, skim it off daily, and rinse off the brine bag.

3 The pickles should be ready within a week, when they taste sour and when the tiny bubbles have stopped rising. Skim off any scum at the top of the jar, and store the pickles in the refrigerator for about 3 days, after which time they should be an even olive-green throughout. They are best eaten within about 3 weeks.

"A cucumber should be well sliced, and dressed with pepper and vinegar, and then thrown out, as good for nothing."

—*Samuel Johnson*

HUNGARIAN SUMMER PICKLES, BY THE QUART

MAKES 1 QUART

THIS IS A PICKLE FOR THE IMPATIENT. It's another half-sour, with a fermentation hastened by sunshine. Although most recipes tell you to ferment pickles in a cool, dark place, this isn't really necessary. Until recently, in fact, commercial picklers fermented cucumbers in open outdoor vats so that ultraviolet rays could control the growth of mold; some companies still make their pickles this way. In this recipe, using sunshine lets you do without a brine bag or other weight. For insurance, though, I recommend using a narrow-mouth jar and wedging the cucumbers in tightly to keep them from floating.

PREPARING CUCUMBERS FOR PICKLING

Begin processing American-type pickling cucumbers within two days of picking, and cornichons within one day. The smaller the cucumber, the quicker it will soften and shrivel as it waits for its brine bath.

Wash the cucumbers gently, but do make sure you remove all dirt. Be sure to remove all traces of the blossoms, too; they may contain fungi, as well as enzymes and hormones that can soften pickles. The USDA recommends cutting $\frac{1}{16}$ inch off the blossom end of the cucumber; I often just scrape the end with my fingernail. Leave the spines if you're using American-type cucumbers. Gently rub off the many tiny prickles on cornichons.

Many people prick or slit cucumbers before fermenting them; others slice off both ends. If you're using a low-salt brine—say, 2½ to 4 percent—any of these measures will promote even fermentation. For slow-fermented cucumbers, pricking, slitting, or stabbing allows gas to escape, which may reduce the number of "bloaters." Bloating isn't normally a problem, though, if the cucumbers are of moderate size and the brine of moderate strength.

Food scientists have found that cucumbers soften when temperatures rise above 80°F during fermentation. This hasn't been a problem for me. Still, on very hot days you may want to move your pickle jar to a cooler place.

So that cucumbers will ferment evenly during a brief cure, and to reduce their tendency to float, eastern Europeans often poke or slit them. This recipe calls for slitting, but you might prefer to poke a bamboo skewer through one end of the cucumber and out the other.

June Meyer, who published a recipe like this one on the Internet, remembers the "sun pickles" of her childhood. "We kids would eat them like Popsicles," she writes. "The envy of all the neighborhood kids."

> 1 quart 3- to 5-inch pickling cucumbers, blossom ends removed
> 1 tablespoon pickling salt
> 2 tablespoons white or red wine vinegar
> 1 dill head and 1 dill sprig
> About 2 cups water

1. Using a knife, slit the cucumbers through lengthwise, leaving their ends intact. Put the salt, vinegar, and dill into a narrow-mouth quart jar. Pack the cucumbers into the jar so they won't float, leaving 1 inch headspace. Cover the cucumbers with water. Cap the jar with a nonreactive lid, and give the jar a shake to dissolve the salt. Loosen the lid. Place the jar outdoors in the sun or in a sunny window, in a dish if seeping brine might do some damage. If you set the jar outdoors, bring it in at night.

2. Within 3 days you should see tiny bubbles rising in the jar; they tell you that fermentation has begun. The pickles should be ready within 5 days, when the tiny bubbles have stopped rising.

3. Chill the jar. The cucumbers are ready to eat. They will keep well in the refrigerator for a few weeks.

LOWER EAST SIDE
FULL-SOUR DILLS

SINCE THE PUBLICATION of the first edition of this book, several New Yorkers (or former New Yorkers) have asked me why I failed to include any sour cucumber pickles. The first time I heard this question I was bewildered. All the pickles in this book are sour; pickles are by definition sour. But the New Yorkers were looking at recipe titles for the term *sour* or *full-sour*—or maybe *New York* or *kosher*—anything to reassure them that the pickles would turn out like the ones from their favorite sidewalk shop in Lower Manhattan. They all urged me to go to one of these shops and taste the pickles and peer into the barrels, and I did. For all you New Yorkers, here's a recipe for pickles as close as I can get to the ones you pine for.

About 4 pounds 3- to 5-inch pickling cucumbers, blossom
    ends removed
4 to 6 dill heads
2 small fresh or dried hot peppers, such as japonés or
    de árbol, slit lengthwise
8 garlic cloves, sliced
1 tablespoon whole allspice berries
1 teaspoon whole black peppercorns
2 tablespoons whole coriander seeds
½ cup pickling salt
3 quarts water

1. Layer the cucumbers in a gallon jar with the dill, hot peppers, garlic, allspice, peppercorns, and coriander. Dissolve the salt in the water, and pour enough brine over the cucumbers to cover them.

TROUBLESHOOTING GUIDE: FERMENTED CUCUMBER PICKLES

Hollow middle	The cucumbers grew this way, perhaps because of inadequate watering. (You can pick out cucumbers like this when you wash them—they float.) Or the cucumbers were held too long before brining. This is mainly a problem with larger, more mature cucumbers.
Pale skins	The cucumbers grew this way; perhaps they were sun-scalded (grape, sour cherry, or black currant leaves may help deepen the green of pale cucumbers), or the pickles were exposed to light during storage.
Dark pickles	Your water contains a lot of iron or is alkaline, or your canning lids are corroded, or you used reactive metal pans or utensils in processing the pickles.
Shriveled pickles	The cucumbers were held too long before brining, or the brine was too strong at the beginning of the curing.
Small brown spots on pickles	The cucumbers were held too long before brining.
Slightly soft pickles	The cucumbers were held too long before brining, or the temperatures were too high during fermentation. The pickles were overheated during processing; try low-temperature pasteurization.
White sediment	Yeast grew on the brine and settled to the bottom of the container (yeast isn't a problem if it's regularly skimmed off during fermentation and if the pickles are heat-processed or refrigerated afterward). Or table salt was used.
Slippery, mushy pickles	Undesirable microbes grew, for any of these reasons: Blossoms weren't removed before fermentation, too little salt was used, some cucumbers weren't completely submerged in the brine, the brine wasn't skimmed, or the pickles were canned without adequate heat treatment or an airtight seal. Don't eat these!
Off-flavor	Undesirable microbes grew, for one or more of the reasons just above. But the pickles are safe to eat if they are sour, firm, and mold-free.

Push a gallon-size freezer bag into the jar, pour the remaining brine into the bag, and seal the bag. Keep the jar at room temperature.

2 Within 3 days you should see tiny bubbles in the brine. If scum forms on top of the brine, skim it off daily and rinse off the brine bag.

3 The pickles should be ready in about 2 weeks, when they are sour and olive-green throughout. At this point, remove the brine bag and any scum, cap the jar, and store it in the refrigerator, where the pickles will keep for several months or longer.

ROBERT'S TEA PICKLES

MAKES 2 QUARTS

M Y HUSBAND WAS INSPIRED to suggest this recipe after he tasted my cucumbers pickled with black currant leaves. Currant leaves add a subtle smoky flavor, and he wanted even more smokiness. Lapsang souchong tea does indeed provide this extra smokiness.

1 small fresh hot pepper, such as serrano or jalapeño, halved lengthwise

6 garlic cloves, sliced

2 teaspoons whole Sichuan peppercorns, crushed

2 teaspoons lapsang souchong tea leaves

2 quarts 3- to 5-inch pickling cucumbers, blossom ends removed

3 tablespoons pickling salt

1 quart water

1 Put the hot pepper, garlic, peppercorns, and tea into a 2-quart jar. Pack the cucumbers into the jar. Dissolve the salt in the water and cover the cucumbers with the brine, leaving at least 1½ inches head-

space. Push a quart-size freezer bag into the mouth of the jar, pour the remaining brine into the bag, and seal the bag. Keep the jar at about room temperature, with a dish underneath if seeping brine might do some damage.

2 Within 3 days you should see tiny bubbles rising in the jar; this shows that fermentation is under way. If scum appears at the top of the jar, skim it off and rinse off the brine bag. If so much brine bubbles out that the pickles aren't well covered, add some more brine in the same proportion of salt to water.

3 The pickles should be ready in 2 to 3 weeks; they will be sour and olive-green throughout. If you plan to eat them within a few weeks, simply remove the brine bag, cap the jar, and store it in the refrigerator. If you want the pickles to keep longer, strain off the brine into a saucepan, bring it to a boil, simmer it for 5 minutes, and let it cool. Rinse the pickles in cold water, pack them into a clean jar (with fresh garlic and Sichuan peppercorns, if you like), and cover them with the boiled and cooled brine before refrigerating them.

WAYS TO USE PICKLE BRINE

In *Polish Heritage Cookery* (2005), Robert and Maria Strybel offer about a dozen traditional uses for pickle brine. One is a hangover remedy: Fill a glass with equal parts chilled pickle brine and ice-cold club soda, and drink the mixture down at once. The Strybels also suggest adding pickle brine to various soups, including a *barszcz* (borscht) made of grated pickles sautéed in butter and combined with bouillon, smoked kielbasa, grated baked beets, and sour cream, and another soup of pickles, potatoes, and pork stock with sour cream.

MUSTARDY
DILL PICKLES

H ERE'S A 1-GALLON RECIPE for those who love the flavors of mustard and horseradish. When I'm not buried in cucumbers, I love fermenting them in gallon glass jars, which are lighter than crocks and give me a clear view of what's happening inside.

1 handful grape or sour cherry leaves

About 4 pounds 3- to 5-inch pickling cucumbers, blossom
    ends removed

Leafy tops of 4 celery stalks

1 large onion, sliced

½ cup chopped fresh horseradish

¼ cup whole yellow mustard seeds

4 to 6 dill heads

6 tablespoons pickling salt

2 quarts water

1 Lay half the leaves in the bottom of a gallon jar. Layer the cucumbers in the jar with the celery tops, onion, horseradish, mustard seeds, and dill. Dissolve the salt in the water and pour enough brine over the cucumbers to cover them. Spread the remaining leaves on top. Push a gallon-size freezer bag into the top of the jar, pour the remaining brine into the bag, and seal the bag. If necessary, add more brine made in the same proportion of salt to water. Store the jar at room temperature.

2 Within 3 days you should see tiny bubbles in the brine, indicating that fermentation has begun. If scum forms on top of the brine, skim it off daily and rinse off the brine bag.

3. The pickles should be ready in 2 to 3 weeks, when the bubbling has stopped and the pickles are sour and olive-green throughout. You can store the pickles in the refrigerator without further processing, provided you'll be eating them within 4 months.

4. For longer storage, in the refrigerator or pantry, pour the cucumbers and brine into a colander set atop a nonreactive pot. Discard the leaves and spices. Bring the brine to a boil and simmer it for 5 minutes, skimming off the scum that forms. Rinse the pickles with cold water and drain them well.

5. If you're storing the pickles in the refrigerator, let the brine cool to room temperature. Pack the pickles into two 2-quart jars or into the washed gallon jar. If you like, add fresh dill, mustard, and horseradish. Pour enough cooled brine over the cucumbers to cover them well.

6. For pantry storage, pack the pickles into quart or pint mason jars. Pour the hot brine over the pickles, leaving ½ inch headspace, and close the jars with two-piece caps. In a boiling-water bath, process pint jars for 10 minutes, quart jars for 15 minutes. Or pasteurize the jars for 30 minutes in water heated to 180° to 185°F. When the jars have cooled, store them in a cool, dry, dark place.

FAVORITE AROMATIC INGREDIENTS FOR THE SOUR CUCUMBER CROCK

Dill heads, sprigs, or seeds	Horseradish root	Cumin seeds
Garlic	Yellow or black mustard seeds	Parsley, tarragon, thyme, and other herbs
Shallots	Coriander seeds	Lemon
Bay leaves	Allspice berries	Celery tops
Fresh or dried hot peppers	Black peppercorns	Black currant leaves
	Fennel seeds	

NO-DILL
CROCK PICKLES

MAKES ABOUT 6 QUARTS

I'M INCLUDING THIS RECIPE for two reasons—to show that a lot of flavors besides dill complement fermented cucumbers, and to provide a set of quantities to fit a 2-gallon crock. Even if you wouldn't consider making pickles without dill, you may want to use the basic quantities here.

2 handfuls grape or sour cherry leaves
About 8 pounds 3- to 5-inch pickling cucumbers, blossom
    ends removed
2 tablespoons whole black peppercorns
1 tablespoon whole allspice berries
Zest of 2 lemons, in strips
8 fennel seed heads, or ¼ cup fennel seeds
8 fennel leaves
1 small bunch fresh parsley
½ cup white wine vinegar
1 gallon water
¾ cup salt

1 Lay half the leaves in the bottom of a 2-gallon crock. Layer the cucumbers in the crock with the peppercorns, allspice, lemon zest, fennel, and parsley. Add the vinegar to the water and dissolve the salt in the liquid. Pour enough brine over the cucumbers to cover them. Spread the remaining leaves on top. Place a plate and weight over the cucumbers, or weight them with a large food-grade plastic bag filled with leftover brine and sealed (if you need more brine, make it with the same proportion of salt to water, omitting the vinegar). Cover the crock with a towel or cloth and store it at room temperature.

2. Within 3 days you should see tiny bubbles in the brine, indicating that fermentation has begun. If a white scum forms on top of the brine, skim it off daily, and rinse off and replace the plate and weight or the brine bag.

3. The pickles should be ready in 2 to 3 weeks, when the tiny bubbles stop rising and the pickles are sour and olive-green throughout. Skim off any scum. Pour the pickles and brine into a colander set on top of a nonreactive pot. Discard the leaves and spices. Remove the colander from the pot and transfer the pot to the stovetop. Bring the brine to a boil, reduce the heat to low, and simmer the brine for 5 minutes. Skim off the scum that forms. Rinse the pickles with cold water and drain them well.

4. To store the pickles in the refrigerator, let the brine cool to room temperature. Pack the pickles into 2-quart or gallon jars. If you like, add fresh lemon zest, fennel, and spices. Pour enough cooled brine over the cucumbers to cover them well. Cap the jars and store them in the refrigerator for up to 6 months.

5. For pantry storage, pack the pickles into quart or pint mason jars. Cover the pickles with hot brine, leaving ½ inch headspace. Close the jars with two-piece caps. In a boiling-water bath, process pint jars for 10 minutes, quart jars for 15 minutes. Or pasteurize the jars for 30 minutes in water heated to 180° to 185°F. When the jars have cooled, store them in a cool, dry, dark place.

SPICY CROCK PICKLES

MAKES ABOUT 10 QUARTS

THIS IS MY CHILDREN'S FAVORITE dill pickle recipe. The leaves keep the cucumbers firm and crunchy, and the mixed pickling spices render them indefinably flavorful. I use a minimal amount of dill, but don't hesitate to use a lot if you like your pickles really dilly.

This recipe will fill a 3-gallon crock.

2 handfuls grape leaves or sour cherry leaves

About 12 pounds 3- to 5-inch pickling cucumbers, blossom ends removed

2 tablespoons Mixed Pickling Spices (page 15)

1 garlic head, cloves separated and peeled

4 to 8 dill heads

6 quarts water

1 cup cider vinegar

1¼ cups pickling salt

1. Line the bottom of a 3-gallon crock with half the leaves. Layer the cucumbers, spices, garlic, and dill heads in the crock. Combine the water and vinegar, and dissolve the salt in the liquid. Pour the brine over the cucumbers to cover them, and lay the remaining leaves on top. Keep the leaves and cucumbers submerged by weighting them with a plate topped with a clean rock or a water-filled jar, or with a large food-grade plastic bag filled with additional brine and sealed. Cover the crock with a towel or cloth and store the crock at room temperature.

2. Within 3 days you should see tiny bubbles in the brine, indicating that fermentation has begun. If a white scum forms on top of the brine, skim it off daily, and rinse and replace the plate and weight or the brine bag.

"Chichikov stepped up to kiss her hand, and she almost shoved it inside his mouth, giving him the opportunity to notice that she washed her hands in pickle brine."

—Nikolai Gogol, Dead Souls

3 The pickles should be ready in 2 to 3 weeks, when the pickles are sour and olive-green throughout. Skim off any scum.

4 Pour the pickles and brine into a colander set on top of a nonreactive pot. Discard the leaves and spices. Remove the colander from the pot and transfer the pot to the stovetop. Bring the brine to a boil, reduce the heat to low, and simmer the brine for 5 minutes. Skim off the scum that forms. Rinse the pickles with cold water and drain them well.

5 To store the pickles in the refrigerator, let the brine cool to room temperature. Pack the pickles into 2-quart or gallon jars. If you like, add fresh garlic, dill, and spices. Pour enough cooled brine over the cucumbers to cover them well. Cap the jars and store them in the refrigerator for up to 6 months.

6 For pantry storage, pack the pickles into quart or pint mason jars. Cover the pickles with hot brine, leaving ½ inch headspace. Close the jars with two-piece caps. In a boiling-water bath, process pint jars for 10 minutes, quart jars for 15 minutes. Or pasteurize the jars for 30 minutes in water heated to 180° to 185°F. When the jars have cooled, store them in a cool, dry, dark place.

"I once asked my grandmother, then seventy-two years old, how she kept her skin so wrinkle-free. The secret, she explained, was a daily dose of the fermented brine from the pickle barrel, rubbed into her skin. This treatment explained the unusual smell I'd always associated with my grandmother, but the astringent quality of the brine did seem to work wonders."

—*Darra Goldstein,* A Taste of Russia *(1983)*

RUSSIAN DILL PICKLES

MAKES ABOUT 10 QUARTS

IN EASTERN EUROPE, a slice of rye bread is often placed at the top of the pickle crock. All-wheat bread is never substituted, for rye, unlike wheat, attracts yeasts that contribute a desired flavor. The bread should not, of course, contain any preservatives.

Russians prefer to ferment their cucumbers in oak barrels, usually only about 1 gallon in size. But you can do without the barrel and just use oak leaves for their tannin, or substitute sour cherry or grape leaves, which also help keep pickles firm. I've designed this recipe to fill a 3-gallon crock.

> 2 to 4 handfuls oak, sour cherry, or grape leaves
> About 12 pounds 3- to 5-inch pickling cucumbers,
>   blossom ends removed
> 3 handfuls dill heads and sprigs
> 3 garlic heads, cloves separated and peeled
> 8 small dried hot peppers, such as japonés or de árbol, slit
>   lengthwise
> 8 Mediterranean bay leaves
> 1 tablespoon whole black peppercorns
> 1 tablespoon whole coriander seeds
> 2 teaspoons whole yellow mustard seeds
> 1¼ cups pickling salt
> 6 quarts water
> 1 thick slice rye bread

1 Spread a handful of leaves on the bottom of a 3-gallon crock. Layer the cucumbers in the crock with the dill, garlic, hot peppers, bay leaves, peppercorns, coriander, and mustard seeds, lining the crock with more leaves if you have plenty. Dissolve the salt in the water

and pour the brine over the cucumbers to cover them well. Lay the rye bread on top and spread the rest of the leaves over it. Put a plate on top and weight it with a clean rock or a water-filled jar. Cover the crock with a towel or cloth and store the crock at room temperature.

2. Within 3 days you should see tiny bubbles in the brine. This means that fermentation has begun. If a white scum forms on top of the brine, skim it off daily and rinse off and replace the plate and weight.

3. Fermentation should be complete within 4 weeks, when the tiny bubbles have stopped rising and the pickles are sour and olive-green throughout. Skim off the scum.

4. Pour the pickles and brine into a colander set on top of a nonreactive pot. Discard the leaves and spices. Remove the colander from the pot and transfer the pot to the stovetop. Bring the brine to a boil, reduce the heat to low, and simmer the brine for 5 minutes. Skim off the scum that forms. Rinse the pickles with cold water, and drain them well.

5. To store the pickles in the refrigerator, let the brine cool to room temperature. Pack the pickles into 2-quart or gallon jars. If you like, add fresh dill, garlic, and spices. Pour enough cooled brine over the cucumbers to cover them well. Cap the jars, and store them in the refrigerator for up to 6 months.

6. For pantry storage, pack the pickles into quart or pint mason jars, adding fresh dill and garlic, if you like. Cover the pickles with hot brine, leaving ½ inch headspace. Close the jars with two-piece caps. In a boiling-water bath, process pint jars for 10 minutes, quart jars for 15 minutes. Or pasteurize the jars for 30 minutes in water heated to 180° to 185°F. When the jars have cooled, store them in a cool, dry, dark place.

"Supper that night began with water glasses of vodka, with pickles and home-baked black bread. . . . And at two-thirty in the morning we had the following meal: glasses of vodka, and pickles again, and fried fish which had been caught in the village pond. . . ."

—John Steinbeck,
  A Russian
  Journal

BRINED SNAP BEANS

INEGAR-PICKLED BEANS are justifiably popular, but if you want to enhance the delicate flavor of snap beans without disguising it, give this recipe a try. Don't bother with tough, overgrown store-bought beans; use tender young ones from the garden or farmers' market.

2 pounds tender young snap beans, trimmed
6 small dried hot peppers, such as japonés or de árbol
6 garlic cloves, chopped
12 whole black peppercorns, crushed
6 dill heads
½ cup pickling salt
3 quarts water

1. Layer the beans, hot peppers, garlic, peppercorns, and dill in a gallon jar. Dissolve the salt in the water and pour enough brine over the beans to cover them well. Push a gallon-size freezer bag into the top of the jar, pour the remaining brine into the bag, and seal the bag. Store the jar at room temperature.

2. Fermentation, indicated by tiny bubbles, should begin within 3 days. If any scum appears at the top of the jar, skim it off and rinse the brine bag.

3. The beans should be ready in about 2 weeks, when they taste sour and the bubbling has stopped. Remove the brine bag and cap the jar. Store it in the refrigerator.

4. The pickled beans should keep in the refrigerator for several months.

MIXED FERMENTED PICKLES

....

MAKES ABOUT 3 QUARTS

A PICKLE LIKE THIS is especially practical if your garden is small, and you have only a handful of this, a handful of that to ferment at any particular time. But I like to make mixed pickles, fermented and stored in glass gallon jars, because they're beautiful to look at and an adventure to eat. Vary the vegetables according to what you have on hand and where your whimsy takes you.

1 pound cauliflower or broccoli florets

2 sweet green or red peppers, such as bell or pimiento, cut into
squares or strips

½ pound asparagus spears, cut into thirds, or whole young
snap beans

½ pound shallots, or regular onions, cut into chunks or rings

¼ pound tiny carrots, or larger carrots (no larger than
½ inch in diameter) cut into rounds or thin sticks

3 garlic cloves, slivered

2 to 3 tarragon sprigs

2 to 3 thyme sprigs

½ cup pickling salt

3 quarts water

2 tablespoons red wine vinegar

1 Toss all of the vegetables together and pack them into a gallon jar, distributing the garlic and herbs among them. Dissolve the salt in the water and pour enough brine over the vegetables to cover them. Add the vinegar.

2. Push a gallon-size freezer bag into the top of the jar, pour the remaining brine into the bag, and seal the bag. Store the jar at room temperature.

3. Within 3 days you should see tiny bubbles in the brine. If a white scum forms on top of the brine, skim it off and rinse and replace the brine bag.

4. The pickles should be ready in 2 to 3 weeks, when the bubbling has stopped and the vegetables taste sour. Remove the brine bag, cap the jar, and store it in the refrigerator.

5. The pickled vegetables should keep in the refrigerator for several months.

TURKISH MIXED PICKLE

MAKES ABOUT 2 QUARTS

THIS IS A FERMENTED VERSION of Pepper "Mangoes," or pickled stuffed peppers (page 139). It's my favorite mixed pickle—at the moment, at least—because all of the vegetables are permeated with the flavor of lemon. Although they're supposed to ferment for 2 to 3 weeks, I like them best when the lemon flavor is strongest, after about 5 days.

If your peppers are too wide to fit through the jar opening, use a gallon jar or crock and double the quantities or slice all of the vegetables instead of mincing some and stuffing them into others.

1 cup shredded head cabbage or kohlrabi

2 tablespoons coarsely grated carrot

2 tablespoons minced red bell pepper

3 garlic cloves, minced

1 tablespoon minced fresh dill leaves

2½ tablespoons pickling salt

3 small bell or other sweet peppers, green or red, cored

About 3 cups mixed prepared vegetables, including any of the
    following: 1- to 2-inch pickling cucumbers, blossom ends
    removed; cauliflower florets; snap beans, trimmed, and cut
    in half if they're long; carrots, sliced into rounds; whole small
    sweet peppers, pierced with a fork; small green tomatoes

1 small lemon, sliced

4 dill sprigs

4 small dried hot peppers, such as japonés or de árbol

½ cup white wine vinegar

3 cups water

2 teaspoons pickling salt dissolved in 1 cup water

1. In a bowl, mix together the cabbage, grated carrot, minced bell pepper, garlic, minced dill, and ½ teaspoon of the salt. Stuff this mixture into the cored bell peppers. Arrange the peppers in a 2-quart jar and fill the spaces between them with the mixed prepared vegetables, the lemon, the dill sprigs, and the hot peppers.

2. Combine the vinegar and water. Add the remaining salt to the liquid and stir until the salt dissolves. Pour the brine over the vegetables to cover them well. Push a quart-size freezer bag into the mouth of the jar and pour in the additional brine made from 2 teaspoons pickling salt stirred into 1 cup water. Seal the bag.

3. Store the jar at room temperature for 2 to 3 weeks or until the vegetables taste sour and the bubbling has stopped. Remove the brine bag, cap the jar, and store it in the refrigerator.

4. Refrigerated, the pickled vegetables should keep well for a few months.

"In the summer [my mother] festooned our house with strings of drying cabbages and turnips; whatever other vegetables we couldn't eat fresh were laid down in big earthenware jars with brine and aromatic spices. In the winter the jars would be opened and we ate pickled vegetables every day. For breakfast we had rice or congee sprinkled with dried, pickled, or salted vegetables, and pickled vegetables were often served at lunch and dinner as well. We ate pickles for snacks, and my mother added them to some dishes, like soups, for pungent flavoring."

—Jung-Feng Chiang, Mrs. Chiang's Szechwan Cookbook, 1976

SICHUAN SOURED VEGETABLES

MAKES 2 QUARTS

ALTHOUGH THE CHINESE are expert at extending the gardening season, in Sichuan Province and elsewhere people traditionally rely on dried, pickled, and salted vegetables to get through the cold winters. This is a mild Sichuan pickle, cured only long enough to sour the liquid; the vegetables don't actually ferment.

This recipe appeals to me particularly because it doesn't require mixing salt and water in a separate container. You make the brine right in your pickle jar and then put in the vegetables, plus a little more salt so the vegetables on top add their own brine to the jar.

Chinese cooks don't throw out the brine when the pickles are gone; they just add a little more rice wine, salt, and sugar, and another batch of vegetables. This time the jar goes right into the refrigerator; since the liquid is already sour, the fermentation isn't repeated. Later batches of pickles are said to be tastier than the first.

1½ tablespoons whole Sichuan peppercorns, crushed

2 tablespoons rice wine

1½ tablespoons rice vinegar

1 tablespoon sugar

3 cups water

3 tablespoons pickling salt

2 quarts prepared vegetables, including any of the following: head of Chinese cabbage, cut into 2-inch squares; turnips, halved and sliced ³⁄₁₆ inch thick; 1- to 1½-inch-long pickling cucumbers, or larger ones, cut into chunks; snap beans, trimmed, and halved if long; summer squash, cut into chunks; whole small carrots (up to ½ inch thick), or larger carrots cut diagonally ¼ inch thick, then lengthwise into ¼-inch-wide sticks; broccoli stems, peeled and halved lengthwise

10 small dried hot peppers, such as japonés or de árbol, some snipped in half or slit lengthwise for added heat

One 2-inch piece fresh ginger, thinly sliced

1 In a 2-quart jar, combine the Sichuan peppercorns, rice wine, rice vinegar, sugar, water, and 2 tablespoons salt. Stir well to dissolve the salt, or cap the jar and shake it. Pack the vegetables firmly into the jar, layering them with the hot peppers and ginger, and sprinkle the remaining 1 tablespoon salt on top. Seal the jar loosely. Let it stand at room temperature for about 3 days, until the vegetables are soured to your taste.

2 Store the jar in the refrigerator.

SAUERRUBEN

MAKES ABOUT 2 QUARTS

THIS GERMAN fermented turnip pickle is made almost exactly like sauerkraut (see pages 179–189). Make *sauerruben* in the fall or spring, using fresh, sweet young turnips or rutabagas. I've shredded turnips with the 2¼-inch-wide blade of an ordinary grater, but this is tiring work and hazardous to the fingertips, so use a kraut board or food processor if you have one.

As with sauerkraut, you can add flavorings such as caraway seeds to *sauerruben*. I'm tempted to add hot pepper and garlic, but then I'd have a sort of kimchi, wouldn't I? Anyway, *sauerruben* is delicious without adornment. I like it even better than sauerkraut.

5 pounds turnips, peeled and shredded
3 tablespoons pickling salt, plus more for the brine

1 In a large bowl, mix the turnips with 3 tablespoons pickling salt. Pack the mixture firmly into a 3-quart or gallon jar. Push a gallon-size freezer bag into the jar, and fill it with a brine made of 1½ tablespoons pickling salt to each quart of water. Seal the bag. Set the jar in a place where the temperature remains between 60° and 75°F.

2 After 24 hours, check to make sure that the turnips are well submerged in their own brine. If they aren't, add some fresh brine (1½ tablespoons pickling salt per 1 quart water) to cover them well. If any scum forms within the jar, skim it off and rinse and replace the bag.

3 After 2 weeks, begin tasting the *sauerruben*. It will be fully fermented in 2 to 4 weeks at 70° to 75°F, or within 4 to 6 weeks at 60°F. When it's ready, remove the bag, cap the jar, and store it in the

refrigerator or another very cool place (at about 38°F), tightly covered.

4. For pantry storage, pack the *sauerruben* and juices into pint or quart mason jars, leaving ½ inch headspace. Close the jars with two-piece caps. Immerse the jars in water heated to 165°F in a canner. Bring the water to a boil and adjust the heat to maintain a gentle boil. Process pint jars for 20 minutes, quart jars for 25 minutes.

5. When the jars have cooled, store them in a cool, dry, dark place.

KAKDOOKI (FERMENTED DAIKON)

MAKES ABOUT 1 QUART

IN KOREA, householders traditionally ferment vast quantities of vegetables every fall. They pack the vegetables into enormous ceramic jars, which they bury in the ground until needed. Modern food preservation methods and imports haven't weakened this tradition much, because Koreans *really* love their pickles.

This is a simple version of Korean fermented daikon; for a slightly fancier one, see the next recipe.

> 1½ pounds daikon, peeled and cut into ¾-inch cubes
> 6 scallions, cut into thin rounds
> 8 garlic cloves, minced
> 2 teaspoons pickling salt
> 2 teaspoons sugar
> 2 teaspoons Korean ground dried hot pepper

1. In a bowl, mix all of the ingredients. Let the bowl stand, covered with a cloth, for 6 to 12 hours.

2 Transfer the contents of the bowl to a quart jar and firmly push down the daikon cubes so the liquid rises to cover them. Cap the jar loosely. Let it stand at room temperature.

3 After 3 to 7 days, when the daikon is sour enough to suit you, tighten the cap and refrigerate the jar.

4 Refrigerated, the *kakdooki* will keep for several weeks.

KAKDOOKI WITH SHRIMP AND APPLE

MAKES ABOUT 1 QUART

K OREANS OFTEN ADD salted shrimp, oysters, and anchovies to fermented vegetables, for both added nutrients and enriched flavor. You can buy salted shrimp at many Asian markets.

2 pounds daikon, peeled and cut into ¾-inch cubes

4 teaspoons pickling salt

2 tablespoons Korean ground dried hot pepper

1 apple, peeled, cored, and coarsely grated

2 tablespoons salted dried shrimp

2 garlic cloves, minced

2 thin slices fresh ginger, peeled and minced

1 scallion, cut into thin rounds

1 Put the daikon cubes into a bowl and toss them with the salt. Let the daikon stand for 1 hour.

2 Drain the daikon. Sprinkle it with the hot pepper and add the remaining ingredients. Mix well. Lay a piece of plastic wrap over the mixture, and then lightly weight the mixture with a dish that just fits inside the bowl. Let the bowl stand at room temperature.

3 The pickle should be sour enough in about 3 days. Transfer it to a quart jar. Cap the jar and store it in the refrigerator. Refrigerated, the *kakdooki* will keep for several weeks.

CHINESE FERMENTED DAIKON

MAKES 1 QUART

 THIS CHINESE COUSIN of *kakdooki* uses whole rather than ground peppers.

1 pound daikon, peeled
4 thin slices fresh ginger
2 small dried hot peppers, such as japonés or de árbol, slit
    lengthwise
1½ tablespoons pickling salt
2 cups water

1 Cut the daikon into quarters or eighths lengthwise (the strips should be about ½ inch thick), and then crosswise into 1½-inch lengths. Layer the daikon, ginger, and hot peppers in a quart jar.

2 Dissolve the salt in the water and pour enough brine over the vegetables to cover them. Push a pint-size freezer bag into the mouth of the jar and pour the remaining brine into the bag. Seal the bag. Let the jar stand at room temperature.

3 After 2 to 3 days, when the daikon is as sour as you like, remove the brine bag and cap the jar. Store the pickle in the refrigerator, where it should keep for several weeks.

KOREAN PICKLED TURNIPS

 *S*unmukimchi, or brined turnips, is a popular and delicious Korean pickle.

> 1 pound (about 6) small turnips, peeled
> 1½ tablespoons pickling salt
> 1 to 2 teaspoons hot pepper flakes
> 3 scallions, minced
> 8 garlic cloves, minced
> 1 teaspoon sugar

1. Slice the turnips very thinly crosswise. (If they are bigger than about 2 inches across, halve them lengthwise first.) Put the slices into a bowl and rub them with 1 tablespoon of the salt. Let them stand at room temperature for about 3 hours, occasionally turning them in their brine.

2. Drain and rinse the turnip slices, and then drain them again. Add the remaining ½ tablespoon salt and the remaining ingredients. Mix well. Put the mixture into a quart jar and pour water over the contents so they are covered by about 1 inch. Cap the jar loosely and let it stand at room temperature.

3. After 6 to 8 days, when the turnips are as sour as you like, cap the jar tightly. Store the jar in the refrigerator, where the pickle should keep for several weeks.

VIETNAMESE PICKLED BEAN SPROUTS

MAKES ABOUT 1½ QUARTS

THESE MILD-FLAVORED, lightly fermented sprouts are a lovely complement to spicy or rich foods. According to Bach Ngo and Gloria Zimmerman, authors of *The Classic Cuisine of Vietnam* (1986), pickled bean sprouts are traditionally served with pork cooked in coconut water or simmered with five-spice powder. Because pickled sprouts are so mild in flavor, you can use them in many ways that you might use fresh sprouts. My children like them in soft tacos.

3 cups water
1 tablespoon pickling salt
½ teaspoon sugar
1 pound mung bean sprouts, rinsed and drained
1 medium-size carrot, shaved with a vegetable peeler
  into thin strips

1 In a saucepan, bring the water, salt, and sugar to a boil. Immediately remove the pan from the heat, and let the brine cool to room temperature.

2 Toss the bean sprouts and carrot strips together in a bowl and then pack them into a 2-quart jar. Pour the brine over the vegetables. It will not cover them completely at first, but within an hour or so the levels of liquid and vegetables should be about equal. Press the vegetables down with a spoon, if necessary, to cover them completely with the brine. Cap the jar loosely and let it stand at room temperature.

3 After 3 days, the sprouts should be sour enough. Cap the jar tightly and refrigerate it. The sprouts will keep well for several weeks, at least.

VIETNAMESE SOURED MUSTARD GREENS

MAKES ABOUT 6 CUPS

T HE PREFERRED MUSTARD variety for this pickle has broad, fleshy leaf stalks and may be sold as "mustard cabbage" or *gai choy*. Like Vietnamese pickled bean sprouts, this pickle is mild and refreshing.

1½ pounds mustard greens, cut into 2-inch lengths
6 scallions, cut into 2-inch lengths
5½ teaspoons pickling salt
1½ teaspoons sugar
1 quart water

1. Spread the mustard greens and scallions on a tray and dry them in the sun (I put them in the greenhouse) for several hours, or set the tray in a very slow oven until the vegetables are quite wilted.

2. Dissolve the salt and sugar in the water. Pack a handful of the greens into a 2-quart jar, add enough brine to cover them, and repeat this process until all the greens are in the jar and well covered with brine. Push a quart-size freezer bag into the mouth of the jar, pour the remaining brine into the bag, and seal the bag. Let the jar stand at room temperature.

3. After 3 to 4 days, the greens should be sour enough. Remove the brine bag, cap the jar, and store it in the refrigerator, where the pickle should keep for several weeks.

STUFFED CUCUMBER KIMCHI

MAKES ABOUT 1 QUART

THIS IS A MILD and very pretty kimchi. To avoid the trouble of cutting daikon and carrots into slivers, you can instead slice them very thin with a vegetable peeler. To avoid slivering scallions, use chives instead.

2 cups water

5 teaspoons pickling salt

¾ pound (about 8) 4-inch pickling cucumbers, blossom ends removed

½ pound daikon, peeled, sliced thinly crosswise, and slivered

3 scallions, cut into 1-inch lengths and slivered

One 2-inch-long piece of a medium-size carrot, halved crosswise and slivered

2 garlic cloves, slivered

2 teaspoons slivered fresh ginger

1 teaspoon hot pepper flakes

1 teaspoon sugar

1. Pour the water into a medium-size bowl and stir in 4 teaspoons salt until it dissolves. Make three deep diagonal slashes in each cucumber, cutting three-quarters of the way through. Put the cucumbers into the bowl of brine and let them stand at room temperature for 2 to 4 hours.

2. Drain the cucumbers, reserving the brine. Squeeze each cucumber gently to remove excess water.

3. In a bowl, mix the remaining 1 teaspoon salt and the other remaining ingredients. Stuff the slits of the cucumbers with the mixture and put the stuffed cucumbers into a bowl. Add any remaining stuffing. Cover the bowl with a cloth and let it stand at room temperature for 6 to 10 hours.

4. Pack the stuffed cucumbers into a 1- to 1½-quart wide-mouth jar and push the extra stuffing down between them. Pour some of the reserved brine over the cucumbers to cover them. Cap the jar loosely and let it stand at room temperature.

5. After 2 to 3 days, the kimchi should be sour enough. Cap the jar tightly and store it in the refrigerator, where the kimchi should keep for several weeks.

6. Serve the cucumber pieces separated and sprinkled with the stuffing.

BRINED PEPPERS

MAKES ABOUT 2 QUARTS

YOU CAN STORE THESE PEPPERS in the refrigerator to use in place of fresh peppers in cooking. Or, if your brined peppers are piquant, you can blend them into Brined Chile Relish (page 339) or puree them into Brined Chile Sauce (page 339).

For extra flavor, you might brine peeled garlic cloves, a bay leaf, and allspice berries along with the peppers.

>   2 pounds ripe peppers, hot or mild, stemmed and halved but
>   not seeded
>   5 tablespoons pickling salt
>   2 quarts water

1. Put the peppers into a jar with a capacity of about 3 quarts. Dissolve the salt in the water and pour 1 quart of the brine over the peppers. Push a gallon-size freezer bag into the mouth of the jar, pour the remaining brine into the bag, and seal the bag. Let the jar stand at room temperature.

2 The next day, check to make sure that the brine covers the peppers. If it doesn't, add more, in the original proportion of salt to water.

3 After a few days the brine should begin to look a little cloudy. If a scum develops in the jar, skim it off, rinse off the bag, and replace the bag carefully.

4 After 3 weeks, begin tasting the peppers (carefully, if they are hot). When they are as sour as you like, drain the brine into a nonreactive saucepan, bring it to a boil, skim off the scum, and let the brine cool. Put the peppers into a clean jar and pour the cooled brine over them. Tightly cap the jar and refrigerate it. The peppers should keep in the refrigerator for several months.

GREEN CHILE PICKLE

MAKES ABOUT 1 PINT

THIS INDIAN-STYLE PICKLE is very spicy and hot. You'll like it with Indian foods, and your chile-head friends will eat it with anything.

> ½ pound small hot green peppers, such as serrano, stemmed
>   and sliced thin
> 2 tablespoons pickling salt
> 1 pint water
> ¼ cup whole black mustard seeds, ground
> One 1-inch piece fresh ginger, minced
> 1 teaspoon ground turmeric
> 3 tablespoons lime juice
> 2 tablespoons mustard oil (page 154) or
>   other vegetable oil

1. Put the peppers and 1 tablespoon salt into a bowl. Using a spoon or gloved hands, mix them well. Pack the peppers into a quart jar. Dissolve the remaining 1 tablespoon salt in the water. Push a quart-size freezer bag into the top of the jar and add enough brine to weight the peppers and seal out air. Seal the bag. Let the jar stand at room temperature.

2. Begin tasting the peppers after 3 weeks. When they are as sour as you like, transfer them to a bowl and stir in the mustard seeds, ginger, turmeric, and lime juice, and then the mustard oil. Pack the mixture into a pint jar. Close the jar tightly with a nonreactive cap and store the jar in the refrigerator.

3. Refrigerated, the pickle will keep well for a year or longer.

BRINED CHERRY TOMATOES

MAKES ABOUT 2 QUARTS

TOMATOES MAY BE BRINED at any stage of ripeness. The red ones have a sweeter flavor, of course, but they get mushy when they're fermented. Very green tomatoes keep their appealing firm texture, and you might also like their moderate bitterness. Partially ripe tomatoes, just beginning to show their color, are perhaps best of all for brining; after fermentation, they're a little bitter, a little sweet, and still quite crisp. As important as the stage of ripeness, though, are the aromatics that accompany the tomatoes. Be generous with the garlic, horseradish, and herbs, and you'll be rewarded with a very satisfying pickle.

This recipe comes from Russia.

"So in our pride we ordered for breakfast an omelet, toast and coffee and what has just arrived is a tomato salad with onions, a dish of pickles, a big slice of watermelon and two bottles of cream soda."

—*John Steinbeck,* A Russian Journal

1¾ pounds half-ripe cherry tomatoes

About 6 dill heads

¼ cup coarsely grated or chopped horseradish

4 or 5 garlic cloves, halved

Leafy tops of 2 celery stalks

3 parsley sprigs

3 tarragon sprigs

½ fresh hot pepper, such as jalapeño, seeded

Several dill sprigs

2 tablespoons pickling salt

1 quart water

1 Put the tomatoes into a 2-quart jar, interspersing all of the aromatics among them, and curling some dill sprigs on top. Dissolve the salt in the water and pour enough brine over the tomatoes to cover them well. Push a quart-size freezer bag into the top of the jar, pour the remaining brine into the bag, and seal it. Let the jar stand at room temperature for about a week, until fermentation has slowed.

2 Remove the brine bag and cap the jar tightly. Store the jar in the refrigerator for about a week before eating the tomatoes. Refrigerated, they will keep for about 3 weeks more.

"At the markets, white tubs filled with brined apples interspersed with cranberries lined the long counters, and a Moscow student chomped a cold, golden apple unreservedly, showing with pride his affiliation: eating brined apples during the Butterweek had been a time-honored tradition among students in Moscow."

—*Aleksandr Kuprin,* The Cadets

PICKLED APPLES

MAKES 1 GALLON

ANOTHER RUSSIAN SPECIALTY, brined apples retain their crispness but acquire a flavor like that of sparkling wine. The variety I've seen pickled in Russian markets appears to be Golden Delicious.

3 quarts water
¼ cup honey
8 teaspoons pickling salt
2 to 3 handfuls sour cherry leaves
4 to 6 tarragon sprigs
3 pounds small green or yellow apples

1. Bring to a boil the water, honey, and salt, stirring to dissolve the salt. Let the brine cool.

2. Spread some of the cherry leaves and 1 or 2 tarragon sprigs in the bottom of a gallon jar. Add a layer of apples placed on their sides; three should just fit. Layer more leaves, tarragon, and apples, and then repeat again for a third layer. Top with the rest of the leaves and tarragon. Pour enough of the brine over the apples to cover them well. Push a gallon-size freezer bag into the top of the jar, pour the remaining brine into the bag, and seal the bag. Let the jar stand at room temperature for 5 to 6 days, until fermentation slows.

3. Remove the brine bag, cap the jar tightly, and set it out of direct sun where the temperature doesn't rise about 50°F (I have used a refrigerator with good results). After 30 to 40 days, the apples will be ready to eat. Refrigerated, the apples will keep well for at least a week longer.

RUSSIAN-STYLE PICKLED LEMONS

RUSSIAN COOKS PRESERVE LEMONS by brining them whole. This is not a uniquely Russian method, though; I have bought whole brined lemons imported from Thailand.

The quantities here will depend not only on how many lemons you wish to brine, but also on what you can use to keep the lemons immersed. When I want to brine just three lemons, I use a narrow 12-ounce jelly jar and stack plastic milk-jug caps between the top lemon and the jar cap. If you want to brine more lemons, you might use a quart jar, and weight the lemons with a plastic bag filled with brine and sealed. Or you might use a crock, and weight the lemons with a plate topped with a clean rock or a water-filled jar.

Russian cooks serve these lemons in thin slices with fish and game. You might also try them with pork chops, rice dishes, stewed chickpeas, or thinly sliced raw red onion.

Whole lemons, preferably thin-skinned, washed and dried
Brine made of 1 tablespoon salt to each cup water

1. Put the lemons into a jar or crock and cover them with the brine. Weight them in whichever way is practical so that the lemons are fully submerged in the brine. If you're not using a brine bag as the weight, cap the jar loosely, or cover the crock and weight with a cloth.

2. Store the jar or crock in the refrigerator or another cool place. The lemons will be ready to eat in about 3 weeks.

3. Serve the lemons thinly sliced. Refrigerated in their brine, they should keep for a year or longer.

"It's nothing but limes now, for everyone is sucking them in their desks in school-time, and trading them off for pencils, bead-rings, paper dolls, or something else at recess. If one girl likes another she gives her a lime; if she's mad with her she eats one before her face, and don't offer even a suck. They treat by turns; and I've had ever so many, but haven't returned them; and I ought, for they are debts of honour, you know."

So explains Amy March in *Little Women* as she begs her sisters for money to pay for pickled limes. Several people have asked me what these limes were and how to prepare them. Those who grew up in New England before World War II, however, ask only the second question, because they understand exactly how Amy felt. They loved pickled limes as children. One remembers always buying pickled limes on the way to the beach; another remembers her mother buying them at a fish shop. Strangely, old New England cookbooks never tell how to pickle limes—although pickled limes are called for in recipes for sweet relishes, with green tomatoes or just sugar and vinegar.

Some historical sleuthing has finally cleared up this mystery. In the West Indies, in the nineteenth and early twentieth centuries, ripe (yellow) limes were packed whole in sea water or fresh-made brine and shipped to northeastern U.S. ports in barrels. In 1838, according to the Royal Horticultural Society of Great Britain, there was "a fair demand in the New York market for pickled limes," but by the late nineteenth century pickled limes were invariably sent to Boston. There they were sold from glass jars on top of candy-store counters, and some families even bought them by the barrel. Because the import tariff for pickled limes was quite low—importers fought to keep them classed as neither fresh fruit nor pickle—children could buy them cheaply, often for a penny apiece. Kids chewed, sucked, and traded pickled limes at school (and not just at recess) for decades, making the limes the perennial bane of New England schoolteachers. Doctors tended to disapprove of the limes, too; in 1869 a Boston physician wrote that pickled limes were among the "unnatural and abominable" substances consumed by children with nutritional deficiencies. Parents, however, seemed generally content for children to indulge themselves in the pickled-lime habit.

To make pickled limes as Amy loved them, get some Mexican (Key, West Indian) limes, both as fresh and as ripe as possible. Brine them as for Russian-Style Pickled Lemons (opposite page). Then wrap a few in brown paper, put them into your lunch box, and consider who in your acquaintance might deserve one—or at least a suck.

3

FRESH PICKLES

CUCUMBERS ARE JUST THE BEGINNING in this very large category of pickles. In this chapter you'll find recipes for pickled peppers, cauliflower, mushrooms, eggplant, artichokes, baby corn, okra, mixed vegetables, and much more.

These pickles are all "fresh" in that they're not fermented. The acid that preserves the vegetables and fruits comes from vinegar, usually, or from citrus juice or citric acid. The chapter includes canned pickles, which typically aren't very sour, since the vinegar is usually cut with an approximately equal amount of water. Other pickles here are truly fresh—in the sense that they're not cooked at all—but very sour, since they're preserved in pure vinegar. A third type of fresh pickle, typically packed in diluted vinegar, is intended for short or long keeping in the refrigerator.

Pickles that are usually canned can be stored in the refrigerator instead, if you're making a small batch or simply don't want to bother with a boiling-water bath and two-piece caps. Use jars of any size, and any caps that won't react with salt and vinegar.

After the jars are opened, all of the pickles in this chapter should be stored in the refrigerator. A jar that is processed but fails to seal should be stored in the refrigerator as well.

"On a hot day in Virginia, I know of nothing more comforting than a fine spiced pickle, brought up troutlike from the sparkling depths of the aromatic jar below stairs in Aunt Sally's cellar."

—*Thomas Jefferson*

TROUBLESHOOTING GUIDE: FRESH CUCUMBER PICKLES

PROBLEM	CAUSES
Hollow middle	The cucumbers grew this way, perhaps because of inadequate watering (you can pick out cucumbers like this when you wash them—they float). Or the cucumbers were held too long before processing.
Pale skins	The cucumbers grew this way, perhaps because of sun-scald (grape or black currant leaves added to the jars may help deepen the green of pale cucumbers). Or the pickles were exposed to light during storage.
Dark pickles	Your water contains a lot of iron, or the canning lids were corroded, or you used reactive metal pans or utensils in processing the pickles. Or you used loose ground spices.
Shriveled pickles	The cucumbers were held too long before processing, or you overcooked the cucumbers or heat-processed the jars for too long. Or you used too much salt, sugar, or vinegar in the liquid at the beginning of the pickling process.
Small brown spots on pickles	The cucumbers were held too long before processing.
White sediment	You used table salt.
Soft pickles	The cucumbers were held too long before processing, or overheated during processing. Try low-temperature pasteurization next time.

SHORT-BRINED DILL PICKLES

MAKES ABOUT 8 QUARTS

BEFORE I STARTED fermenting cucumbers, I made these pick-les every summer. The recipe is very flexible; as long as you stick with the proportions of vinegar, water, salt, and sugar given here, you can vary the seasonings as you like. Add yellow mustard seeds, for example (about 2 teaspoons per quart), some grated or sliced horseradish, some bay leaves, or more hot peppers. Or be a little more daring: Try adding some black currant leaves or shallots, or even leave out the dill and use fennel or cumin instead. Grape or sour cherry leaves can help keep the pickles firm, but they aren't essential, either.

If you have just one or two cucumber vines, you may prefer to make your pickles by the quart. In this case, drop into the jar 2 sliced garlic cloves, 4 peppercorns, and a slit hot pepper. Pack the cucumbers into the jar along with 2 to 3 dill heads, and pour over the cucumbers a hot solution of 1 cup each vinegar and water with 1½ teaspoons sugar and 2 teaspoons salt. Process and store the jar as described in steps 4 and 5.

12 pounds 3- to 5-inch pickling cucumbers, blossom ends removed

1½ cups pickling salt

2 gallons plus 2 quarts water

7⅓ cups cider vinegar or distilled white vinegar

¼ cup sugar

16 garlic cloves, sliced

32 whole black peppercorns

16 to 24 dill heads

8 small dried hot peppers, such as japonés or de árbol, slit lengthwise (optional)

24 to 32 grape leaves or 48 to 64 sour cherry leaves (optional)

1. Halve or quarter the cucumbers lengthwise, if you like, or leave them whole. In a large bowl or crock, dissolve ¾ cup pickling salt in 2 gallons water. Add the cucumbers and weight them with a heavy plate that just fits inside the container. Let them stand in the brine at room temperature for 8 to 12 hours.

2. Drain the cucumbers. If you like less salty pickles, rinse the cucumbers and drain them well again.

3. In a nonreactive pot, bring to a boil the remaining ¾ cup pickling salt, the remaining 2 quarts water, the vinegar, and the sugar. While the mixture heats, divide the garlic and peppercorns among 8 quart or 16 pint mason jars. Pack the jars with the cucumbers, dill, and, if you're using them, the hot peppers and grape or cherry leaves.

4. Pour the hot liquid over the cucumbers, leaving ½ inch headspace. Close the jars with two-piece caps. In a boiling-water bath, process pint jars for 10 minutes, quart jars for 15 minutes. Or pasteurize the jars for 30 minutes by immersing them in water heated to 180° to 185°F.

5. Store the cooled jars in a cool, dry place for at least a month before eating the pickles. After opening a jar, store it in the refrigerator.

BEYOND DILL

If you're not crazy about dill, or if you just want to try some different flavorings in your fresh pickles, here are some ideas. For each quart of pickles, use ½ teaspoon Mixed Pickling Spice (page 15), ½ teaspoon cumin seeds, 2 Mediterranean bay leaves, or a fennel head or two in place of the dill. For mildly sweet, spicy pickles, omit the dill and add 1 teaspoon Mixed Pickling Spice and 2 tablespoons sugar.

REALLY QUICK DILL PICKLES

MAKES 3 QUARTS

AFTER MAKING SHORT-BRINED cucumber pickles for years, I was surprised to find that I like pickles made by this no-brine method.

For firmer pickles, add 2 to 3 grape leaves or 6 to 8 sour cherry leaves for each quart of pickles.

You can double or triple this recipe to suit the size of your harvest. To make a single quart of pickles, you'll need 1 cup water, ⅞ cup vinegar, 8 peppercorns, 2 garlic cloves, 2 dried hot peppers, and 2 dill heads.

4 pounds 4-inch pickling cucumbers, blossom ends removed
24 whole black peppercorns
1 garlic head, cloves separated, peeled and chopped
6 small dried hot peppers, such as japonés or de árbol,
    slit lengthwise (optional)
6 dill heads, with sprigs
2¾ cups cider vinegar, white wine vinegar, or
    distilled white vinegar
3 cups water
¼ cup pickling salt

1. Halve or quarter the cucumbers lengthwise, if you like, or leave them whole. Divide the peppercorns, garlic, and hot peppers (if you're using them) among 6 pint or 3 quart mason jars. Pack a portion of the cucumbers into each jar along with some dill.

2. In a saucepan, bring the vinegar, water, and salt to a boil, stirring to dissolve the salt. Pour the hot liquid over the cucumbers, leaving ½ inch headspace. Close the jars with two-piece caps. In a boiling-water bath, process pint jars for 10 minutes, quart jars for 15 minutes.

Or pasteurize the jars for 30 minutes by immersing them in water heated to 180° to 185°F.

3 Store the pickles for at least 1 month in a cool, dry place before eating them. After opening a jar, store it in the refrigerator.

DON'T KNOCK IT TILL YOU'VE TRIED IT

Northerners may laugh when they first hear of this favorite Southern snack, but fried cucumber pickles are a real delicacy. This recipe, from Pickle Packers International, produces a thin, crisp, tempura-like coating that complements the intense flavor of the hot pickle. Try these pickles with Hot Orange Ketchup (page 347).

Although the recipe calls for sliced pickles, I fry small ones whole.

FRIED DILL PICKLES

1 cup all-purpose flour

¼ cup cornstarch

1 teaspoon baking powder

¼ teaspoon salt

1 cup ice water

1 egg yolk

2 tablespoons pickle brine

8 medium to large dill pickles, such as Short-Brined Dill Pickles (page 84) or Really Quick Dill Pickles (opposite page), sliced ¼ inch thick (about 4 cups)

Vegetable oil for deep-frying

In a bowl, stir together the flour, cornstarch, baking powder, and salt. Make a well in the center and add the water, egg yolk, and pickle brine. Whisk the ingredients together to form a smooth batter. Cover the bowl and refrigerate it for 30 minutes.

In a heavy pot, heat at least 2 inches of oil to 375°F. In batches, dip the pickle slices in the batter, slip them into the oil, and fry them without crowding until the coating is crisp and golden, 1½ to 2 minutes. Drain the pickle slices on paper towels and serve them immediately.

OLD-FASHIONED
BREAD-AND-BUTTERS

MAKES ABOUT 8 PINTS

NOT LONG BEFORE PUBLICATION of the first edition of this book, I learned that bread-and-butter pickles had gone upscale. At a benefit for Citymeals-on-Wheels at Rockefeller Center in New York City, Alice Waters, chef and owner of Chez Panisse in Berkeley, served bread-and-butter pickles with smoked salmon and watercress on toasted walnut bread. (Afterward, though, she said she regretted not choosing miniature hamburgers instead of the salmon to go with the pickles.)

These bread-and-butters are a little less sweet than most; you can increase the sugar, if you like. Some people also add a little ground cloves, and you might try some diced red pepper in place of some of the onions. One of my pickling correspondents, Mark Cravens, uses a teaspoon or more of whole coriander seeds for "a little floral flavor."

6 pounds 4- to 5-inch pickling cucumbers

2 pounds small onions, sliced into thin rounds

½ cup pickling salt

4½ cups cider vinegar

3 cups sugar

2 teaspoons ground turmeric

2 teaspoons whole celery seeds

2 tablespoons whole yellow mustard seeds

1 Slice the cucumbers crosswise 3/16 inch thick, discarding both ends. In a large bowl, toss the cucumbers and onions with the salt. Empty

2 trays of ice cubes over the vegetables and let them stand at room temperature for 3 to 4 hours.

2 Drain the vegetables. In a large nonreactive pot, bring the remaining ingredients to a boil. Add the vegetables and slowly return the contents to a boil. With a slotted spoon, transfer the vegetables to pint mason jars, leaving ½ inch headspace. Divide the liquid evenly among the jars. Close the jars with two-piece caps. In a boiling-water bath, process the jars for 10 minutes. Or pasteurize the jars for 30 minutes by immersing them in water heated to 180° to 185°F.

3 Store the cooled jars in a cool, dry, dark place for at least 1 month before eating the pickles. After opening a jar, store it in the refrigerator.

BREAD-AND-BUTTERS
MY WAY

MAKES 4 PINTS

BECAUSE I FIND traditional bread-and-butter pickles cloying, I've developed a lighter version, using only a quarter as much sugar, some water to cut the vinegar, and a little hot pepper for zing.

> About 3½ pounds 3- to 5-inch pickling cucumbers
> ¼ cup pickling salt
> 4 teaspoons whole yellow mustard seeds
> 1 teaspoon whole celery seeds
> 1 teaspoon hot pepper flakes
> 2 cups cider vinegar
> 2 cups water
> ½ cup sugar
> 1 teaspoon ground turmeric

1. Slice the cucumbers ³⁄₁₆ inch thick, discarding both ends. You should have 2 quarts. In a large bowl, toss the cucumber slices with the salt. Top the cucumbers with ice cubes from 2 ice trays. Let the cucumbers stand at room temperature for 3 to 4 hours.

2. Drain the cucumbers well. Toss them with the mustard seeds, celery seeds, and hot pepper flakes. Pack the cucumbers into 4 pint mason jars.

3. In a saucepan, bring the vinegar, water, sugar, and turmeric to a boil. Pour the hot liquid over the cucumber slices, leaving ½ inch headspace. Close the jars with two-piece caps. In a boiling-water bath, process the jars for 10 minutes. Or pasteurize the jars for 30 minutes by immersing them in water heated to 180° to 185°F.

4. Store the cooled jars in a cool, dry, dark place for at least 3 weeks before eating the pickles. After opening a jar, store it in the refrigerator.

LIMED BREAD-AND-BUTTERS

If you like your bread-and-butters crisp, you can treat the cucumbers with pickling lime. Mix the salt and 1 cup pickling lime with 1 gallon cold water in a large bowl or nonreactive pot. Soak the cucumber slices for 12 to 24 hours, stirring occasionally. Drain and rinse the cucumbers and then soak them in fresh water for 1 hour. Drain them again. Repeat the rinsing, soaking, and draining two more times before continuing with the recipe. Handle the cucumber slices carefully, because they will be brittle.

DUTCH LUNCH SPEARS, BY THE QUART

MAKES 1 QUART

THIS IS MY VARIATION of an old Mennonite recipe. I've cut the vinegar and sugar substantially, but these pickles will still please people who like strong flavors.

If you'd like to put some of these pickles on the pantry shelf, multiply the quantities by four. Give the jars a 10-minute boiling-water bath, or immerse them in water heated to 180° to 185°F for 30 minutes.

> 1¼ pounds 4- to 5-inch pickling cucumbers, blossom ends removed
> 3 tablespoons plus 2 teaspoons pickling salt
> 1 quart plus ¾ cup water
> 1 garlic clove
> 1 small onion
> 1 dill head
> 2 grape leaves (optional)
> ¾ cup cider vinegar
> ¼ cup sugar
> 1 teaspoon Mixed Pickling Spices (page 15)

1 Quarter the cucumbers lengthwise and put them into a bowl or crock. Dissolve 3 tablespoons salt in 1 quart water, and pour the brine over the cucumbers. Top the cucumbers with a heavy plate that just fits inside the crock or bowl. Let the cucumbers stand at room temperature for 8 to 12 hours.

2 Drain the cucumbers, rinse them, and drain them again. Pack them into a quart jar with the garlic, onion, and dill. Add the grape leaves, if you have them; they will help keep the cucumbers firm and green.

3. In a nonreactive saucepan, combine the remaining ¾ cup water and 2 teaspoons salt with the vinegar, sugar, and spices. Bring the mixture to a boil. Pour the hot liquid over the cucumbers and seal the jar. Let it cool.

4. Store the jar in the refrigerator for at least 1 week before eating the pickles. Refrigerated, they will keep for several months, at least.

SANDWICH-SLICED DILL PICKLES

MAKES 6 PINTS

I**N THE** 1990s commercial pickle packers discovered old-fashioned "tongue pickles," which were reborn as "stuffers" and "sandwich builders." These are all simply names for cucumber pickles sliced lengthwise into slabs.

5 pounds 4-inch pickling cucumbers, blossom ends removed
6 tablespoons pickling salt
2 quarts plus 3 cups water
12 garlic cloves, coarsely chopped
1½ teaspoons hot pepper flakes
24 whole black peppercorns
6 dill heads
2¾ cups cider vinegar

1. Slice the cucumbers lengthwise ³⁄₁₆ inch thick, discarding a narrower slice at either side. Put the cucumbers into a bowl. Dissolve 3 tablespoons salt in 2 quarts water, pour this brine over the cucumbers, and weight them with a heavy plate that just fits inside the bowl. Let them stand at room temperature for 12 hours.

2 Drain the cucumbers. Divide the garlic, hot pepper flakes, and peppercorns evenly among 6 pint mason jars. Pack the cucumber slices into the jars, along with a dill head in each jar.

3 In a saucepan, combine the vinegar with the remaining 3 cups water and 3 tablespoons salt. Bring the contents to a boil, stirring to dissolve the salt. Pour the hot liquid over the cucumber slices, leaving ½ inch headspace. Close the jars with two-piece caps. In a boiling-water bath, process the jars for 10 minutes. Or pasteurize the jars for 30 minutes by immersing them in water heated to 180° to 185°F.

4 Store the cooled jars in a cool, dry, dark place for at least 3 weeks before eating the pickles. After opening a jar, store it in the refrigerator.

HONEYED SUNSHINE PICKLES

MAKES 7 PINTS

OVERSIZED, YELLOWED, tough-skinned cucumbers can still make good pickles if you peel and seed them. (Until late in the summer, however, you should avoid letting any cucumbers ripen, or

PICKLES: A KEY TO LONGEVITY?

Susie Potts Gibson died in 2006 at the age of 115. Born in Mississippi, she had lived in the same house in Alabama for 80 years. When she died, her daughter told National Public Radio her mother's three secrets to longevity: pickles, vinegar, and avoidance of medicine. Susie lived for her pickles, her daughter said, and she had vinegar on everything. She drank pickle juice, soaked her feet in it, and put it on any part of her body that hurt.

the plants may stop fruiting prematurely.) Ripe cucumbers are often pickled like watermelon rind. For this mildly sweet, pretty yellow pickle I use crescents of ripe lemon cucumbers—which look much like navel oranges—but you might use chunks of ripe pickling cucumbers instead.

7 pounds ripe cucumbers, peeled, seeded, and
   cut into crescents or 1-inch chunks (about 3½ pounds
   prepared cucumbers)
1 pound onions, halved and sliced
¼ cup pickling salt
21 thin slices fresh ginger
3½ cups cider vinegar
1 cup water
1¼ cups honey
¼ cup minced fresh hot pepper, such as jalapeño or Fresno
2 tablespoons whole yellow mustard seeds
1 teaspoon whole celery seeds
1 teaspoon ground turmeric
1 cup golden raisins

1 In a large bowl, toss the cucumbers and onions with the salt, and cover the vegetables with ice cubes from 2 ice trays. Let the vegetables stand at room temperature for 3 to 5 hours.

2 Drain the vegetables, rinse them, and then drain them well again.

3 Put 3 ginger slices into each of 7 pint mason jars.

4 In a large, nonreactive pot, bring the remaining ingredients to a boil, stirring to dissolve the honey. Add the drained vegetables and slowly bring the mixture to a boil. Ladle the hot vegetables and liquid into the jars, leaving ½ inch headspace. Close the jars with two-piece caps. In a boiling-water bath, process the jars for 10 minutes. Or pasteurize the jars for 30 minutes by immersing them in water heated to 180° to 185°F.

5 Store the cooled jars in a cool, dry, dark place for at least 3 weeks before eating the pickles. After opening a jar, store it in the refrigerator.

SENFGURKEN

MAKES 4 PINTS

I ADAPTED THIS RECIPE from one sent to me by Dick Schaefer, who inherited it from his German grandmother. *Senfgurken*, or mustard pickles, are made with ripe cucumbers, the ones that are overlooked in the garden or field until they are huge, yellow, tough-skinned, and watery. Once peeled, they are still good for pickling, and you can save their seeds for next year's crop.

> 5 pounds ripe cucumbers (about 4), peeled
> ¼ cup pickling salt
> 3 cups cider vinegar
> 1½ cups sugar
> 1½ tablespoons whole yellow mustard seeds
> 2 teaspoons Mixed Pickling Spices (page 15)

1 Slice the cucumbers in half vertically and scrape the seed cavities clean. Slice each half into strips about 1 inch by 2 inches. Mix the strips in a bowl with the salt. Cover the bowl and leave it at room temperature for 4 to 12 hours.

2 Drain the cucumber strips well; do not rinse them. In a nonreactive pot, stir together the vinegar, sugar, mustard seeds, and spices. Add half the cucumber strips and bring the mixture to a boil over medium heat. Reduce the heat, and simmer the cucumbers for 1 minute.

3. Ladle the cucumbers into hot pint mason jars and cover them with the hot liquid, leaving ½ inch headspace. Close the jars with two-piece caps. In the same way, heat the remaining cucumber strips in the liquid remaining in the pot, ladle them into jars with the liquid, and cap the jars. In a boiling-water bath, process the jars for 10 minutes. Or pasteurize the jars for 30 minutes by immersing them in water heated to 180° to 185°F.

4. Store the cooled jars in a cool, dry, dark place for at least 3 weeks before eating the pickles. After opening a jar, store it in the refrigerator.

THE MYSTERIOUS CHRISTMAS PICKLE

A typical German family hides a blown-glass cucumber-pickle ornament in the Christmas tree for the children to search for, and the one who finds it gets good luck or an extra present. Or so believe many Americans. Strangely, few Germans have any knowledge of the Christmas-pickle tradition. At least one German manufacturer exports glass pickle ornaments to the United States, and some of these ornaments are sold in Germany today. But glass pickles are rare in Germany, and they have no special status among German Christmas ornaments.

According to Internet folklore, the tradition is German-American. It arose when one John Lower, who emigrated from Bavaria in 1842 and became a Union soldier, was captured and sent to the Confederate prison in Andersonville, Georgia. Sick and starving, he begged the guard for just one pickle before he died. When the guard took pity on him and gave him the pickle, it provided John the strength to live on. Once reunited with his family, he began a tradition of hiding a pickle ornament on the Christmas tree. Whoever found it would be blessed with a year of good fortune.

In fact, German blown-glass ornaments weren't imported to the United States until the 1880s, after Christmas trees became popular here. The Christmas-pickle tradition may have originated as a simple marketing ploy. No matter—a tradition it now is, in many American families. In my house, though, the pickle isn't hidden in the tree. Instead, it hangs proudly at the end of a branch, where everyone can admire it.

CORNICHONS À CRU

MAKES 1 QUART

FOR THIS CLASSIC FRENCH PICKLE, harvest very small cornichons (European gherkins) or American pickling cucumbers, and start processing them the same day.

French recipes for *cornichons à cru* can vary a lot. Frequent additions are garlic, cloves, and thyme, and I have sometimes added mustard, coriander, allspice, or even cinnamon. The French often use red wine vinegar, which makes for a delicious if less pretty pickle. I sometimes use cider vinegar, and once I pickled cornichons with ginger, hot pepper, garlic, and cold rice vinegar, to create what I called *Cornichons à l'Orientale*, a pungent, clean-tasting pickle.

Traditionally, *cornichons à cru* always accompany pâté. My husband loves them with fried ham.

If you like, use two pint jars instead of one quart jar.

> 1 quart 1¹/₂- to 2-inch cornichons or 1- to 1¹/₂-inch
>   American pickling cucumbers (about 1¹/₄ pounds),
>   blossom ends removed
> 3 tablespoons pickling salt
> 4 shallots, peeled
> 1 Mediterranean bay leaf
> 10 whole black peppercorns
> 2 small dried hot peppers, such as japonés or de árbol
> 1¹/₂ to 2 cups white wine vinegar

1 Wash the cucumbers gently and rub off the tiny spines if you're using cornichons. In a bowl, mix the cucumbers with the salt. Let them stand at room temperature for 3 to 5 hours.

2 Drain the cucumbers, rinse them in cold water, and pat each one dry with a clean towel. Put the cucumbers into a sterilized quart jar, interspersing among them the shallots, bay leaf, peppercorns, and hot peppers. Fill the jar with vinegar to cover the cucumbers well, and close the jar with a nonreactive cap (you can use a two-piece mason jar cap if you line it with two layers of plastic wrap). Store the jar in a cool, dark place.

3 The cornichons will be ready to eat in about a month, and will keep well for about a year. After opening the jar, store it in the refrigerator.

OLIVE OIL PICKLES

MAKES 1 QUART

THIS RECIPE IS REALLY FOUR IN ONE. You can use small whole cucumbers or sliced medium-size ones. In either case, you can add mustard seed, if you like, or leave it out. All of these versions have been popular in this country since the time of Mary Randolph (*The Virginia Housewife*, 1824) or earlier. The olive oil not only provides a floating barrier against spoilage but also deliciously coats each pickle as it's drawn from the jar. The pickles are uncooked, uncanned, and very tasty.

About 1¼ pounds small or medium-size pickling cucumbers,
    blossom ends removed
2 small onions, thinly sliced
4 teaspoons pickling salt
½ teaspoon hot pepper flakes
2 tablespoons whole yellow mustard seeds (optional)
About 1½ cups white wine vinegar or cider vinegar
2 tablespoons olive oil

1. If the cucumbers are 2 to 3 inches long, leave them whole; if they are 4 to 5 inches long, slice them into ³⁄₁₆-inch-thick rounds. In a bowl, toss the cucumbers and onions with the salt. Let them stand at room temperature for 3 to 5 hours.

2. Drain the vegetables well. Layer them in a sterilized quart jar with the hot pepper flakes and, if you like, the mustard seeds. Cover the vegetables well with vinegar, then cover the surface with the olive oil. Seal the jar with a nonreactive lid (if you don't have an all-plastic jar cap, line a metal lid and rim with plastic wrap). Store the jar in a cool, dark place.

3. The pickles will be ready to eat in about 2 weeks, and will keep well for at least 6 months. After opening the jar, store it in the refrigerator.

"Grandmother lived to be ninety, she thought, and she never missed a dinner without the proverbial 'seven sours.'"

—*Mary Emma Showalter,* Mennonite Community Cookbook *(1957)*

PAUL'S SALT-FREE DILLS

MAKES 1 QUART

U NTIL MY NEIGHBOR Paul asked it, I had always brushed off the question of how to make salt-free pickles. Why would people want to make pickles at all, I wondered, if their diets didn't allow salt? But when Paul asked the question, I took it seriously. When a pickle-loving man cooks for a wife with a malfunctioning kidney, compromise becomes necessary.

Could a pickle taste good without salt? I decided to find out. I made a quart of cucumber pickles in a more or less standard way, but without the salt and with a few grape leaves added to firm the cucumbers. And I rather liked the result. If you're accustomed to a sodium-free diet, you probably won't miss the salt at all.

4 medium-size grape leaves

2 garlic cloves, chopped

8 whole black peppercorns

¼ teaspoon whole coriander seeds

1 quart (1 to 1¼ pounds) 3- to 4-inch pickling cucumbers,
blossom ends removed

1 dill head

1 dried hot pepper, such as japonés or de árbol, slit
lengthwise

1 cup cider vinegar

1 cup water

1 tablespoon sugar

1. Push two of the grape leaves to the bottom of a quart jar. Drop the garlic, peppercorns, and coriander into the jar, and then pack in the cucumbers, dill, and hot pepper.

2. Stir together the vinegar, water, and sugar. Pour the liquid over the cucumbers, covering them well and leaving about ¼ inch headspace. Fold the remaining grape leaves to fit in the top of the jar. Close the jar tightly with a nonreactive cap.

3. Refrigerate the jar for at least 2 weeks before eating the pickles. I found them best after about 4 months.

BREAD-AND-BUTTER ZUCCHINI

MAKES ABOUT 5 PINTS

 UCCHINI STANDS IN WELL for cucumbers in bread-and-butter pickles.

4 pounds zucchini, 1 inch in diameter, sliced into
$\frac{3}{16}$-inch rounds (about 2 quarts)
¾ pound small onions, sliced into thin rounds (about 2 cups)
¼ cup pickling salt
2¼ cups cider vinegar
1¼ cups sugar
1 tablespoon whole yellow mustard seeds
1 teaspoon whole celery seeds
1 teaspoon ground turmeric

1. Put the zucchini and onions into a bowl and toss the vegetables with the salt. Cover the vegetables with ice cubes from 2 ice trays. Let the vegetables stand at room temperature for 2 hours.

2. Drain the vegetables well. In a nonreactive pot, bring to a boil the vinegar, sugar, and spices. Add the vegetables and, over medium heat, slowly bring them to a boil, stirring frequently. Simmer them for 5 to 7 minutes, until the bright skin of the zucchini turns olive. Ladle the vegetables and liquid into pint mason jars, leaving ½ inch headspace. Close the jars with two-piece caps. In a boiling-water bath, process the jars for 10 minutes. Or pasteurize the jars for 30 minutes by immersing them in water heated to 180° to 185°F.

3. Store the cooled jars in a cool, dry, dark place for at least 3 weeks before eating the pickles. After opening a jar, store it in the refrigerator.

JARDINIÈRE

T HIS IS A GLORIOUS WAY to show off fresh garden produce that money can't buy—little cornichons, tiny pattypan squash, and real baby carrots. But you needn't stick with the vegetables here; alternative ingredients might include cauliflower florets, onion chunks, green beans in 2-inch lengths, zucchini cut into sticks or thick rounds, and celery pieces. You'll need 5 pints of prepared vegetables.

2 medium-size red bell peppers, cut into squares or strips
½ pound shallots
¼ pound carrots, cut into thin sticks
1¼ pounds 1- to 3-inch whole pickling cucumbers,
    blossom ends removed
½ pound whole 1-inch-wide pattypan squashes, or
    slightly larger ones, halved
5 large garlic cloves
1¼ teaspoons whole black peppercorns
20 whole allspice berries
5 tarragon sprigs
5 thyme sprigs
5 small fresh hot peppers, such as japonés (optional)
2¾ cups white wine vinegar
2 cups water
1 tablespoon pickling salt

1 Combine the prepared vegetables in a large bowl. Into each of 5 pint mason jars, put 1 garlic clove, ¼ teaspoon peppercorns, and 4 allspice berries. Fill each jar with vegetables, adding a tarragon sprig, a thyme sprig, and a hot pepper, if you like. Shake the jar to settle the vegetables.

2. In a nonreactive saucepan, bring to a boil the vinegar, water, and salt, stirring to dissolve the salt. Pour the hot liquid over the vegetables, leaving ½ inch headspace. Close the jars with two-piece caps. In a boiling-water bath, process the jars for 20 minutes.

3. Store the cooled jars in a cool, dry, dark place for at least 3 weeks before eating the pickles. After opening a jar, store it in the refrigerator.

GIARDINIERA

MAKES ABOUT 6 PINTS

THIS IS AN ITALIAN VERSION of *jardinière*, gardener's pickle. Again, you can vary the ingredients. You'll need a total of 3 quarts prepared vegetables.

½ pound pickling cucumbers, about ¾ inch in diameter,
    trimmed and sliced crosswise into ½-inch chunks
2 celery stalks, cut crosswise into ¾-inch pieces
5 teaspoons pickling salt
½ small cauliflower head, broken and cut into florets
1 large carrot, sliced into ³⁄₁₆-inch rounds
1 cup whole shallots or very small onions
½ pound long sweet peppers, seeded and cut into
    ¾-inch rings, or whole sweet cherry peppers,
    slit twice lengthwise
6 Mediterranean bay leaves
12 garlic cloves
1½ teaspoons whole black peppercorns
6 oregano sprigs
2¾ cups white wine vinegar
2½ cups water
6 tablespoons olive oil

1. Put the cut cucumbers and celery into a bowl, and toss them with 1 teaspoon salt. Let them stand at room temperature for 1 to 2 hours, then drain them well. Combine them in a large bowl with the remaining vegetables.

2. Into each of 6 pint jars, put 1 bay leaf, 2 garlic cloves, and ¼ teaspoon peppercorns. Pack the jars with the vegetables, add 1 oregano sprig to each jar, and shake the jars to settle the vegetables.

3. In a saucepan, bring to a boil the vinegar, water, and remaining 4 teaspoons salt, stirring to dissolve the salt. Pour the hot liquid over the vegetables, leaving just a bit more than ½ inch headspace. Top each jar with 1 tablespoon olive oil and seal the jar. Process the jars in a boiling-water bath for 20 minutes.

4. Store the cooled jars in a cool, dry, dark place for at least 3 weeks before eating the pickles. After opening a jar, store it in the refrigerator.

"There never was a more indefatigable preserver, pickler, curer, spicer, or canner than the Dutch housewife. Very little escapes her expert touch—and as a consequence she got in the habit centuries ago of loading every table with many 'sweet and sours.' To such an extent that over the centuries it became a fixed tradition of Dutch hospitality for her to put on the table (especially for 'company') precisely seven sweets and seven sours. The 'company' would often count them! Indeed would gaily demand them if missing."

—*J. George Frederick*, Pennsylvania Dutch Cook Book *(1935)*

ARMENIAN PICKLED MIXED VEGETABLES

MAKES 2 QUARTS

 ERE'S A BEAUTIFUL, hot-pink mixed pickle to put up in a big jar in the refrigerator.

2 quarts mixed vegetables, including any or all of the following:
   2- to 3-inch whole pickling cucumbers, blossom ends removed; sweet green peppers, cut into wide strips; small carrots, cut into thin 3- to 4-inch-long sticks; whole green cherry tomatoes; cauliflower florets; small radishes, halved or quartered if larger than 1 inch in diameter
1 small beet, peeled and sliced
2 large garlic cloves, sliced
8 cilantro sprigs
8 basil sprigs
8 tarragon sprigs
1 cup white wine vinegar
3 cups water
3 tablespoons pickling salt
6 whole black peppercorns
3 Mediterranean bay leaves
One 1-inch cinnamon stick

1 Pack the vegetables, including the beet, into a 2-quart jar, interspersing the herbs and half the garlic. Shake the jar to settle the vegetables. In a saucepan, bring the remaining ingredients, including the rest of the garlic slices, to a boil. Cover the vegetables well with the hot liquid, and seal the jar.

2 When the jar has cooled, store it in the refrigerator. The pickle will be ready after 1 month, and will keep for at least another month thereafter.

GINGERY SWEET PICKLED VEGETABLES

MAKES 2 QUARTS

I FIRST TASTED THIS Cantonese pickle in a commercial version that I bought in Seattle's International District. The pickle included stem ginger, in thick pieces so tender that you could eat them right along with the other vegetables. If you can get stem ginger, by all means use it in this recipe.

The children I know who have tasted this pickle love it as much as their parents do.

½ pound 2- to 3-inch pickling cucumbers, both ends trimmed, cut into 1-inch lengths
1 teaspoon pickling salt
½ cup thin slices fresh ginger
2 small dried hot peppers, such as japonés or de árbol
1½ cups rice vinegar
1½ cups water
1½ cups sugar
2 cups ⅛-inch-thick diagonal carrot slices
1 large sweet pepper, such as bell or pimiento, cut into 1-inch squares
¾ pound onions (1 large or 2 medium-size), cut into 1-inch chunks

1 Put the cucumbers into a bowl and toss them with ½ teaspoon salt. Let them stand at room temperature for 1 to 2 hours.

2 In a nonreactive pot, bring to a boil the ginger, hot peppers, vinegar, water, sugar, and remaining ½ teaspoon salt, stirring to dissolve the sugar and salt. Remove the pot from the heat and add the carrots. Let the mixture cool.

3. Drain the cucumbers, rinse them, and drain them again. Add them to the pot with the pepper and onion pieces. Mix well, then transfer the vegetables and liquid to a 2-quart jar. Close the jar with a nonreactive cap and store the jar in the refrigerator.

4. The pickles will be ready to eat after about 3 days. Refrigerated, they will keep for at least 2 months.

APPLE AND ONION PICKLE

MAKES ABOUT 3 CUPS

"What are they doing to those poor little vegetables?"

—Michelle, age 10, at the Oregon State Fair, 1998, on seeing jars of various pickles

I FOUND THIS RECIPE in an interesting old cookbook, Marion Harris Neil's *Canning, Preserving, and Pickling* (1914). The sweet, tart, and spicy apple and onion slices make a delightful relish for a holiday feast.

1 firm-fleshed apple (about ½ pound), peeled, cored, and thinly sliced

1 large sweet onion (about ¾ pound), thinly sliced

2 teaspoons slivered fresh ginger

One 3-inch cinnamon stick, broken into pieces

6 whole allspice berries, crushed

¼ teaspoon blade (unground) mace

1 generous pinch hot pepper flakes

About 1¾ cups cider vinegar

Choose a jar that will hold the apple and onion slices horizontally (I use a wide, 0.75-liter European canning jar). Alternate layers of apple and onion in the jar, distributing the aromatics among the layers. Cover the apple and onion well with cider vinegar and close the jar with a nonreactive cap. Store the jar in a cool, dark place. The pickle will be ready to eat in about 2 weeks and will keep well for several months. After opening the jar, store it in the refrigerator.

PICKLED ASPARAGUS

THIS LOVELY PICKLE has become so popular in recent years that you can find it in almost any supermarket. But you can save money by making your own, even if you don't have an asparagus patch.

I pickle asparagus in 12-ounce jelly jars, which are a little taller than pint jars—just right for the tender portion of an asparagus stalk.

Some people like to pack asparagus into jars with the tips down, so that the spears are easy to remove without breaking them, but others think that asparagus looks more attractive with the tips up. Pack your pickles either way, as you choose.

> 5 large garlic cloves, sliced
> 15 whole allspice berries
> 30 whole black peppercorns
> 20 whole coriander seeds
> 5 small pieces of mace or nutmeg
> ½ teaspoon hot pepper flakes (optional)
> About 3 pounds asparagus, trimmed to fit into
>   12-ounce jars
> 2½ cups white wine vinegar
> 2½ cups water
> 2½ teaspoons pickling salt
> 2 tablespoons sugar

1 Divide the garlic, allspice, peppercorns, coriander, mace or nutmeg, and hot pepper flakes (if you're using them) among five 12-ounce jelly jars. Pack the asparagus vertically in the jars, tips down or up.

2. In a nonreactive saucepan, bring to a boil the vinegar, water, salt, and sugar, stirring to dissolve the salt and sugar. Pour the hot liquid over the asparagus, leaving ½ inch headspace. Close the jars with two-piece caps. Process the jars for 10 minutes in a boiling-water bath, or pasteurize the jars for 30 minutes in water heated to 180° to 185°F.

3. Store the cooled jars in a cool, dry, dark place for at least 3 weeks before eating the asparagus. After opening a jar, store it in the refrigerator.

BASIC PICKLED BEETS

MAKES ABOUT 8 PINTS

FOR SOME FAMILIES I know, pickled beets are a must at every special dinner. This is a typical recipe, except that I use brown sugar for extra flavor, and cider vinegar instead of harsher-tasting distilled vinegar. Pickle very small beets whole, and slice larger ones.

7 pounds beets, with their rootlets and 2 inches of their tops, well scrubbed
Two 4-inch cinnamon sticks, broken into pieces
1 tablespoon whole allspice berries
1 teaspoon whole cloves
1 cup granulated sugar
1 cup firmly packed light brown sugar
2 teaspoons pickling salt
1 quart cider vinegar
2 cups water

1. Put the beets into a large pot and pour enough boiling water over them to cover them. Return the water to a boil and boil the beets for 15 to 35 minutes, depending on their size, until they are just tender.

2. Drain the beets and cover them with cold water. When they are cool, trim them and slip off their skins. If they are large, halve or quarter them—or, if you like, slice all the beets into ¼-inch-thick rounds.

3. Tie the spices in a spice bag or scrap of cheesecloth. Put this into a nonreactive pot with both sugars, salt, vinegar, and water. Bring the contents to a boil, stirring to dissolve the sugar. Reduce the heat and simmer the liquid, uncovered, for 10 minutes.

4. While the liquid simmers, pack the beets into pint or quart mason jars. Pour the hot liquid over the beets, leaving ½ inch headspace. Close the jars with two-piece caps. Process the jars for 30 minutes in a boiling-water bath.

5. Store the cooled jars in a cool, dry, dark place for at least 3 weeks before eating the beets. After opening a jar, store it in the refrigerator. When you finish a jar, consider saving the liquid for Eggs Pickled in Beet Juice (page 393).

PICKLED BEETS WITH RED WINE

MAKES 7 TO 8 PINTS

 THESE HAVE NONE OF THE HARSHNESS of typical pickled beets. Even people who usually scorn beets may love these.

6 pounds beets, with their rootlets and 2 inches of their tops,
    well scrubbed

1 teaspoon whole cloves

Two 4-inch cinnamon sticks, broken into pieces

One 1-inch piece fresh ginger, thinly sliced

3 cups sugar

2 cups red wine

3 cups red wine vinegar

1 tablespoon pickling salt

1. Put the beets into a large pot and pour enough boiling water over them to cover them. Return the water to a boil and boil the beets 15 to 35 minutes, depending on their size, until they are just tender.

2. Drain the beets and cover them with cold water. When they are cool, trim them and slip off their skins. If they are large, halve or quarter them—or, if you like, slice all the beets into ¼-inch-thick rounds.

3. Tie the cloves, cinnamon, and ginger in a spice bag or scrap of cheesecloth. Put this into a nonreactive pot with the sugar, wine, vinegar, and salt. Bring the contents to a boil, stirring to dissolve the sugar and salt. Simmer the syrup, uncovered, for 10 minutes.

4. While the syrup simmers, pack the beets into pint mason jars.

5. Remove the spice bag from the pan and pour the hot syrup over the beets, leaving ½ inch headspace. Close the jars with two-piece caps. Process the jars for 30 minutes in a boiling-water bath.

6. Store the cooled jars in a cool, dry, dark place for at least 3 weeks before eating the beets. After opening a jar, store it in the refrigerator.

PICKLED OKRA

O KRA ISN'T JUST FOR Southern gardeners; I've seen it thriving in a Boston community garden. But I've had little luck with this vegetable in my Oregon garden, where cucumber beetles ravage the plants. Shriveled, browning supermarket okra won't do. Fortunately, Asian markets sometimes carry beautiful fresh green okra pods, and they are just what you want for this pickle.

4 large garlic cloves, sliced

2 to 4 small dried or fresh hot peppers, such as
    japonés or de árbol

2 teaspoons whole dill seeds

2 quarts (about 2 pounds) fresh small okra pods,
    stems trimmed

1 quart cider vinegar

1 quart water

¼ cup pickling salt

1. Divide the garlic, hot peppers, and dill evenly among 4 pint mason jars. Pack the okra into the jars. In a saucepan, bring to a boil the vinegar, water, and salt, stirring to dissolve the salt. Ladle the hot liquid over the okra, leaving ¼ inch headspace. Close the jars with two-piece caps. Process the jars for 15 minutes in a boiling-water bath.

2. Store the cooled jars in a cool, dry, dark place for at least 3 weeks before eating the okra. After opening a jar, store it in the refrigerator.

PICKLED BROCCOLI

ALTHOUGH THIS PICKLE has Indian roots, it isn't heavily spiced. The seasonings enhance the flavor of the broccoli without disguising it.

1½ pounds broccoli florets and peeled, sliced stems
2 tablespoons chopped garlic
1 tablespoon coarsely grated fresh ginger
1 tablespoon whole dill seeds
1 tablespoon whole black mustard seeds
1 tablespoon vegetable oil
2½ cups white wine vinegar
2½ cups water
1 teaspoon pickling salt

1. In a large bowl, toss the broccoli with the garlic, ginger, dill, mustard seeds, and oil. Pack the mixture into a 2-quart jar.

2. Combine the vinegar and water, and stir the salt into the liquid until it dissolves. Pour the liquid over the broccoli. Cap the jar and store it in the refrigerator for 1 week before eating the broccoli. Refrigerated, the pickle will keep well for at least several weeks.

TARRAGON OR BASIL BEANS

MAKES 6 PINTS

I LIKE TO PICKLE slender little French filet beans—my favorite variety is Vernandon—or yellow Cherokee Wax beans. Sometimes I combine the two in a single jar.

For an interesting variation, suggests my friend Mary Ann Baclawski, try cilantro in place of the tarragon or basil.

6 garlic cloves, sliced
36 whole black peppercorns, crushed
3 pounds young, tender snap beans, trimmed, if needed,
   to 4 inches
6 tarragon sprigs or 12 basil sprigs
3½ cups white wine vinegar
3½ cups water
2 tablespoons pickling salt

1 Divide the garlic and peppercorns evenly among 6 pint mason jars. Pack the beans vertically into the jars, adding 1 tarragon sprig or 2 basil sprigs to each.

2 In a saucepan, bring to a boil the vinegar, water, and salt. Pour the hot liquid over the beans, leaving ½ inch headspace. Close the jars with two-piece caps. Process the jars for 5 minutes in a boiling-water bath, or pasteurize them for 30 minutes by immersing them in water heated to 180° to 185°F.

3 Store the cooled jars in a cool, dry, dark place for at least 3 weeks before eating the beans. After opening a jar, store it in the refrigerator.

ZYDECO BEANS

es haricots verts are here pickled with flavors of Louisiana—garlic, mustard, hot peppers, and of course salt *(ces haricots sont bien salés!)*. Omit one or both peppers if you don't like the heat. For traditional dilly beans, omit the mustard.

In New Orleans, I'm told, a Bloody Mary is often served with a pickled bean instead of a celery stick.

6 garlic cloves, sliced
6 teaspoons whole yellow mustard seeds
3 pounds young, tender filet beans, trimmed, if needed, to 4 inches
6 to 12 small fresh or dried hot peppers, such as japonés or de árbol
6 dill heads (optional)
3½ cups white wine vinegar
3½ cups water
2 tablespoons pickling salt

1. Into each of 6 pint jars, put 1 sliced garlic clove and 1 teaspoon mustard seeds. Pack the beans vertically into the jars. To each jar, add 1 or 2 hot peppers and, if you like, a dill head.

2. In a saucepan, bring to a boil the vinegar, water, and salt. Pour the hot liquid over the beans, leaving ½ inch headspace. Close the jars with two-piece caps. Process the jars for 5 minutes in a boiling-water bath, or pasteurize them for 30 minutes by immersing them in water heated to 180° to 185°F.

3. Store the cooled jars in a cool, dry, dark place for at least 3 weeks before eating the beans. After opening a jar, store it in the refrigerator.

CRISP PICKLED PUMPKIN OR SQUASH

MAKES 4 PINTS

T HIS MILDLY SWEET PICKLE may especially please people who like the flavor but not the mushy texture of cooked pumpkin or squash. The texture of the pumpkin remains firm and crisp, and the pumpkin flavor is enhanced but undisguised.

3½ pounds pumpkin or winter squash, peeled, seeded, and cut
  into ¾-inch cubes (about 9 cups)
2 tablespoons pickling salt
4 whole cloves
8 whole black peppercorns, crushed
1 Mediterranean bay leaf, crumbled
2 cups cider vinegar
1 cup sugar
4 thin slices fresh ginger, slivered
3 garlic cloves, chopped

1. In a bowl, toss the pumpkin or squash cubes with the salt. Let the cubes rest for 2 to 3 hours.

2. Drain the cubes, rinse them, and drain them again. Pack them into 4 pint mason jars.

3. Tie the cloves, peppercorns, and bay leaf in a spice bag or scrap of cheesecloth. In a saucepan, combine the spice bag with the vinegar, sugar, ginger, and garlic. Bring the mixture to a boil, stirring to dissolve the sugar. Reduce the heat, cover the pan, and simmer the liquid 10 minutes.

4. Remove the spice bag from the pan and pour the hot liquid over the pumpkin or squash cubes, leaving ½ inch headspace. Close the jars

with two-piece caps. Process the jars for 10 minutes in a boiling-water bath. Store the cooled jars in a cool, dry, dark place for at least 3 weeks before eating the pickle. After opening a jar, store it in the refrigerator.

PICKLED CAULIFLOWER

MAKES 4 PINTS

THIS IS A LOVELY PICKLE for an antipasti platter. The same recipe works well with Brussels sprouts.

For this recipe and the ones on pages 120 and 121, your pickle will look prettier if you avoid slicing through the florets. Cut through the cauliflower core lengthwise from the base, stopping before your knife reaches the florets. Break the head in half, and then break or cut off the florets. Divide each large floret just as you have divided the head, by cutting lengthwise from the base of the stem and then breaking apart the floret.

> 1 teaspoon whole cumin seeds
> 2 teaspoons whole coriander seeds
> 2 teaspoons whole fennel seeds
> 1 medium-size cauliflower head (1½ pounds), divided into
>   small florets (you should have 7 cups)
> 1 cup diced sweet, or mixed sweet and hot, red peppers
> 2 cups white wine vinegar
> 2 cups water
> 2 tablespoons pickling salt

1. Put ¼ teaspoon cumin and ½ teaspoon each of coriander and fennel into each of 4 pint mason jars. Toss the cauliflower and peppers together and pack the vegetables firmly into the jars (the brine will loosen the vegetables).

2. In a nonreactive saucepan, bring the vinegar, water, and salt to a boil. Pour the liquid over the cauliflower, leaving ½ inch headspace. Close the jars with two-piece caps and process the jars for 10 minutes in a boiling-water bath.

3. Store the cooled jars in a cool, dry, dark place for at least 3 weeks before eating the cauliflower. After opening a jar, store it in the refrigerator.

PICKLED PLUM TOMATOES

Besides cherry tomatoes, also good for pickling whole are meaty plum tomatoes, from green to ripe (but still firm). You may see jars of these pickled tomatoes in Russian markets, with dill, as in Pickled Green Cherry Tomatoes (opposite page), or with warmer spices such as cloves. Experiment with a quart or more of these larger tomatoes, multiplying the quantities of vinegar, water, and salt as needed and varying the spices to suit your taste.

PICKLED GREEN CHERRY TOMATOES

MAKES 1 PINT

T HESE CRUNCHY, SLIGHTLY BITTER pickled tomatoes have a taste that may grow on you. They will soften if processed with heat, so store them in the refrigerator.

For the best flavor, pick your tomatoes when they are barely beginning to redden.

1 to 2 dill sprigs
1 garlic clove, sliced
One ½-inch cube of horseradish, thinly sliced
¼ teaspoon whole yellow mustard seeds
½ teaspoon Mixed Pickling Spices (page 15)
1 small dried hot pepper, such as japonés or de árbol
1 pint (about 14 ounces) green cherry tomatoes
½ cup cider vinegar
½ cup water
½ teaspoon pickling salt

1. Put the aromatics into a sterilized pint jar. Fill the jar with the tomatoes. Combine the vinegar and water, and stir in the salt until it dissolves. Pour the liquid over the tomatoes, right to the brim of the jar. Close the jar tightly with a nonreactive cap (you can use a two-piece mason jar cap if you line it with two layers of plastic wrap).

2. Store the jar in the refrigerator. The tomatoes will be ready to eat in about 1 week, and will keep, refrigerated, for 2 months or longer.

PINK PICKLED CAULIFLOWER AND CABBAGE

MAKES 2 QUARTS.

I N THIS POPULAR Middle Eastern pickle, the cauliflower is tinted pink by the red cabbage. If you'd like to use white head cabbage instead, just add a few slices of raw or pickled beet to get the pink color.

1 small cauliflower head (1 to 1½ pounds),
   divided into small florets (page 117)
½ small red cabbage (about ¾ pound), cut in
   two directions to make 1-inch squares
1 to 2 small dried hot peppers, such as japonés or
   de árbol, slit lengthwise
1 teaspoon whole caraway seeds
1 Mediterranean bay leaf
2¼ cups white wine vinegar
2¼ cups water
2 tablespoons pickling salt

1. In a sterilized 2-quart jar, combine the cauliflower, cabbage, hot pepper(s), caraway seeds, and bay leaf. Combine the vinegar and water, and stir in the salt until it dissolves. Pour the liquid over the vegetables. Cap the jar and let it stand at room temperature for 10 days.

2. If you don't eat the pickle right away, refrigerate the jar. The pickle will keep well in the refrigerator for 4 to 6 weeks, after which time it may lose its crispness.

INDIAN-INSPIRED PICKLED CAULIFLOWER

T HIS STARTED AS AN INDIAN RECIPE, but I have increased the quantities of vinegar and water to avoid having to shake the jar daily, and I've included only a very little oil.

    1 medium-size cauliflower head (1 ¾ to 2 pounds), divided into
        small florets (page 117)
    2 fresh hot peppers, such as jalapeños, seeded and chopped
    6 to 8 garlic cloves, chopped
    1 teaspoon ground turmeric
    1 teaspoon whole cumin seeds
    One 2-inch piece fresh ginger, grated
    1 tablespoon vegetable oil
    2 teaspoons pickling salt
    2½ cups white wine vinegar
    2½ cups water

1 In a bowl, toss together the cauliflower, hot peppers, garlic, tur-
   meric, cumin, ginger, and oil. Pack the mixture into a 2-quart jar.
   Combine the vinegar and water, and stir in the salt until it dissolves.
   Pour the liquid over the cauliflower. Cap the jar.

2 Store the jar in the refrigerator for a week or more before eating the
   cauliflower. Refrigerated, the pickle will keep well for several
   weeks, at least.

PINK PICKLED TURNIPS

MAKES ABOUT 2 QUARTS

I NEVER LIKED TURNIPS until I tried this Middle Eastern pickle, which is now one of my favorites. In their pink brine, colored by the beet, the turnips are as pretty as they are delicious.

When I don't have a fresh beet on hand, I use a pickled one in this recipe.

2 pounds small turnips, peeled and quartered
Leafy tops of 2 to 3 celery stalks
4 garlic cloves
1 small beet, peeled and sliced
2 cups white wine vinegar
2 cups water
3 tablespoons pickling salt

1 Put the turnips, celery leaves, garlic, and beet into a sterilized 2-quart jar. Combine the vinegar and water, and stir in the salt until it dissolves. Cover the turnips with this liquid. Cap the jar and let it stand at room temperature for 10 days.

2 Eat the turnips right away, or refrigerate the jar. The pickle will keep well in the refrigerator for about 1 month.

SWEET PICKLED DAIKON

MAKES 1 PINT

THE STRONG, RATHER FOUL ODOR of this Japanese pickle makes it especially fun to serve to friends. It tastes much, much better than it smells.

The sun-drying is traditional and preserves the daikon longer, but I have skipped this step with good results.

> ¾ pound daikon, dried in the sun until limp (for 3 to 4 days)
> ¼ cup rice vinegar
> ½ cup water
> ½ cup sugar
> 1½ tablespoons pickling salt

1. Cut the daikon in half lengthwise, then slice it crosswise as thinly as you can. Put the daikon into a pint jar. In a saucepan, bring to a boil the remaining ingredients, stirring until the sugar and salt dissolve. Pour the hot syrup over the daikon and cap the jar. Let the jar cool.

2. Store the jar in the refrigerator for at least 3 days before eating the pickle. Refrigerated, it should keep for several weeks. Keep the jar tightly covered to keep the aroma from escaping.

PICKLED RADISH PODS

MAKES 1 PINT

WHEN YOUR RADISHES GROW tough or wormy, don't despair; you may get better use from the pods. This may be a little-known pickle today, but it was popular in 1824, when Mary

Randolph (*The Virginia Housewife*, 1824) offered a recipe. Even today, one radish variety, called rat tail, is grown just for its pods. For this pickle, I've used both rat tail pods and the pods of a French white radish whose roots were a disappointment.

Be sure to pick your pods before they toughen.

> 1 pint fully formed but still tender radish pods, stems trimmed to ¼ inch
> 1 small fresh hot pepper, such as serrano, cut into rings, or 1 dried hot pepper, such as japonés or de árbol, slit vertically
> 1 tarragon sprig
> 1 large garlic clove, sliced
> ½ cup cider vinegar
> ½ cup water
> 1 teaspoon pickling salt
> 1 tablespoon olive oil

1. Pack a pint jar with the radish pods, hot pepper, tarragon, and garlic. Stir together the vinegar, water, and salt, and pour the liquid over the pods, covering them well and leaving only about ⅛ inch headspace. Add the olive oil and cap the jar tightly with a nonreactive lid (you can use a two-piece mason jar cap if you line it with two layers of plastic wrap).

2. Store the jar in a cool, dry, dark place for at least 3 weeks before eating the pods. Tightly covered and refrigerated, or not, they should keep well for a year. After opening the jar, store it in the refrigerator.

PICKLED SNAP PEAS

MAKES 1 QUART

THE BEST WAY TO EAT snap peas is raw, right off the vine. This recipe ranks a close second, though. I pickle snap peas whenever I'm lucky enough to have a heavy crop, and continue to enjoy them for weeks after the pea vines have wilted away.

1¼ cups white wine vinegar
1¼ cups water
1 tablespoon pickling salt
1 tablespoon sugar
1 pound snap peas, stemmed and strung
4 garlic cloves, sliced
1 to 2 small dried hot peppers, such as japonés or de árbol,
   slit lengthwise
2 tarragon sprigs

1 In a nonreactive saucepan, bring to a boil the vinegar, water, salt, and sugar, stirring to dissolve the salt and sugar. Let the liquid cool.

2 Pack the peas into a quart jar along with the garlic, hot pepper(s), and tarragon. Pour the cooled liquid over the peas and close the jar with a nonreactive cap.

3 Store the jar in the refrigerator for at least 2 weeks before eating the peas. Refrigerated, they will keep for several months.

PICKLED PURSLANE

MAKES 1 PINT

EVEN IF YOU'VE NEVER HEARD the word *purslane*, you probably know this plant; it's a succulent, ground-hugging weed that seems to find a home in most vegetable gardens. In Italy, France, and other European countries, it's also a well-loved vegetable. Frankly, I don't much like the invasive form of purslane. Better, I think, are the upright, thick-stalked varieties whose seeds are available from catalogs. These purslanes are tart and crunchy, and they are said to be excellent sources of vitamin E and omega-3 fatty acids.

Popular in eighteenth-century England and America, pickled purslane deserves to come back in style. Don't discard the leaves—they're very good in salads.

About ½ pound purslane stalks, cut to fit vertically
    in a pint jar
1 dill head
1 small fresh or dried hot pepper, such as japonés or
    de árbol, split lengthwise (optional)
⅔ cup white wine vinegar
⅔ cup water
1½ teaspoons pickling salt
1 garlic clove, sliced
4 whole black peppercorns

1. Pack the purslane stalks vertically in a pint jar, slipping the dill head and hot pepper (if you're using it) down the side. In a saucepan, combine the vinegar, water, salt, garlic, and peppercorns. Bring the contents to a boil, stirring to dissolve the salt, then pour the hot liquid over the purslane. Close the jar with a nonreactive cap.

2 Store the cooled jar in the refrigerator. The purslane will be ready to eat in 1 week and will keep, refrigerated, for at least several months.

LIMED GREEN TOMATO PICKLE

MAKES ABOUT 6 PINTS

WHEN FROST THREATENS and you rush to the garden to rescue the last of the tomatoes, take the yellowish and pink ones to ripen indoors, but don't leave behind the very green ones. They are the ones you want for this pickle.

This is a Southern-style green tomato pickle: The tomato slices are treated with lime so they stay very crisp. They are also sweet—but not too sweet, since I've called for less sugar than is traditional. This pickle complements baked beans, burgers, pork chops, and roasts.

4 pounds fleshy green tomatoes (such as paste types)
½ cup pickling lime (page 17)
2 quarts water
1 quart cider vinegar
1 cup firmly packed light brown sugar
1 cup granulated sugar
1½ tablespoons pickling salt
2 teaspoons whole yellow mustard seeds
1 teaspoon whole allspice berries
1 teaspoon whole cloves
One 1-inch cinnamon stick, broken into pieces
¾ pound onions, sliced into rounds (about 2 cups)

1. Cut the tomatoes crosswise into ¼-inch slices, discarding a narrow slice from each end. In a large bowl, stir the pickling lime into the water, and add the tomatoes. Let them soak in the limewater at room temperature for 12 to 24 hours.

2. Drain the tomatoes, rinse them, and cover them with cold water. Let them soak for 1 hour, then drain, rinse, and soak them for 1 hour more. Repeat this process a third time, then drain the tomatoes.

3. In a large nonreactive pot, combine the vinegar, both sugars, salt, and mustard seeds. Tie the other spices in a spice bag or scrap of cheesecloth, and add this to the pot. Bring the mixture to a boil, stirring to dissolve the sugars and salt. Add the tomatoes and onions. Bring the contents to a boil, then reduce the heat. Let the pickle simmer for 15 minutes, while you occasionally stir the vegetables and push them under the liquid.

4. Remove the spice bag, then ladle the vegetables and pickling liquid into pint mason jars, leaving ½ inch headspace. Close the jars with two-piece caps, and process the jars for 10 minutes in a boiling-water bath.

5. Store the cooled jars in a cool, dry, dark place for at least 3 weeks before eating the tomatoes. After opening a jar, store it in the refrigerator.

"So I merely slammed the door behind me and went down and made some green-tomato pickle. Somebody had to do it."

—*Eudora Welty, "Why I Live at the P.O."*

CURRIED GREEN TOMATO PICKLE

MAKES ABOUT 3 PINTS

THIS GREEN TOMATO PICKLE, with its unusual spices, is one of my favorites. According to an old Mennonite cookbook, the recipe is French in origin.

2½ pounds fleshy green tomatoes, such as paste types, sliced
 3/16 inch thick (about 2 quarts tomato slices)
1 medium-size onion, thinly sliced
2 tablespoons pickling salt
2 cups cider vinegar
½ cup firmly packed light brown sugar
1 ½ teaspoons curry powder
1 teaspoon ground turmeric
½ teaspoon dry mustard
½ teaspoon ground cinnamon
½ teaspoon ground ginger
½ teaspoon ground allspice

1. Combine the green tomatoes and onion in a large bowl or a crock. Add the salt and mix gently. Let the mixture stand at room temperature for 8 to 12 hours.

2. Drain the vegetables, rinse them, and drain them again. In a large nonreactive pot, combine the vinegar, sugar, and spices. Bring the mixture to a boil and add the vegetables. Bring the contents to a boil again, then reduce the heat. Simmer the vegetables gently, stirring occasionally, about 3 minutes, or until the vegetables are just heated through. Pack the mixture into pint mason jars, leaving ½ inch headspace, and close the jars with two-piece caps. Process the jars for 10 minutes in a boiling-water bath.

3. Store the cooled jars in a cool, dry, dark place for at least 3 weeks before eating the pickle. After opening a jar, store it in the refrigerator.

SOUR GRAPES

MORE TART THAN SWEET, this pickle is more like cornichons than like the fruit pickles in Chapter 6. If you grow your own table grapes, put some up this way for gifts; they'll look beautiful in their jars, ornamented by tarragon sprigs. This recipe is based on one created by Helen Witty (*Fancy Pantry*, 1986).

Serve the pickled grapes with pâté or cold meat, or cut them in half and add them to salads.

3½ cups red and/or green seedless grapes
   (such as Flame, Thompson, or Canadice),
   stemmed, rinsed, drained, and patted dry
4 tarragon sprigs
3 tablespoons sugar
1½ teaspoons pickling salt
1¾ cups white wine vinegar, or more if needed

1 Pack the grapes into a quart jar, slipping the tarragon sprigs in along the side. Stir the sugar and salt into the vinegar until the sugar and salt dissolve, then pour this liquid over the grapes. If the grapes are not well covered, add a little more vinegar. Close the jar with a non-reactive cap and store the jar in a cool, dry, dark place.

2 The grapes will be ready to eat in about 1 month and will keep for 1 year or more. After opening the jar, store it in the refrigerator.

PICKLED JERUSALEM ARTICHOKES

MAKES 2 PINTS

THIS IS A FAVORITE SOUTHERN PICKLE. Native to North America, the Jerusalem artichoke plant is a perennial sunflower grown for its edible tubers. (The Italian word for sunflower, *girasole*, sounded like "Jerusalem" to English speakers.) It was once hoped that these tubers would prove as useful as potatoes, and many people still eat Jerusalem artichokes cooked and mashed. But they were found difficult to digest and so came to be used mainly as hog feed.

Today, under the new name "sunchokes," Jerusalem artichokes are regaining some popularity. They are pleasant to eat, for their crunchy texture if not their bland flavor, and they should produce no uncomfortable aftereffects if eaten in modest quantities. So don't let the hogs have them all—pickle a couple of jars for yourself.

1½ pounds Jerusalem artichokes, scrubbed and
    sliced ¼ inch thick
¼ cup plus 1 teaspoon pickling salt
1 quart water
4 thin slices fresh ginger
2 large garlic cloves, sliced
2 small dried hot peppers, such as japonés or de árbol
½ teaspoon whole coriander seeds
1 teaspoon whole cumin seeds
2 cups cider vinegar
3 tablespoons light brown sugar

1. Put the artichokes into a bowl. Stir ¼ cup salt into 1 quart water until the salt dissolves, and pour the brine over the artichokes. Let them stand at room temperature for 12 to 18 hours.

2. Drain the artichokes, rinse them, and drain them again.

3. Divide the ginger, garlic, hot peppers, coriander, and cumin evenly between 2 pint mason jars. Add the artichokes. In a saucepan, bring to a boil the vinegar, the sugar, and the remaining 1 teaspoon salt. Pour the hot liquid over the artichokes, leaving ½ inch headspace. Close the jars with two-piece caps. Process the jars for 15 minutes in a boiling-water bath.

4. Store the cooled jars in a cool, dry, dark place for at least 3 weeks before eating the artichokes. After opening a jar, store it in the refrigerator.

PICKLED WALNUTS

MAKES ABOUT 2 QUARTS

VERY POPULAR ON BOTH SIDES of the Atlantic in the nineteenth century, this strange-sounding pickle is still widely enjoyed in England today. This is the basic method: You pick unripe English (or Persian) walnuts—not black walnuts—between late June and mid-July, before they have formed a hard shell. Soak the walnuts in brine for several days, let them blacken in the sun, and then cover them with spiced vinegar. My recipe is based on that of Mary Randolph (*The Virginia Housewife*, 1824).

In England, pickled walnuts are eaten with brown bread, cold cuts, and ale and added to salads and stews.

> 2 pounds green English walnuts, in their husks
> 6 tablespoons pickling salt
> 2 tablespoons whole black peppercorns
> 1 tablespoon whole allspice berries
> ½ teaspoon whole cloves
> 1 teaspoon whole yellow mustard seeds
> 2 garlic cloves, sliced
> 4 thin slices fresh ginger
> 4 to 5½ cups white wine vinegar or cider vinegar

1. Pierce each nut about six times with a large needle and put the nuts into a 2-quart jar. Dissolve 2 tablespoons of the salt in 1 quart boiling water and pour the water over the nuts. Cover the jar and leave it at room temperature for 3 days.

2. Drain off the water. Dissolve another 2 tablespoons salt in 1 quart boiling water, and pour this over the nuts. Repeat the process 3 days later.

3. Nine days after first putting the nuts in the jar, drain them and leave them in a colander in the sun for 2 to 3 days to blacken. Turn them occasionally.

4. Pack the nuts and spices into a sterilized 2-quart jar (or divide them among smaller jars). Cover the nuts well with the vinegar. Close the jar tightly with a nonreactive cap and store the jar in a cool, dry, dark place.

5. The pickled walnuts will be ready to eat in 3 months, and they should keep well for about 1 year. After opening the jar, store it in the refrigerator.

PICKLED ROASTED PEPPERS

MAKES 3 PINTS

T HIS IS MY FAVORITE WAY to preserve ripe pimiento peppers, which I highly recommend for this recipe. Their skins and seeds are easy to remove, and, with their attractive heart shape, they will often lie flat in a wide-mouth canning jar.

To roast and peel peppers, put them under a broiler, on a screen or fork over a gas flame, or in a pan in an oven heated to 500°F. Turning the peppers frequently, let them blacken. As soon as their skins are charred and blistered over most of the surface, remove the peppers from the heat and lay a damp cloth over them. When they have cooled, their skins will come off easily. Pull or cut out their stems and use a spoon to scrape out their seeds.

These peppers are delicious in sandwiches and they will keep their appeal in a make-ahead lunch. They also make a delicious instant salad: Slice them in halves, quarters, or narrow strips, dribble them with olive oil, and, if you like, sprinkle them with chopped anchovy.

> 2¼ cups white wine vinegar or distilled white vinegar
> 1 tablespoon sugar
> 1 tablespoon pickling salt
> 3 garlic cloves
> 4 pounds pimiento, bell, or Anaheim peppers
>   (red, yellow, green, or a of mix of colors),
>   roasted, peeled, cored, and seeded

1 Combine the vinegar, sugar, and salt in a nonreactive saucepan and bring the mixture to a boil. Remove the pan from the heat.

2 Put a garlic clove into each of 3 pint mason jars. Pack the peppers loosely in the jars. Pour the hot liquid over the peppers, leaving ½ inch headspace. Run a narrow spatula around the inside edge of each jar to release any bubbles, and then add a little more of the liquid if needed. Close the jars with two-piece caps. Process the jars for 10 minutes in a boiling-water bath, or immerse them for 30 minutes in water heated to 180° to 185°F.

3 Store the cooled jars in a cool, dry, dark place for at least 3 weeks before eating the peppers. After opening a jar, store it in the refrigerator.

MARINATED SWEET PEPPERS

MAKES 3 PINTS

IN THIS RECIPE the peppers are softened by blanching, not roasting, so no peeling is necessary. The pickling liquid makes a good salad dressing.

> 2¼ pounds pimiento or bell peppers
>   (green, red, yellow, or a mix of colors)
> 3 small garlic cloves
> 3 thyme, marjoram, or oregano sprigs
> 1 cup white wine vinegar, or more if needed
> 1½ teaspoons pickling salt
> 1 cup olive oil

1 Put the peppers into a large bowl and cover them with boiling water. Let them stand for 3 minutes or until they are flexible.

2 Drain the peppers and cover them with ice water. When they have thoroughly cooled, drain them well. Put a garlic clove and an herb

sprig into each of 3 pint mason jars. If the peppers are very long, cut them in half. Pack the peppers into the jars.

(3) In a nonreactive saucepan, heat the vinegar and salt. As soon as the liquid comes to a boil, add the olive oil. Bring the contents to a boil again. Immediately pour the hot mixture over the peppers, leaving ½ inch headspace. The liquid should just cover the peppers; if it doesn't, add a little more vinegar. Close the jars with two-piece caps. Process the jars for 10 minutes in a boiling-water bath, or immerse them for 30 minutes in water heated to 180° to 185°F.

(4) Store the cooled jars in a cool, dry, dark place for at least 3 weeks before eating the peppers. After opening a jar, store it in the refrigerator.

SHORT-BRINED PICKLED PEPPERS

MAKES 6 PINTS

B RINING PEPPERS BEFORE PICKLING them in vinegar intensifies their flavor. Use this recipe to pickle whole small peppers to serve as appetizers, or large peppers, cut into pieces, to use in stews, salsas, pasta sauces, and so on. The peppers can be green or ripe, sweet or hot.

4 pounds peppers, slit twice if you're using them whole, or
　　cored, seeded, and halved or quartered
1¼ cups pickling salt
1 gallon plus 1½ cups water
2 tablespoons sugar
2 garlic cloves, chopped
1 tablespoon coarsely grated horseradish
5½ cups white wine vinegar or distilled white vinegar

1. In a large bowl, crock, or nonreactive pot, stir the salt into 1 gallon water until the salt dissolves. Add the peppers and weight them with a heavy plate. Let them stand in the brine at room temperature for 12 to 18 hours.

2. Drain the peppers, rinse them, and drain them again. In a saucepan, combine the sugar, garlic, horseradish, vinegar, and remaining 1½ cups water. Bring the contents to a boil, then cover the pan and reduce the heat. Simmer the liquid, covered, for 10 minutes.

3. Pack the peppers into pint mason jars. Pour the hot liquid over the peppers, leaving ½ inch headspace. Close the jars with two-piece caps. Process the jars for 10 minutes in a boiling-water bath, or immerse them for 30 minutes in water heated to 180° to 185°F.

4. Store the cooled jars in a cool, dry, dark place for at least 3 weeks before eating the peppers. After opening a jar, store it in the refrigerator.

PICKLED SWEET GREEN PEPPER STRIPS

MAKES 4 PINTS

THESE SWEET, SOUR, CRUNCHY STRIPS are a wonderful addition to salads or accompaniment for dips such as hummus and baba ghanoush.

4 thin slices fresh ginger

4 small garlic cloves

2 teaspoons pickling salt

2 pounds green bell or pimiento peppers, cut into ½-inch lengthwise strips

2 cups white wine vinegar or distilled white vinegar

2 cups water

1¼ cups sugar

1. Divide the ginger, garlic, and salt evenly among 4 pint mason jars. Pack the pepper strips snugly into the jars.

2. In a saucepan, combine the vinegar, water, and sugar. Bring the contents to a boil, stirring to dissolve the sugar, then reduce the heat and cover the pan. Simmer the liquid, covered, for 5 minutes.

3. Pour the hot liquid over the pepper strips, leaving ½ inch headspace, and close the jars with two-piece caps. Process the jars for 10 minutes in a boiling-water bath, or immerse them for 30 minutes in water heated to 180° to 185°F.

4. Store the cooled jars in a cool, dry, dark place for at least 3 weeks before eating the peppers. After opening a jar, store it in the refrigerator.

REFRIGERATOR PICKLED PEPPERS

MAKES 2 QUARTS

 FLAVORED WITH FENNEL, celery, and bay leaf, this is a delightfully unusual pepper pickle.

2 pounds bell or pimiento peppers, preferably of mixed colors,
    cut into strips or 1- to 1½-inch squares
1 large celery stalk with leaves, chopped
3 garlic cloves, chopped
1 tablespoon whole fennel seeds
1 Mediterranean bay leaf
3 cups water
1½ cups white wine vinegar
2½ tablespoons pickling salt

1. In a large bowl, toss the peppers with the celery, garlic, and fennel. Pack the vegetables and seeds with the bay leaf into a 2-quart jar.

2. Combine the water and vinegar, and dissolve the salt in the liquid. Pour the brine over the vegetables. Close the jar with a nonreactive cap and refrigerate the jar.

3. The peppers will be ready in about 8 days. Refrigerated, they will keep well for 6 to 8 weeks.

PEPPER "MANGOES"

MAKES 2 QUARTS

"MANGOES"—not the tropical fruit but any fruit or vegetable stuffed with cabbage or seasonings and then pickled in vinegar—were popular throughout the United States and England in the nineteenth century. These pickles were most often made with melons—small, thin-skinned, white-fleshed melons that were pickled green, and so were more like plump cucumbers than like the muskmelons, honeydews, and casabas we know today. Although melons of the mango type are still popular in places such as Asia and Italy, even their seeds are hard to come by in the United States. Also delicious, however, are pepper mangoes, or pickled cabbage-stuffed peppers, and these are easy to make with modern produce.

To make a pepper mango, some nineteenth-century cooks cored and stuffed the pepper through a slit in the side, leaving the stem end intact. Others cut off the stem end like a jack-o'-lantern top, then fastened it back on with toothpicks after stuffing the pepper. My technique is easier: Just cut out the stem and core, stuff the pepper, and leave the opening alone.

These pickles make a pretty accompaniment to a winter meal.

12 small green bell or pimiento peppers, cored and seeded

1 cup plus 1 teaspoon pickling salt

1 gallon plus 2 cups water

1½ pounds white or green head cabbage (about 1 small head), shredded

2 tablespoons minced garlic

2 tablespoons minced dill sprigs

2 teaspoons whole yellow mustard seeds

2 small dried hot peppers, such as japonés or de árbol

2 small Mediterranean bay leaves

2 cups cider vinegar

1. Put the peppers into a large bowl, crock, or nonreactive pot. Dissolve 1 cup of the salt in 1 gallon of the water and pour the brine over the peppers. Weight the peppers with a plate. Let them stand at room temperature for 24 hours.

2. Drain the peppers, rinse them, and drain them again thoroughly. In a large bowl, mix the cabbage with the remaining 1 teaspoon salt, garlic, dill, and mustard seeds. Stuff this mixture into the peppers.

3. Pack the stuffed peppers into a sterilized 2-quart jar, tucking the hot peppers and bay leaves around them. Combine the vinegar and remaining 2 cups water. Cover the peppers well by 1 inch or more with the liquid and close the jar tightly with a nonreactive cap.

4. Store the jar in the refrigerator. The mangoes will be ready to eat in about 1 week and will keep well for a few months.

HONEYED JALAPEÑO RINGS

MAKES 8 HALF-PINTS

I LOVE JALAPEÑO PEPPERS because they're meaty and usually mild—mild, that is, compared with really hot peppers, such as serrano, cayenne, and, especially, habanero. (For the appearance and taste of jalapeños with scarcely any heat, try the hybrid Señorita pepper.) You can use this pickle as a table condiment, to spoon right into your tacos or black bean soup.

This pickle will be particularly appealing if you mix green and red jalapeños. Remember, though, that jalapeños get soft and mushy if left on the plant after ripening; pick the red ones when they're still quite firm.

You can seed the peppers or not, as you wish. After I cut the peppers into rings, I take out most of the seeds with the help of a grapefruit spoon (a pointed teaspoon with serrated sides). Then I put the rings into a colander and rinse off the seeds still clinging to the peppers.

Be sure to wear rubber gloves while you're handling jalapeños.

24 whole black peppercorns
8 small garlic cloves, sliced
2 tablespoons Mixed Pickling Spices (page 15)
1 quart cider vinegar
2 tablespoons honey
2 teaspoons pickling salt
2¼ pounds jalapeño peppers, cut into
⅜₁₆-inch rings and, if you like, seeded
4 tablespoons olive oil

1 Divide the peppercorns and garlic evenly among 8 half-pint mason jars.

2 Tie the spices in a spice bag or scrap of cheesecloth and put it into a saucepan with the vinegar, honey, and salt. Bring the contents to a boil. Add the pepper rings, and bring the contents back to a simmer.

3 Divide the peppers among the jars, and pour the hot liquid over them, leaving a little more than ½ inch headspace. Discard the spice bag. Pour about 1½ teaspoons olive oil into each jar and close the jars with two-piece caps. Process the jars for 10 minutes in a boiling-water bath, or immerse them for 30 minutes in water heated to 180° to 185°F.

4 Store the cooled jars in a cool, dry, dark place for at least 3 weeks before eating the peppers. After opening a jar, store it in the refrigerator.

PICKLED WHOLE HOT PEPPERS

MAKES 4 PINTS

FOR THIS PICKLE I LIKE to use Cascabella peppers, in their glorious colors of yellow, orange, and red. But you can use any small hot fleshy pepper, such as Floral Gem (a similar wax-type pepper), jalapeño, or hot cherry. Give a jar of these pickled peppers to some chile-head friends and stick around to watch them expire.

8 small garlic cloves
8 whole allspice berries
16 whole black peppercorns
2 small Mediterranean bay leaves, torn in half
2 pounds small, fleshy fresh hot peppers,
	such as Cascabella, each slit twice lengthwise,
	stems trimmed to about ¼ inch

2 cups cider vinegar, white wine vinegar, or
   distilled white vinegar
2 cups water
4 teaspoons pickling salt
¼ cup olive oil

1 Divide the garlic, allspice, peppercorns, and pieces of bay leaf among 4 pint mason jars. Add the hot peppers.

2 In a nonreactive saucepan, bring to a boil the vinegar, water, and salt. Pour the hot liquid over the peppers, leaving slightly more than ½ inch headspace, and then pour 1 tablespoon olive oil into each jar. Close the jars with two-piece caps (make sure the rims are free of oil, which could prevent a good seal). Process the jars for 10 minutes in a boiling-water bath, or immerse them for 30 minutes in water heated to 180° to 185°F.

3 Store the cooled jars in a cool, dry, dark place for at least 3 weeks before eating the peppers. After opening a jar, store it in the refrigerator.

PEPERONCINI

MAKES 4 PINTS

THIS RECIPE IS MUCH LIKE the preceding one, except that here I simplify the seasonings and use thin, straight, mild-flavored, yellow-green peppers that are just long enough to fit into a pint mason jar. You may have seen them pickled in jars in gourmet shops. Since these peppers may be labeled simply *peperoncini* in seed catalogs, you need to look at the picture and read the description to be sure you're getting the variety you want. Japanese *fushimi* peppers and some Spanish *guindilla* varieties make good substitutes.

8 small garlic cloves

2 small Mediterranean bay leaves, torn in half

2 pounds straight green *peperoncini*, each slit once lengthwise,
stems trimmed to about ¼ inch

2 cups cider vinegar, white wine vinegar, or distilled white
vinegar

2 cups water

4 teaspoons pickling salt

¼ cup olive oil

1. Divide the garlic and pieces of bay leaf evenly among 4 pint jars. Pack the peppers vertically in the jars.

2. In a nonreactive saucepan, bring the vinegar, water, and salt to a boil. Pour the hot liquid over the peppers, leaving slightly more than ½ inch headspace, and then pour 1 tablespoon olive oil into each jar. Close the jars with two-piece caps (make sure the rims are free of oil, which could prevent a good seal). Process the jars for 10 minutes in a boiling-water bath, or immerse them for 30 minutes in water heated to 180° to 185°F.

3. Store the cooled jars in a cool, dry, dark place for at least 3 weeks before eating the peppers. After opening a jar, store it in the refrigerator.

PICKLED TOMATILLOS

MAKES 1 QUART

MANY GARDENERS HAVE A LOVE-HATE relationship with tomatillos. These fruits are lovable in that they're easy to grow; you plant them once, and they come up on their own year after year. But a plant that acts like a weed is no joy to a vegetable gardener unless the fruits get eaten, and most gardeners can't think what to do with tomatillos besides turning them into salsa. And how much salsa can you eat?

Here's another great use for tomatillos: Have these pickles with grilled meat or fish, or with tacos or tostadas and beans. Once you try them, you may eat them up faster than salsa.

1 pound husked green tomatillos, halved if small, quartered
 if large
2 sweet or mild peppers, such as bell, pimiento, or Anaheim,
 cut into strips or 1-inch squares
2 or 3 jalapeño peppers, seeded and sliced into rings
3 large garlic cloves, sliced
3 oregano sprigs
1 cup white wine vinegar
1 cup water
2 teaspoons pickling salt
1 teaspoon sugar
½ teaspoon whole cumin seeds

1 In a quart jar, combine the tomatillos, peppers, garlic, and oregano. Bring the remaining ingredients to a boil in a saucepan, and pour the hot liquid over the vegetables. Let the contents cool.

2 Close the jar with a nonreactive cap. Refrigerate the jar for about 1 week before eating the pickles. They will keep, refrigerated, for at least 2 months.

ENGLISH PUB–STYLE PICKLED ONIONS

MAKES 1 QUART

THIS PICKLE is made the traditional way, with a short-brining step to keep the onions crisp, and with cool rather than hot vinegar. If you'd like to can the onions, though, use 2 pint or 4 half-pint mason jars instead of a quart jar, and pour the spiced vinegar over the onions while the vinegar is hot. Close the jars immediately with two-piece caps, and process the jars in a boiling-water bath for 10 minutes.

Sharp-tasting, brown malt vinegar is available at some supermarkets. If you can't find it, or if you'd like a milder pickle, use white wine vinegar.

½ cup pickling salt
2 quarts water
1½ pounds very small onions or shallots, unpeeled
2 tablespoons light brown sugar
2 cups malt vinegar
1 teaspoon whole black peppercorns
¼ teaspoon whole allspice berries
¼ teaspoon hot pepper flakes
1 Mediterranean bay leaf, crumbled

1 In a bowl, dissolve ¼ cup salt in 1 quart water. Add the onions. Weight them gently with a plate that fits inside the bowl. Let them stand at room temperature for 8 to 12 hours.

2 Drain the onions and peel them. Return them to the bowl. Make a brine with the remaining salt and water, pour it over the onions, and weight them gently again. Let them stand at room temperature for 2 days.

3 In a saucepan, bring the sugar and vinegar to a boil. Let the liquid cool.

4. Drain the onions, rinse them, and drain them well again. In a sterilized quart jar, layer them with the peppercorns, allspice, hot pepper flakes, and bay. Cover them with the cooled, sweetened vinegar. Close the jar with a nonreactive cap and refrigerate the jar for at least 1 month before eating the onions.

5. Refrigerated, the onions should keep for at least 6 months.

PICKLED MUSHROOMS IN OLIVE OIL

MAKES 4 HALF-PINTS

THIS MAY SEEM a very extravagant recipe, since the pickling liquid is discarded before the mushrooms are put into jars, and a great deal of precious olive oil is then required to cover the mushrooms. But the marinated mushrooms are really delicious. Besides, you can use the vinegar solution for making a quick pickle, and the olive oil for dressing salads or for sautéing. This recipe is based on one developed by Dr. George York, a microbiologist at the University of California, Davis.

½ cup lemon juice
1 quart plus 1 cup water
1½ pounds (about 6 cups) small button mushrooms
2 garlic cloves, sliced
4 thyme sprigs
4 marjoram sprigs
1 cup white wine vinegar
1½ teaspoons pickling salt
2 Mediterranean bay leaves, torn in half
About 1¾ cups olive oil

1. In a large saucepan, combine the lemon juice and 1 quart water. Add the mushrooms, garlic, and herbs. Bring the ingredients to a boil, reduce the heat, and simmer them for 5 minutes.

2. Drain the mushrooms and put them into a bowl. Combine the vinegar, the remaining 1 cup water, and the salt. Pour the liquid over the mushrooms and let them stand at room temperature for 10 to 12 hours.

3. Drain the mushrooms (you can save the liquid for a quick pickle). Pack them into half-pint jars, dividing the herb sprigs and bay leaves among the jars. Cover the mushrooms with olive oil, leaving ½ inch headspace. Close the jars with two-piece caps (make sure the rims are free of oil, which could prevent a good seal). Process the jars for 20 minutes in a boiling-water bath.

4. Store the cooled jars in a cool, dry, dark place for at least 1 week before eating the mushrooms. After opening a jar, store it in the refrigerator.

PICKLED MUSHROOMS WITH GINGER AND RED WINE

MAKES ABOUT 1 PINT

FRESH GINGER gives these mushrooms an unexpected, delightful flavor. They make an appealing side dish for lamb or game.

1 pound small button mushrooms
2 teaspoons pickling salt
6 tablespoons red wine vinegar
⅔ cup red wine
½ teaspoon sugar

4 whole cloves

8 whole black peppercorns

One 1-inch piece fresh ginger, thinly sliced

1 Mediterranean bay leaf

1. Toss the mushrooms with the salt. Put them into a flat-bottomed dish and cover the dish with plastic wrap. Let the mushrooms stand at room temperature for 8 to 12 hours.

2. Put the mushrooms and their juice into a nonreactive pan. Cook them over medium heat until all the juice has evaporated, 8 to 10 minutes. Add the remaining ingredients. Simmer the mixture for 5 minutes. Remove the pan from the heat and let the mushrooms cool.

3. Pack the mushrooms into a 2- to 3-cup jar. Pour the liquid over the mushrooms. Cap the jar and refrigerate it for at least 2 days before eating the mushrooms.

4. The mushrooms should keep for about 2 months in the refrigerator.

HERBED MARINATED MUSHROOMS

MAKES 1 PINT

SHIITAKES INTENSIFY THE MUSHROOM FLAVOR of this pickle. I use dried shiitakes, which are quite inexpensive in Chinese markets, rather than the high-priced fresh ones sold in supermarkets.

Neither too sour nor too salty, this pickle makes a fine antipasto to serve along with cheese and pickled peppers.

12 dried shiitake mushrooms

½ cup olive oil

1 pound small button mushrooms

2 garlic cloves, sliced

2 shallots, minced

¼ cup balsamic vinegar

Leaves from 2 thyme sprigs, or ½ teaspoon dried thyme

3 fresh sage leaves, chopped, or ½ teaspoon dried sage

4 teaspoons chopped fresh parsley

1 Mediterranean bay leaf, crumbled

½ teaspoon pickling salt

1. Put the shiitake mushrooms into a bowl and pour boiling water over them. Let them soak for 5 minutes and then drain them (save the liquid to add to soup).

2. In a skillet, heat 2 tablespoons of the olive oil. Add the shiitake and button mushrooms and sauté them until the mushrooms are tender, about 15 minutes. Transfer the mushrooms to a bowl.

3. In a small nonreactive saucepan, simmer the garlic, shallots, and vinegar. Add the herbs, bay, salt, and remaining 6 tablespoons olive oil, and heat the mixture briefly. Pour the mixture over the mushrooms and toss them.

4. Pack the mushrooms and their liquid into a pint jar. Cap the jar and let it cool. Store the mushrooms in the refrigerator for about a week before eating them. Bring the jar to room temperature before serving the mushrooms.

5. Refrigerated, they should keep for several weeks, at least.

POLISH PICKLED MUSHROOMS

MAKES 1 PINT

THIS MUSHROOM PICKLE, my favorite, is also the least trouble to make. I fell in love with the recipe after trying it with some fried-chicken mushrooms (*Lyophyllum decastes*) that I found growing near the house one day. If you can't find fried-chicken mushrooms or identify them with certainty, use button or any other firm-fleshed edible mushrooms.

This spicy pickle would be very good with game.

    1 pound mushrooms
    ½ cup chopped onion
    2 Mediterranean bay leaves
    2 teaspoons whole black peppercorns
    1 teaspoon whole allspice berries
    2 teaspoons pickling salt
    ½ cup water
    ¼ cup white wine vinegar

1 Combine all of the ingredients in a nonreactive saucepan. Bring them to a boil, reduce the heat, and simmer them for 15 minutes.

2 Put the mushrooms and their liquid into a pint jar. Let the jar cool, then cap it. Store the jar in the refrigerator for several days before eating the mushrooms.

3 Refrigerated, the mushrooms will keep for about 3 weeks.

MANGO PICKLE I

MAKES ABOUT 3 CUPS

Most indian mango pickles are made with the green fruit of varieties that have little sweetness until they ripen. Since these mangoes aren't commercially available in the United States, I haven't included any recipes that call for them. For this recipe and the next one, however, you can use the big, green-to-red mangoes commonly available in U.S. supermarkets; when underripe, their flesh is firm but bright orange and quite sweet.

This pickle is deliciously hot. Have it with curry, with grilled or roasted meat, or even with plain rice.

3 slightly underripe mangoes, peeled and sliced lengthwise
3 fresh green hot peppers, such as serrano or jalapeño, one cut
    into thin lengthwise strips, the others minced
1½ teaspoons pickling salt
½ cup white wine vinegar
1 teaspoon whole coriander seeds
¾ teaspoon whole fenugreek seeds
1 teaspoon whole cumin seeds
1½ teaspoons whole black mustard seeds
⅓ cup mustard oil (page 154) or other vegetable oil
2 tablespoons grated fresh ginger
1 tablespoon minced garlic
1 teaspoon whole yellow mustard seeds

1. In a bowl, mix the mango slices, hot pepper strips, salt, and vinegar.
2. Grind the coriander, fenugreek, cumin, and black mustard seeds in a spice or coffee grinder.

③ In a skillet, heat the oil. Fry the minced hot peppers, ginger, and garlic for 2 to 3 minutes. Remove the skillet from the heat, and stir in the ground spices and the yellow mustard seeds. Mix the seasonings with the mango slices and pepper strips. Transfer the mixture to a jar and let the mixture cool.

④ Close the jar tightly with a nonreactive cap. Let the jar stand at room temperature for several days, shaking the jar at least once a day.

⑤ If you don't eat the pickle at once, store it in the refrigerator, where it will keep for at least 2 months.

MANGO PICKLE II

MAKES ABOUT 1 QUART

EVERY REGION OF INDIA, and perhaps every family, has its own mango pickle recipe. This recipe is much like the preceding one, but the seasonings are different enough that you may want to try both pickles and see which you like best.

4 slightly underripe mangoes (about 4 pounds), peeled and
    sliced lengthwise
4 whole small fresh hot peppers, such as serrano or jalapeño,
    cut into thin lengthwise strips
4 teaspoons pickling salt
1⅓ cups cider vinegar
2 large garlic cloves, chopped
2 teaspoons ground coriander
2 teaspoons whole black mustard seeds
1 teaspoon hot pepper flakes
2 teaspoons dry mustard
½ cup mustard oil (page 154) or other vegetable oil
2 Mediterranean bay leaves

1. In a bowl, toss the mango slices and hot pepper strips with the salt. Let the mixture stand at room temperature for 6 to 12 hours.

2. Drain the mangoes and peppers. Add the remaining ingredients and stir well. Pack the mixture into a quart jar and close the jar tightly with a nonreactive cap. Let the jar stand at room temperature for 4 days, shaking it at least once a day.

3. If you don't eat the pickle at once, store it in the refrigerator, where it will keep for at least 2 months.

THE LOWDOWN ON MUSTARD OIL

The oil extracted from mustard seeds is available at Indian groceries and many natural foods stores in the United States, but it is always labeled "for external use only." This is because in 1989 the U.S. Food and Drug Administration (FDA) banned the sale of mustard oil for culinary use, since it contains erucic acid, which "in laboratory studies with test animals . . . has been associated with nutritional deficiencies as well as cardiac lesions." Canola oil, which is extracted from a rapeseed cultivar, also contains erucic acid, although in much smaller amounts; so, of course, do mustard seeds and prepared mustard, on whose use and sale the government imposes no restrictions.

According to a 1999 U.S. Department of Agriculture (USDA) study, mustard oil also contains the pungent antimicrobial chemical allyl isothiocyanate, as does horseradish. Mustard oil and horseradish, says the USDA, "pack a punch against *Listeria monocytogenes*, *E. coli*, *Staphyloccus aureus* and other food pathogens you definitely don't want in your sandwich."

For centuries Indians have favored mustard oil for their oil-based pickles, and in much of India this oil is also used for deep frying. But because of a huge recent increase in imports of edible oils (especially palm oil), India's mustard-oil industry is now in severe crisis. Without the unique, strong flavor of mustard oil, Indian-style pickles will still taste good, but not quite traditional—not in India, and not at your table. And they may not be as good for you, either.

MARINATED
ARTICHOKE HEARTS

MAKES 1 PINT

ALTHOUGH ALMOST ALL of the artichokes sold in the United States come from California's central coast region, artichokes will grow well wherever summers are cool and winters mild. In Seattle, Angelo Pellegrini raised all the artichokes his family could eat, and shared extra shoots with any friends, neighbors, or strangers who expressed interest in the plants. In *The Unprejudiced Palate* (1948), he recommended freezing artichokes, after trimming them, halving them, and blanching them for 3 to 4 minutes.

I have much less success in growing artichokes, so I used commercially canned artichoke hearts to develop this recipe (a can weighing 13¾ ounces holds 1 pint artichoke hearts). If you can't grow artichokes yourself, frozen artichoke hearts are preferable to canned ones, though harder to find. Boil frozen artichoke hearts for 5 minutes and drain them well before proceeding with the recipe.

1 pint canned, frozen, or home-cooked artichoke hearts
⅓ cup white wine vinegar
⅓ cup water
6 whole black peppercorns, crushed
1 garlic clove, sliced
1 thyme sprig
1 marjoram or oregano sprig
1 teaspoon pickling salt
1 pinch hot pepper flakes
⅓ cup olive oil

1. Pack the artichoke hearts into a pint jar. In a nonreactive saucepan, bring the vinegar, water, peppercorns, garlic, herbs, salt, and hot pepper flakes to a boil. Pour the hot liquid over the artichokes, then add the olive oil. Close the jar tightly with a nonreactive cap, and let the jar cool.

2. Store the jar in the refrigerator for at least 1 week before eating the artichokes. During this period, turn the jar occasionally from top to bottom to mix the seasonings.

3. Refrigerated, the artichokes should keep well for several weeks.

MOROCCAN-STYLE PRESERVED LEMONS

MAKES 1½ CUPS

THIS RECIPE AND VARIATIONS on it are popular in much of North Africa, the Middle East, and India. Sometimes the lemon segments are separated rather than kept attached at the base. Paprika may be added for color as well as flavor; in India turmeric is sometimes used in the same way. Whole bay leaves, cinnamon sticks, and peppercorns may also be added to the jar.

To use preserved lemons, remove the pulp, wash the rind, and chop it into small pieces. Add the pieces to soups, stews, salads, and steamed potatoes, sprinkle them on roast poultry, or stew them with chicken and green olives.

3 small lemons (about ½ pound), washed and well dried

5 teaspoons pickling salt

Juice of 1 to 2 lemons

2 tablespoons olive oil

1. With your palms, roll the lemons on your work surface until they feel soft; this will help to release their juices. Cut the lemons lengthwise into eighths, leaving ¼ inch intact at the stem end. Squeeze the lemons over a bowl to extract as much juice as possible. Rub 1 teaspoon salt into the interior of each lemon. Pack the lemons into a sterilized narrow 12-ounce mason jar, wedging the last one in so it won't float.

2. Add the juice of a fourth lemon to the juice in the bowl and stir in the remaining 2 teaspoons salt. Pour this mixture over the lemons. If it doesn't cover them, add the juice of another lemon. Top with the olive oil. Close the jar with a nonreactive cap and let the jar stand at room temperature for 3 weeks, shaking the jar occasionally and turning it over once or twice during this period.

3. After 3 weeks, store the jar in the refrigerator. The lemons can be eaten right away but will keep well for months.

SWEET PICKLED LEMONS

MAKES 1 PINT

PLENTY OF SUGAR and strong spices balance the bitterness of lemon peel in this Indian pickle, making it a good choice for people who have never tasted pickled lemon. I suggest cutting the lemons into small pieces before serving them as a relish.

3 small lemons (about ½ pound), washed and well dried

1½ teaspoons whole fennel seeds

1½ teaspoons whole cumin seeds

1½ teaspoons whole black peppercorns

1½ tablespoons pickling salt

6 tablespoons lemon juice

1½ cups firmly packed light brown sugar

2 small dried hot peppers, such as japonés or de árbol

1. Cut the lemons lengthwise into eighths, leaving ¼ inch intact at the stem end. In a coffee or spice grinder, grind the fennel, cumin, and peppercorns. Mix the spices with the salt and stuff the mixture into the lemons. Put the lemons into a sterile narrow 12-ounce jelly jar. Cover them with the lemon juice and cap the jar tightly. Let the jar stand at room temperature for 7 days, preferably in a sunny window.

2. On the eighth day, pour the juices from the jar into a nonreactive saucepan, pressing the lemons to extract more liquid. Add the sugar to the pan. Stirring, bring the mixture to a simmer. When the sugar has dissolved, add the lemons. Boil gently for 10 minutes or until the lemons are tender. Stir in the hot peppers.

3. Pack the pickle into a sterilized pint jar and cap the jar tightly. Let it stand at room temperature for at least 1 month before eating the pickle. It will keep for months in the refrigerator.

PRESERVED
GRAPE LEAVES

MAKES 1 PINT

IF YOU LIKE to make *dolma*, stuffed grape leaves, you may be glad to know that you can easily preserve your own leaves for this purpose. And they won't be salty, so you won't have to soak them before stuffing them. You'll want to use large, tender, light green leaves picked early in summer. Leaves from any *Vitis vinifera* grapevine will do (*V. labrusca* cultivars tend to have fuzzy leaves).

You can buy citric acid at a canning or brewing supply store, or order it from online sources. Citric acid is a harmless substance that occurs naturally in foods, especially citrus fruits.

> 2 teaspoons pickling salt
> 1 quart water
> About 30 grape leaves, stemmed
> 1 cup water plus ¼ cup lemon juice *or* 1 ¼ cups water plus
> ½ teaspoon citric acid

1. Combine the salt and 1 quart water in a large saucepan and bring the water to a boil. Add the leaves and blanch them for 30 seconds. Drain them.

2. Stack the leaves in small piles of about six each, and roll the stacks loosely from the side (not from the stem end or tip). Pack the rolls into a pint mason jar, folding over the ends if necessary.

3. In a small saucepan, bring to a boil 1 cup water and the lemon juice. Cover the rolled leaves with the hot liquid, leaving ½ inch headspace. Close the jar with a two-piece cap. Process the jar for 15 minutes in a boiling-water bath, or store it in the refrigerator.

JAPANESE PICKLED GINGER

USE FRESH YOUNG GINGER for this pickle. Available in Asian markets, young ginger is pale, almost white, with a very thin skin and pink stem stubs. A mandoline (page 179) may be useful for slicing the root.

Your pickled ginger may turn out faintly pink, but it won't have the hot pink color you'll see in some commercial versions of this pickle; that color comes from food dye.

A traditional accompaniment to sushi, pickled ginger refreshes the palate and cleanses the mouth of fishy tastes.

1 quart water
½ pound fresh ginger, sliced paper-thin
1 teaspoon plus a sprinkle of pickling salt
1 cup rice vinegar
3 tablespoons sugar
1 teaspoon light *(usukuchi)* Japanese soy sauce

1. Bring the water to a boil in a saucepan and add the ginger. Bring the water back to a boil and then drain the ginger well in a colander. Let the ginger cool.

2. Put the ginger into a bowl and sprinkle the ginger lightly with salt.

3. In a saucepan, bring to a boil the vinegar, the sugar, the 1 teaspoon salt, and the soy sauce, stirring to dissolve the sugar and salt. Pour the hot liquid over the ginger and mix well.

4. Store the ginger in a tightly covered container in the refrigerator. It will be ready to use in a day or two and will keep for several months, at least.

PICKLED SCALLIONS

MAKES 1 PINT

I DEVELOPED THIS RECIPE in imitation of a pickle I found in an Asian market. I pickle my scallions in autumn, after frost has ruined most of their green leaves but the scallions have not yet begun to go to seed—although summer scallions, or even green bulbing onions or shallots, should work as well. I trim off almost all of the green parts as well as the roots. I like these scallions in sushi rolls with cold-smoked salmon.

1 thin slice fresh ginger
¼ teaspoon hot pepper flakes
½ cup rice wine vinegar, plus more if needed
6 tablespoons water
1 tablespoon sugar
1 teaspoon pickling salt
2 cups trimmed scallions

1. Put the ginger and hot pepper flakes into a pint jar. In a saucepan, bring the vinegar, water, sugar, and salt to a boil. While the mixture heats, pack the scallions into the jar; I like to arrange them vertically.

2. When the vinegar mixture comes to a boil, pour it over the scallions to fill the jar. If the mixture doesn't reach the top of the jar, add a little more vinegar. Close the jar tightly with a nonreactive cap and store the jar in the refrigerator.

3. The scallions should be ready to eat in a week, and they should keep well for several months.

CHINESE PICKLED GARLIC

THIS RECIPE NOT ONLY MAKES a deliciously hot, crunchy condiment, but it's also a good way to preserve garlic for the times when you've run out of fresh bulbs or are just in a hurry. Although the recipe is Chinese, it includes no soy sauce, so the pickled garlic is suitable for use in all sorts of dishes. The garlicky vinegar is good in dressings and sauces, too.

Pickle garlic in the summer or fall, when the cloves are plump, white, and sweet-smelling.

> 1 cup garlic cloves
> ½ cup rice vinegar, white wine vinegar, or distilled white
>   vinegar
> ½ teaspoon sugar
> ½ teaspoon pickling salt

Put the garlic into a half-pint jar. Stir together the vinegar, sugar, and salt and pour the liquid over the garlic. Cap the jar and store it in the refrigerator or another cool, dark place for at least 1 month before using the garlic. It should keep well for 1 year or more. After opening the jar, store it in the refrigerator.

Many people are horrified to find that their pickled garlic—or a single clove of garlic in another sort of pickle—has turned blue or green. This color change seems to happen most with immature garlic, and at least one study has shown that storing garlic heads for a month at or above 23°C (73.4°F) prevents the production of the greenish pigment.

Other foods also turn color when pickled in vinegar. Asparagus often gets pinkish, or turns its pickling solution pinkish, and Brussels sprouts can do the same thing.

In each of these cases, the pickled food is safe to eat in spite of its strange color.

FRENCH PICKLED GARLIC

MAKES ABOUT 1 CUP

MELLOWED BY brief cooking and wine, this pickled garlic is very mild in flavor. Some recipes call for topping off the jar with olive oil, which would make for a very satisfying appetizer.

½ cup white wine vinegar

½ cup dry white wine

1 small dried hot pepper, such as japonés or de árbol

1 small thyme sprig

1 small rosemary sprig

1 small Mediterranean bay leaf

10 whole black peppercorns

2 teaspoons sugar

½ teaspoon pickling salt

1 cup garlic cloves

1. Put all of the ingredients except the garlic into a nonreactive sauce-pan. Bring the contents to a boil and add the garlic. Return the contents to a boil and boil them for 5 minutes. Cover the pan and let it stand at room temperature for 24 hours.

2. Bring the contents of the saucepan to a boil again, then transfer them to a half-pint jar. Let the jar cool, and then cap it. Store it in the refrigerator or another cool, dark place.

3. The garlic will be ready to eat in about 5 days, and it will keep well for about 1 year.

SPICY PICKLED GARLIC

MAKES 3 HALF-PINTS

WITH ITS CLEAR LIQUID and pretty spices, this is a fine pickle to give as a gift. The recipe makes enough for 3 half-pint jars—one for you, and two for your friends.

2 quarts water

1½ cups white wine vinegar or distilled white vinegar

1 tablespoon sugar

1½ teaspoons pickling salt

3 whole allspice berries

6 whole black peppercorns

12 whole coriander seeds

1 Mediterranean bay leaf, torn into thirds

3 small dried hot peppers, such as japonés or de árbol, slit lengthwise

3 cups garlic cloves

1. In a large saucepan, bring the water to a boil.

2. While the water heats, bring to a boil in another saucepan the vinegar, sugar, and salt, and divide the spices, bay leaf, and hot peppers among 3 half-pint mason jars.

3. When the water comes to a boil, add the garlic cloves. Boil the cloves for 1 minute.

4. Drain the cloves and divide them among the mason jars. When the vinegar mixture comes to a boil, pour it over the garlic, leaving ½ inch headspace in each jar. Close the jars with two-piece caps and process the jars in a boiling-water bath for 10 minutes.

5. Store the jars in a cool, dry, dark place for at least 2 weeks before eating the garlic. After opening a jar, store it in the refrigerator.

PICKLED NASTURTIUM PODS

MAKES ABOUT 1¾ CUPS

STOPPING HIS TRUCK in my driveway to ask directions, an old man was distracted by the sight of nasturtiums growing around my dogwood tree. "Excuse me—do you mind?" he said, as he reached down to pluck a vermilion blossom. Munching the flower, he reached for a couple of the saucer-like leaves. "Do you know," he asked, chewing them with relish, "that every part of this plant is edible? Even the seeds." He knelt on the ground to search out several that were still green and plump. "They're hot as peppers," he declared, eating them one at a time. "Here, try one."

As we stood there munching nasturtium seeds, I asked the old man if he'd ever had them pickled. He had not, preferring to eat them right in the garden, warm from the summer's sun. But the old man didn't know what he was missing. Despite the unpleasant, sulphurous smell the plump seeds release when brined, pickled nasturtium seeds (or pods, or buds, as they are variously called) taste very much like pickled capers, except that they are crunchier and a bit peppery. "Nasturtium buds make better capers than capers do," noted Euell Gibbons. My family likes them in pasta sauces; they are also good in salads.

Nasturtium pods need no seasoning besides salt and vinegar, but they're even better with a little spice. Here I use the seasonings Eliza Smith called for, in her 1727 cookbook *The Compleat Housewife*.

4½ tablespoons pickling salt

3 cups water

1 pint fresh, green, plump nasturtium pods

4 whole cloves

1 pinch blade (unground) mace

¼ nutmeg kernel

1 slice horseradish (about 1½ inches in diameter x ³⁄₁₆ inch
    thick), cut into thin strips

1 shallot

About 1 cup white wine vinegar

1 Dissolve 1½ tablespoons salt in 1 cup water, and pour this brine over the nasturtium pods. Let them stand at room temperature for 24 hours.

2 Drain the nasturtium pods, make a fresh brine the same way as before, and pour it over the pods. Again, let them stand at room temperature for 24 hours. Do the same on the third day.

3 On the fourth day, drain the pods, put them into a jar with the cloves, mace, nutmeg, horseradish, and shallot, and cover all well with the vinegar. Cover the jar tightly and let it stand at room temperature for at least 1 week.

4 After opening the jar, store it in the refrigerator.

MARINATED DRIED TOMATOES

MAKES ABOUT 1½ CUPS

D RIED TOMATOES ARE WONDERFUL when briefly rehydrated, and then packed in olive oil. But if you add fresh garlic or herbs, food scientists say, you must keep the jar refrigerated, for a maximum of three weeks, or risk contracting botulism. Olive oil solidifies in the refrigerator, which means you must bring the jar to room temperature before eating the tomatoes. My solution is to acidulate the tomatoes—that is, to pickle them. Pickled dried tomatoes taste extra tart, but they are a delicious addition to salads.

1½ cups dried tomatoes
2 cups boiling water
1 tablespoon small fresh basil leaves
¼ teaspoon pickling salt
2 large garlic cloves, thinly sliced
6 tablespoons red wine vinegar
2 tablespoons olive oil

1 Put the tomatoes into a small bowl, cover them with the boiling water, and let them stand for 5 minutes.

2 Drain the tomatoes. Toss them in a bowl with the basil, salt, garlic, and vinegar, then pack the mixture into a 12-ounce to 1-pint jar. Add the olive oil and cap the jar.

3 Store the jar in a cool, dry, dark place. For long-term storage, keep the jar in the refrigerator.

PICKLED
EGGPLANT CUBES

MAKES 3 PINTS

A UBERGINES CERTAINLY ARE INDIGESTIBLE," writes Patience Gray (*Honey from a Weed*, 1986), "especially when conserved in vinegar." She is partially right: For some people, aubergines—that is, eggplants—usually don't go down without causing discomfort and bloating. But such people are delighted with this pickle, which they find they can eat with impunity. I love it in salads and on toasted bread with hummus.

3 cups white wine vinegar
2¼ pounds slender eggplants, peeled and cut into ⅜- to ½-
    inch cubes
2 tablespoons chopped garlic
¼ cup loosely packed small fresh basil leaves
2 teaspoons pickling salt

1. In a nonreactive saucepan, bring the vinegar to a boil. Blanch the eggplant in the vinegar for 2 minutes, in three or four batches. In a bowl, toss the eggplant with the garlic, basil, and salt.

2. Pack the eggplant into pint mason jars and pour the boiling vinegar over, leaving ½ inch headspace. Close the jars with two-piece lids. Process the jars for 10 minutes in a boiling-water bath.

3. Store the jars in a cool, dry, dark place for 1 week or longer before eating the eggplant. After opening a jar, store it in the refrigerator.

ITALIAN PICKLED RAW EGGPLANT

MAKES ABOUT 1 PINT

 AW EGGPLANT, pressed to remove excess moisture and marinated with basil, garlic, and hot pepper, makes a tasty antipasto.

1½ pounds slender eggplants, peeled, sliced crosswise into
   1-inch pieces, then sliced lengthwise ³⁄₁₆ inch thick
2 teaspoons pickling salt
½ cup red wine vinegar
3 garlic cloves, sliced
½ teaspoon hot pepper flakes
8 fresh basil leaves, each torn in half
About ¼ cup olive oil

1. Toss the eggplant strips with the salt and put them into a colander. Let them drain for 6 to 12 hours.

2. Press each eggplant slice between your palms to remove any remaining excess moisture. Put them into a wide bowl and toss them with the vinegar and garlic. Let them stand for 1 hour, turning them occasionally.

3. In a pint jar, layer the eggplant and garlic with the hot pepper flakes and basil, pressing the eggplant down to fit. Add any liquid remaining in the bowl. Pour over the eggplant enough olive oil to cover it well. Cap the jar and refrigerate it.

4. After several hours, add more olive oil if the eggplant isn't well covered.

5. The eggplant will be ready to eat after several days, and it will keep well, refrigerated, for several weeks. Bring it to room temperature before serving it.

LEBANESE PICKLED EGGPLANT STUFFED WITH GARLIC

THE IDEA OF PICKLING WHOLE EGGPLANTS may seem strange if the only eggplants you know are the enormous ones sold in U.S. supermarkets. But eggplants were so named because many varieties are like birds' eggs in both size and shape (and even color—some varieties are white rather than purple). Our giant eggplants would be novelties in most of the world, where little eggplants are the norm. Fruits of the smaller varieties, I've found, generally have a firmer texture and less bitter flavor, and so are well worth seeking out in seed catalogs and farmers' markets.

For this pickle, round eggplants are traditional, but I like to use the elongated Little Fingers variety.

In Lebanon, these pickles are traditionally eaten as part of the *maza*, an assortment of hot or cold appetizers. The *maza* usually features olives and yogurt cheese and always includes spearmint leaves and flat bread rounds.

> 1¼ pounds 3- to 4-inch-long eggplants
> 1 garlic head, cloves separated, peeled, and crushed
> 1 tablespoon plus 1 teaspoon pickling salt
> ½ teaspoon cayenne
> 1 cup plus 2 tablespoons red wine vinegar, plus more if needed
> 1 cup plus 2 tablespoons water

1. Steam the eggplants for 5 to 8 minutes, or until they are tender but not mushy. Let them cool.

2. Mix the garlic with 1 tablespoon salt and the cayenne. Using the tip of a knife, slit each eggplant once lengthwise, cutting most of the way through. Stuff the eggplants with the garlic mixture. Pack the eggplants into a sterilized quart jar.

3. In a nonreactive saucepan, combine the vinegar, water, and remaining 1 teaspoon salt. Bring the contents to a boil, stirring to dissolve the salt. Let the liquid cool.

4. Fill the jar to the brim with the cooled liquid (top the jar off with a little more vinegar, if necessary). Close the jar with a nonreactive cap. Let the jar stand in a cool place for 1 to 2 weeks.

5. If you don't eat the pickles right away, store the jar in the refrigerator. The pickles will keep, refrigerated, for at least several weeks.

"My father has told me that when he was a child visiting relatives in Syria he remembers that the women of the family devoted their time to pickling and to making jams and syrups whenever they had no parties, feasts, or other household activities to occupy them. Large glass jars were filled with turnips, onions, cucumbers, lemons, cauliflowers, eggplants, and peppers. The family could hardly wait to start eating them, and often did so before the pickles were quite ready. A visit to the cellar or store cupboard to see how they were maturing and mellowing to soft pinks, saffrons, mauves, and pale greens was a mouth-watering expedition."

—Claudia Roden, A Book of Middle Eastern Food *(1980)*

ARMENIAN PICKLED EGGPLANT STUFFED WITH PEPPERS AND PARSLEY

MAKES 1 QUART

T HIS ARMENIAN RECIPE is much like the preceding Lebanese one, except that parsley and hot and sweet peppers take the place of the garlic.

1¼ pounds 3- to 4-inch-long eggplants

¼ cup coarsely chopped sweet red pepper,
    such as bell or pimiento

2 tablespoons coarsely chopped sweet green pepper,
    such as bell or pimiento

1 tablespoon minced red hot pepper, such as
    jalapeño or Fresno

2 tablespoons chopped fresh parsley

1 small garlic clove, minced

1 tablespoon plus ¼ teaspoon pickling salt

1 cup plus 2 tablespoons white wine vinegar

1 cup plus 2 tablespoons water

2 tablespoons sugar

1 Steam the eggplants for 5 to 8 minutes, or until they are tender but not mushy. Put them into a colander and lay a heavy dish over them. Press them for 4 to 10 hours.

2 In a small bowl, mix together the peppers, parsley, garlic, and ¼ teaspoon salt. With the tip of a knife, slit each eggplant once lengthwise, cutting most of the way through. Stuff each eggplant with some of the pepper-parsley mixture and squeeze the eggplant gently to close the slit. Pack the eggplants into a sterilized quart jar.

3. In a nonreactive saucepan, combine the vinegar, water, sugar, and remaining 1 tablespoon salt. Bring the contents to a boil, stirring until the sugar and salt have dissolved. Let the liquid cool.

4. Fill the jar to the brim with the cooled liquid (top the jar off with a little more vinegar, if necessary). Close the jar with a nonreactive cap. Let the jar stand in a cool place for 1 to 2 weeks.

5. If you don't eat the pickles right away, store the jar in the refrigerator. The pickles will keep, refrigerated, for at least several weeks.

TURKISH PICKLED EGGPLANT STUFFED WITH CABBAGE AND DILL

MAKES 1 QUART

BECAUSE THE STUFFING in this recipe is bulkier that that in the preceding two recipes, the eggplants are tied shut. If you find celery or dill too awkward to use, you can substitute cotton kitchen string.

1 pound 3- to 4-inch-long eggplants

3 celery stalks or 6 or more dill stems

½ cup shredded white head cabbage

1 small sweet pepper, such as bell or pimiento, minced

¼ cup minced dill sprigs

1½ tablespoons minced garlic

1 tablespoon minced celery leaves

1 cup plus 2 tablespoons red wine vinegar

1 cup plus 2 tablespoons water

1 tablespoon plus ¼ teaspoon pickling salt

1. Steam the eggplants for 5 to 8 minutes, or until they are tender but not mushy. Put them into a colander and lay a heavy dish over them. Press them for 4 to 10 hours.

2. Steam or boil the celery stalks or dill stems until they are quite tender. Let them cool. Quarter the celery stalks lengthwise.

3. In a small bowl, mix together the cabbage, pepper, minced dill, garlic, celery leaves, and ¼ teaspoon salt. With the tip of a knife, slit each eggplant once lengthwise, cutting most of the way through. Stuff each eggplant with some of the cabbage mixture and squeeze the eggplant gently to close the slit. Tie each eggplant closed with 1 or 2 celery strips or dill stems. Pack the eggplants into a sterilized quart jar.

4. In a saucepan, combine the vinegar, water, and remaining 1 tablespoon salt. Bring the contents to a boil, stirring until the salt has dissolved. Let the liquid cool.

5. Fill the jar to the brim with the cooled liquid (top the jar off with a little more vinegar, if necessary). Close the jar tightly with a nonreactive cap. Let the jar stand in a cool place for 1 to 2 weeks.

6. If you don't eat the pickles right away, store the jar in the refrigerator. The pickles will keep, refrigerated, for at least several weeks.

CANNING PICKLED BABY CORN

If you'd like to can pickled baby corn, first blanch it for 30 to 45 seconds in boiling water or steam. Let it cool, and then pack it into pint or half-pint jars, leaving ½ inch headspace. Pour over the pickling liquid, and then immerse the jars for 15 minutes in water heated to 180° to 185°F.

SPICY PICKLED BABY CORN

MAKES 1 QUART

FARMERS SAY YOU CAN MAKE THIS PICKLE with any field corn or sweet corn, if you pick it at the right stage of maturity. Sweeter varieties of corn don't produce sweeter baby corn, because the corn ears are harvested before pollination and before sugar has been stored in the kernels. But special varieties for pickling are available in seed catalogs, and with some of these varieties you can get four ears on most stalks. To grow baby corn, plant the seeds close together, and pick the ears when the silks just begin to show.

1 Mediterranean bay leaf, broken up
8 whole allspice berries
8 whole black peppercorns
20 whole coriander seeds
½ teaspoon whole yellow mustard seeds
1 quart husked baby corn (each ear about 3 inches long)
4 small dried hot peppers, such as japonés or de árbol
1 teaspoon pickling salt
2 teaspoons sugar
1 cup cider vinegar
1 cup water

1 Put the bay leaf, allspice, peppercorns, coriander, and mustard into a quart jar. Add the corn ears, interspersing the hot peppers.

2 In a nonreactive saucepan, bring to a boil the salt, sugar, vinegar, and water. Pour the hot liquid over the corn and cap the jar.

3 Store the jar in the refrigerator for at least 1 week before eating the corn. It will keep, refrigerated, for at least several weeks.

4

SAUERKRAUT, KIMCHI, AND OTHER CABBAGE PICKLES

THIS CHAPTER CELEBRATES that humble cool-weather vegetable that keeps people healthy throughout much of the world. Easy to grow and cheap to buy, cabbage comes in countless varieties. Whereas the other favorite pickling vegetable, the cucumber, has little nutritional value beyond its high water content, cabbage has fairly high levels of vitamin C—high enough to prevent scurvy in sailors—and some Asian cabbages are very rich in vitamin A.

When brined, cabbage is much more digestible than when fresh. Pickled cabbage assists in the digestion of other foods, too, and can be just as rich in vitamins as fresh cabbage. Cabbage kimchi, in fact, has much higher vitamin B levels than unfermented Chinese cabbage.

Along with the recipes for sauerkraut, kimchi, and other forms of brined cabbage, you'll find here a sampling of recipes for vinegar-pickled cabbage.

Although kimchi and Japanese salt-pickled cabbage normally aren't canned, sauerkraut usually is, at least in the United States, and so are some cabbage in-vinegar pickles. The recipes specify when canning is recommended. See Chapter 1 for complete instructions on boiling-water processing and low-temperature pasteurization.

REVIVING THE KRAUT BOARD

The traditional tool for shredding cabbage is a kraut board, also known as a *krauthobel* ("cabbage plane") or mandoline. Today most mandolines sold in stores and catalogs are small and expensive plastic-and-metal or all-metal versions of their wood-and-metal predecessors. But you can buy the real thing—made of tongue-and-groove hardwood and big enough to hold a whole medium-size cabbage—from various Internet vendors.

SAUERKRAUT WITH JUNIPER BERRIES

MAKES 6 QUARTS

T HE BASIC RECIPE for sauerkraut is very simple, since there are only two ingredients: cabbage and salt. Few Americans add anything else. In the past, though, added flavorings were common—juniper berries, caraway, bay, garlic, onions, and wine have all made sauerkraut more interesting, just as ginger, garlic, onions, and hot pepper flavor cabbage kimchi today. If you're going to the trouble of making your own kraut, you may well prefer to make it special.

In this recipe I call for juniper berries, whose balmy aroma and bittersweet flavor always remind me of the forest. Juniper berries aren't sold in many stores, but you can gather your own from wild or cultivated plants or order some from an Internet supplier. Or, of course, you can leave them out.

This recipe uses 15 pounds of cabbage, as much as will fit comfortably in a 3-gallon crock. If you want to make more or less sauerkraut, the adjustments are simple. Just use 3 tablespoons of salt for each 5 pounds of cabbage. You can fit 5 pounds of cabbage in a gallon jar, 25 pounds in a 5-gallon crock or bucket. Before weighing the cabbage, be sure to remove the tough or damaged outer leaves and cores.

If you use freshly harvested cabbage, it will easily release enough liquid to cover itself. If your cabbage has been stored for a few weeks, though, you may have to add brine to the crock.

15 pounds trimmed and cored white head cabbage

9 tablespoons pickling salt

3 tablespoons whole juniper berries

1. Working with 5 pounds of cabbage at a time, quarter the heads and shred the cabbage very thinly, about the thickness of a quarter. I find this easiest to do with a chef's knife, but for very fine shreds you may prefer to use a kraut board (page 179) or a meat slicer. (I don't recommend a food processor, which can easily turn cabbage to mush.)

2. Add 3 tablespoons of the salt and 1 tablespoon of the juniper berries to the cabbage and thoroughly mix the ingredients with your hands. I do this right in the crock, but if you're going to ferment your cabbage in gallon jars, you'll want to do your mixing in a large bowl or nonreactive pot. Pack the cabbage into a crock or bucket. When it has softened and released some liquid—as it probably will have done by the time you've shredded the next 5 pounds of cabbage— tamp it down very firmly, using a potato masher or your hands.

3. When you've mixed and packed all the cabbage, weight it to keep it protected in its brine. The crock I prefer to use, a Gärtopf, comes with its own weights (page 36). You can instead use a food-grade plastic bag, such as one meant for roasting a turkey in, or two or more smaller bags, filled with brine (1½ tablespoons pickling salt for each 1 quart water) in case of a leak. Or you can cover the cabbage with a pie plate or dinner plate a little smaller than the container opening and top the plate with large, clean rocks or two or three quart jars filled with water. Some people cover the shredded cabbage with whole cabbage leaves before adding the plate, and some use a clean piece of muslin or two layers of cheesecloth. These are optional measures, but they are helpful if the brine gets scummy; you can replace the leaves or cloth with fresh ones instead of trying to skim off the scum. Cover the container with a towel or other cloth (I use a pillow case). Put the container in a cool place.

4. Within 24 hours, the cabbage should be submerged in its own brine. If it isn't, dissolve 1½ tablespoons pickling salt in 1 quart

water and pour as much of this as you need over the cabbage. Check the sauerkraut once every day or two to see if scum has formed. If you do find scum, remove it daily and wash the plate and weights.

5. Start tasting the sauerkraut after 2 weeks. The sauerkraut will be fully fermented in 2 to 4 weeks at 70° to 75°F, or in 5 to 6 weeks at 60°F. It will have a pale golden color and a tart, full flavor. Within two days after fermentation is complete, little bubbles will have stopped rising to the surface.

6. When the sauerkraut is ready, you can store it, tightly covered, in the refrigerator or another very cool place (at about 38°F). Or you can freeze it, in either plastic freezer bags or rigid containers; freezing may preserve the vitamin C content better than canning, and it doesn't harm the texture much.

7. If you prefer to can your kraut, pack the sauerkraut and juices into pint or quart mason jars, leaving ½ inch headspace at the top of each jar. Close the jars with two-piece caps. Immerse the jars in a canner of water heated to about 140°F and bring the water to a boil. Keeping the water at a gentle boil, process pint jars for 20 minutes, quart jars for 25 minutes.

8. Store the cooled jars in a cool, dry, dark place.

"Cold as kraut," say people in Appalachia, who used to store their sauerkraut on the back porch through the winter.

APFELKRAUT

Another way to mellow the flavor of kraut a bit, according to my friend Sally White, is to add some grated apple. I make my *apfelkraut* with 3 medium-size apples to 9 pounds cabbage and 6 tablespoons pickling salt.

WINE KRAUT

W HEN MY HUSBAND took a taste of this kraut from the crock, he thought I had the wrong kind of fermentation going on. But the wine had just added its own complex flavors to that of the fermenting cabbage.

As with the basic kraut recipe, you can multiply or divide the quantities here to suit the amount of cabbage you have on hand. Leave out the caraway if you don't like it. You might instead try juniper berries, as in the preceding recipe.

> 15 pounds trimmed and cored fresh white head cabbage
> 9 tablespoons pickling salt
> 6 teaspoons whole caraway seeds
> 1½ cups dry white wine

1. Working with 5 pounds of cabbage at a time, quarter the heads and shred the cabbage very thin, about the thickness of a quarter.

2. Add 3 tablespoons salt and 2 teaspoons caraway seeds to the cabbage, and thoroughly mix the ingredients with your hands. Pack the cabbage into a crock or bucket. When it has softened and released some liquid—as it probably will have done by the time you've shredded the next 5 pounds of cabbage—tamp it down very firmly, using a potato masher or your hands.

3. When you've mixed and packed all the cabbage, weight it to keep it protected in its brine. A Gärtopf (page 36) crock comes with its own weights. You can instead use a food-grade plastic bag, such as one meant for roasting a turkey in, or two or more smaller bags, filled with brine (1½ tablespoons pickling salt to each quart of water). Or you can cover the cabbage with a pie plate or dinner

plate a little smaller than the container opening, and top the plate with large, clean rocks or 2 to 3 quart jars filled with water. Cover the container with a towel or pillowcase and put the container in a cool place.

4. After 24 hours, remove the weights and add the wine. Replace the weights.

5. Check the sauerkraut once every day or two to see if scum has formed. If you do find scum, remove it and wash the bags or the plate and weights before replacing them.

6. Start tasting the sauerkraut after 2 weeks. The kraut will be fully fermented in 2 to 4 weeks at 70° to 75°F, or 5 to 6 weeks at 60°F. It will be pale gold with a tart, full flavor. Within 2 days after fermentation has stopped, little bubbles will have stopped rising to the surface.

7. When the sauerkraut is ready, either store it, tightly covered, in the refrigerator or another very cool place (at about 38°F), freeze it in airtight containers, or can it.

8. To can your kraut, pack it with its juices into pint or quart mason jars, leaving ½ inch headspace at the top of each jar. Close the jars with two-piece caps. Immerse the jars in a canner of water heated to about 140°F, and bring the water to a boil. Keeping the water at a gentle boil, process pint jars for 20 minutes, quart jars for 25 minutes.

9. Store the cooled jars in a cool, dry, dark place.

FERMENTING SAUERKRAUT

Sauerkraut that ferments at cooler temperatures—65°F or lower—has the best flavor and color and highest vitamin C levels. That's why most people make sauerkraut in the fall, using cabbage planted for late harvest. But fermentation is slow at low temperatures; at 60°F, the curing may take five to six weeks. Sauerkraut fermented at 70° to 75°F, however, has very good flavor and is ready in only three weeks or so. At temperatures over 90°F, the kraut will ferment in just eight to ten days, but most of the work will be done by homofermentative bacteria, which produce lactic acid but not acetic acid and other substances that contribute to the complex flavor of really good sauerkraut. If the days are really hot, ferment the kraut in a cellar, an air-conditioned room, or another cool place. I've made good sauerkraut in 85° to 90°F weather by using a stoneware crock set on a concrete floor in a dark corner of a shed.

Full-flavored sauerkraut ferments in stages: *Leuconostoc mesenteroides* produces carbon dioxide to create anaerobic conditions for *Lactobacillus plantarum*, which produces a lot of acid and removes a bitter-flavored compound (mannitol) produced by *Leuconostoc*. Other bacteria may contribute to the process, too, depending on temperature, salt concentration, and how long fermentation is allowed to continue. All this happens with remarkably little intervention on the part of the sauerkraut maker.

SAUERKRAUT IN HISTORY

It's no accident that we use a German name for fermented shredded cabbage; although sauerkraut is popular throughout most of Europe and North America, Germans have long loved it the most. According to Mark Kurlansky (*Salt: A World History*, 2002), by the sixteenth century tradespeople in Alsace called *Surkrutschneider* were slicing cabbage and salting it in barrels with such seasonings as anise seeds, bay leaves, elderberries, fennel, horseradish, savory, cloves, and cumin.

By the seventeenth century, the Dutch were making and eating a lot of sauerkraut, too, and this may partially explain their maritime dominance during that era. Because of its high vitamin C content, raw sauerkraut can prevent scurvy. The many barrels of sauerkraut, or *zuurkool*, on Dutch ships helped them withstand long sea voyages better than other sailors.

When a doctor informed the British admiralty in 1753 that sauerkraut could prevent scurvy, the navy set up special stores in British ports to provision naval vessels with sauerkraut. Captain James Cook had it served to his crew at each meal, and in 1776 he was awarded a medal for demonstrating that the antiscorbutic really worked.

Although sauerkraut remains very popular in central and eastern Europe, its consumption has declined in the United States in recent years. Although three out of every four Americans eat sauerkraut, Americans ate only 1.1 pounds per person in 2003, less than half our 1970 consumption. Younger Americans are eating much less sauerkraut—and cabbage in any form—than their elders are.

SWEET KRAUT

MAKES ABOUT 4 QUARTS

A BUTCHER I ONCE MET told me about this recipe. It's German, he said, and the sauerkraut it produces isn't really sweet, but it has a mellower flavor than other kraut. After trying the method, I agree. You might start with this recipe if you're not sure your family will eat sauerkraut.

> 10 pounds trimmed and cored fresh white head cabbage
> 6 tablespoons pickling salt
> ¾ cup sugar

1 Working with 5 pounds of cabbage at a time, quarter the heads and shred the cabbage very thin, about the thickness of a quarter.

2 Add 3 tablespoons of the salt and 6 tablespoons of the sugar to the cabbage, and thoroughly mix the ingredients with your hands. Pack the cabbage into a crock or 1-gallon jar. When it has softened and released some liquid—as it probably will have done by the time you've shredded the remaining cabbage—tamp it down very firmly. Mix the remaining cabbage with the remaining salt and sugar, and pack the mixture into the crock or into a second gallon jar.

3 When all the cabbage is mixed and packed, weight it to keep it protected in its brine. A Gärtopf (page 36) crock comes with its own weights. With an ordinary crock or a jar, you can use a food-grade plastic bag, or more than one, filled with brine (to make the brine, use 1½ tablespoons pickling salt per 1 quart water). Or cover the cabbage with a pie plate or dinner plate a little smaller than your crock opening; top the plate with large, clean rocks or 2 to 3 quart jars filled with water; and cover the crock with a towel or pillowcase. Put the crock or jars in a cool place.

TROUBLESHOOTING GUIDE: SAUERKRAUT

PROBLEM	POSSIBLE CAUSES
White scum on top	Yeast—the plate or brine bag did not exclude all air during fermentation. Skim off the scum daily.
Sliminess	The temperature was too high during fermentation, or the salt content was too low. Dump this batch.
Dark color at top	Oxidation—the salting was uneven, fermentation temperatures were too high, or the kraut was stored for too long or at too high a temperature. Discard the darkened kraut.
Soft texture	Too little salt was used, the salting was uneven, fermentation temperatures were too high, or the kraut wasn't firmly packed in the crock.
Mold on top	The fermentation temperature was too high, and the kraut wasn't well covered. Remove moldy kraut promptly.
Pink color on top	Yeast—too much salt was used, the salting was uneven, or the kraut wasn't well covered or weighted during fermentation. Skim off pink kraut.

4 Check the sauerkraut once every day or two to see if scum has formed. If you do find scum, remove it and wash the bags or the plate and weights before replacing them.

5 Start tasting the sauerkraut after 2 weeks. The kraut will be fully fermented in 2 to 4 weeks at 70° to 75°F, or in 5 to 6 weeks at 60°F.

6 When the sauerkraut is ready, store it, tightly covered, in either the refrigerator or another very cool place (at about 38°F), freeze it in airtight containers, or can it. To can your kraut, pack it with its juices into pint or quart mason jars, leaving ½ inch headspace at the top of each jar. Close the jars with two-piece caps. Immerse the jars in a canner of water heated to about 140°F and bring the water to a boil. Keeping the water at a gentle boil, process pint jars for 20 minutes, quart jars for 25 minutes.

7 Store the cooled jars in a cool, dry, dark place.

KIMCHI KRAUT

MAKES ABOUT 3 QUARTS

T HERE IS NO REASON your sauerkraut can't have the bright flavors and colors of kimchi. This recipe includes scallions, ginger, and red pepper—hot or mild, as you like.

6¾ pounds trimmed and cored fresh white head cabbage
1¾ cups chopped scallions
⅓ cup minced fresh ginger
¼ cup chopped garlic
½ cup ground dried hot or mild red pepper, or a mixture
4½ tablespoons pickling salt
2 tablespoons sugar

1. Working with half of the cabbage at a time, quarter the heads and shred the cabbage very thinly, about the thickness of a quarter.

2. Add half of the scallions, ginger, garlic, pepper, salt, and sugar to the cabbage, and thoroughly mix the ingredients with your hands. Pack the mixture into a gallon jar. When the shredded cabbage has softened and released some liquid—as it probably will have done by the time you've shredded the rest—tamp it down very firmly. Prepare the remaining half of the ingredients in the same way.

3. When all of the ingredients are packed in the jar, weight them with a food-grade plastic bag filled with brine (to make the brine, use 1½ tablespoons pickling salt per 1 quart water). Put the jar in a cool place.

4. If any scum forms at the top of the kraut, you'll know that air must be getting in around the bag. Remove the scum, wash the bag, and replace the bag carefully in the jar.

5. Start tasting the kraut after 2 weeks. It will be fully fermented in 2 to 4 weeks at 70° to 75°F, or in 5 to 6 weeks at 60°F. When it has a tart, full flavor, store the jar, tightly covered, in either the refrigera-

WHAT DO YOU DO WITH ALL THAT KRAUT?

Here are some popular ways to use sauerkraut:

Eat it on hot dogs.

Add some shredded onion or carrot or minced garlic, dress with olive or sunflower oil, and serve the kraut cold as a salad.

Put it in a Reuben sandwich (rye bread, Swiss cheese, and corned beef or pastrami).

Stuff it into pierogis.

Cook it in a stew with pork, apples, and caraway.

Add ½ cup kraut per loaf to whole wheat or rye bread dough.

Make it into a soup with onion, bacon, potatoes, caraway, and sour cream.

Use 1 cup of kraut, rinsed, in a two-layer chocolate cake (recipes abound).

Cook it with onions, green pepper, and sausage.

Make *choucroûte garnie*, the Alsatian dish of smoked pork on a bed of sauerkraut, braised with white wine.

Put it on pizza (no kidding—some people do).

tor or another very cool place (at about 38°F), freeze the kraut in airtight containers, or can it. To can your kraut, pack it into pint or quart mason jars, leaving ½ inch headspace at the top of each jar. Close the jars with two-piece caps. Immerse the jars in a canner of water heated to about 140°F and bring the water to a boil. Keeping the water at a gentle boil, process pint jars for 20 minutes, quart jars for 25 minutes.

6 Store the cooled jars in a cool, dry, dark place.

RUSSIAN SOURED CABBAGE

MAKES ABOUT 3 QUARTS

THIS RECIPE, based on one in Anne Volokh's book *The Art of Russian Cuisine* (1983), exemplifies the refinement of Russian pickling. The cabbage is fermented for only four to five days with a little less salt than usual, in a sort of half-sour version of sauerkraut. Sweet apple, darkly aromatic caraway, and tart, colorful cranberries all contribute to the beauty of the finished dish.

Serve this kraut as a salad or as an accompaniment for pork, poultry, or game.

> 2 tablespoons pickling salt
> 5 pounds trimmed and cored fresh white head cabbage,
>   2 outer leaves reserved, the rest shredded
> 2 medium-size carrots, coarsely grated
> 1 apple, cored and sliced into 16 wedges
> ¾ cup cranberries
> 2 tablespoons whole caraway seeds
> 1½ tablespoons pickling salt dissolved in 1 quart water,
>   for the brine bag

1. In a large bowl, mix the salt with the shredded cabbage, rubbing the salt into the cabbage with your hands. Gently mix in the carrots, apple, cranberries, and caraway seeds. Pack the mixture in a gallon jar, pressing the cabbage down firmly. Add any liquid that has accumulated in the bowl. Lay the reserved cabbage leaves on top.

2. Push a food-grade plastic bag into the top of the jar and fill it with the brine. Seal the bag. Set the jar out of direct sunlight at a temperature of 65° to 72°F.

3. Two or three times a day during the next 2 to 3 days, push a long chopstick or the handle of a wooden spoon to the bottom of the jar to let gases escape.

4. Let the mixture ferment for 4 to 5 days, until the cabbage is as sour as you like. Remove the brine bag, cap the jar, and refrigerate it. The kraut should be ready to eat in a day or two. "For braising or for stuffing a goose," says Anne Volokh, "it should mature a little longer, about another week in the refrigerator."

TURKISH PICKLED CABBAGE

MAKES ABOUT 1½ QUARTS

ALTHOUGH THIS PICKLE uses shredded white head cabbage, it is more like a typical kimchi than like sauerkraut, in both method and flavorings. The cabbage is briefly brined to reduce its volume, and then fresh brine is added with the flavorings. These flavorings—garlic, ginger, and hot pepper—are very familiar to kimchi fans. The finished pickle is sour, hot, spicy, and delicious.

I've left out one distinctly Turkish ingredient, fresh chickpeas, since they are so rarely available in the United States. If you happen to have a source for them, add a half cup along with the other flavorings.

2¾ pounds trimmed and cored fresh
    white head cabbage, shredded
¼ cup pickling salt
2 tablespoons minced garlic
2 tablespoons minced fresh ginger
2 tablespoons hot pepper flakes
1 teaspoon sugar
3 cups water

1. In a large bowl, mix the cabbage with 2 tablespoons of the salt. Let the cabbage stand at room temperature for 2 to 3 hours.

2. Drain the cabbage, rinse it with cold water, and drain it again well. Mix it with the garlic, ginger, hot pepper flakes, and sugar. Pack the mixture into a 2-quart jar. Dissolve the remaining 2 tablespoons salt in the 3 cups water. Pour enough of this brine over the cabbage to cover it. Push a food-grade plastic bag into the top of the jar, and pour the remaining brine into the bag. Seal the bag. Set the jar out of direct sunlight at a temperature of 65° to 72°F.

3. The next day and each day following, stir the cabbage briefly and then replace the brine bag.

4. In 10 to 14 days, fermentation will have slowed and the pickled cabbage will be ready to eat. Remove the brine bag, cap the jar tightly, and store it in the refrigerator. The cabbage will keep well for months.

BASIC CABBAGE KIMCHI

MAKES ABOUT 1½ QUARTS

KOREANS ARE EVEN MORE ENTHUSIASTIC about their kimchi than Germans are about their sauerkraut. Their favorite kimchi vegetable is Chinese (napa) cabbage, which householders ferment in enormous quantities. They then pack the kimchi into huge earthenware jars, bury the jars in the ground up to their necks, and cover the lids with straw until the kimchi is needed. Or, today, they use appliances that look like chest freezers and that have temperature settings for both fermentation and storage, sometimes in separate compartments.

Kimchi almost always includes hot pepper, usually dried and either ground or flaked. Because much of the ground dried pepper sold in

Korean markets is only mildly hot, Koreans can use generous quantities without burning up. Some of the Mexican and New Mexican ground peppers sold in supermarkets are comparable. If you can't find ground pepper with a moderate heat level, though, you can combine sweet paprika and cayenne to suit your taste.

3 tablespoons plus 1 teaspoon pickling salt
6 cups water
2 pounds Chinese cabbage (1 large head),
    cored and cut into 2-inch squares
6 scallions, cut into 2-inch lengths and
    slivered lengthwise
1½ tablespoons minced fresh ginger
1½ tablespoons minced garlic
2 tablespoons Korean ground dried hot pepper
    (or other mildly hot ground red pepper)
1 teaspoon sugar

1 Dissolve 3 tablespoons salt in the water. Put the cabbage into a large bowl, crock, or nonreactive pot and pour the brine over it. Weight the cabbage with a plate. Let the bowl stand at room temperature for 12 hours.

2 Drain the cabbage, reserving the brine. Mix the cabbage with the remaining ingredients, including the remaining 1 teaspoon salt. Pack the mixture into a 2-quart jar. Cover the cabbage with some of the reserved brine, push a food-grade plastic bag into the mouth of the jar, and pour the remaining brine into the bag. Seal the bag. Let the kimchi ferment in a cool place, preferably at no higher than 68°F, for 3 to 6 days, until the kimchi is as sour as you like.

3 Remove the brine bag and cap the jar tightly. Store the kimchi in the refrigerator, where it will keep for months.

THE KOREAN NATIONAL PASSION

Every autumn, Korean women throughout the country rush to market to buy vegetables for pickle making. They use several kinds of vegetables, including daikon and turnips as well as Chinese cabbage. In fact, Korean pickles come in so many types that a Seoul museum is entirely devoted to the subject; it includes 160 different kinds of kimchi.

Koreans eat kimchi at every meal, including breakfast. At least one and preferably three or four kinds of kimchi are served among the *panchan* (side dishes) at even a simple family dinner. Besides standing as a dish in its own right, kimchi is added to soups, stews, stir-fries, and pancakes. In the winter, a Korean adult consumes as much as a half pound of kimchi per day.

Korean scientists have studied kimchi at least as thoroughly as their Western counterparts have studied sauerkraut. The scientists have found that fresh cabbage kimchi is actually more nutritious than unfermented Chinese cabbage. When kimchi tastes best—before it becomes overly sour—its levels of vitamins B_1, B_2, B_{12}, and niacin are twice what they were initially, and its vitamin C level equals that of fresh cabbage. Scientists have also found that undesirable bacteria and parasites are destroyed during fermentation.

KIMCHI: KOREAN SAUERKRAUT?

Cabbage kimchi differs from sauerkraut in several ways. First, it is usually made from Chinese cabbage rather than white head cabbage, and it is heavily seasoned with hot pepper, ginger, and onions or garlic or both. Kimchi is also a little saltier than sauerkraut, and it's fermented for a much shorter period, so it doesn't get nearly so sour. To preserve nutrients and texture, Koreans do not pasteurize kimchi, although Americans sometimes do. I recommend storing your kimchi in the refrigerator or another dark, cool place.

CABBAGE AND RADISH KIMCHI

MAKES ABOUT 1½ QUARTS

 DAIKON IS OFTEN COMBINED with cabbage in kimchi. The radish slices provide a pleasant crunch.

3 tablespoons pickling salt

5 cups water

1 pound Chinese cabbage (½ large head), cored
 and cut into 2-inch squares

1 pound daikon, cut in half lengthwise and
 thinly sliced crosswise

1 tablespoon minced fresh ginger

1 tablespoon minced garlic

5 scallions, cut into thin rounds

1½ tablespoons Korean ground dried hot pepper
 (or other mildly hot ground dried red pepper)

1 teaspoon sugar

1 Dissolve 2 tablespoons plus 2 teaspoons of the salt in the water. Combine the cabbage and daikon in a large bowl or nonreactive pot and cover them with the brine. Weight the vegetables with a plate and let them stand at room temperature for 12 hours.

2 Drain the vegetables, reserving the brine. Combine them with the remaining ingredients, including the remaining 1 teaspoon salt. Pack the mixture into a 2-quart jar. Pour enough of the reserved brine over the vegetables to cover them. Push a food-grade plastic bag into the jar and pour some or all of the remaining brine into the bag. Seal the bag. Let the kimchi ferment in a cool place, at a temperature no higher than 68°F, for 3 to 6 days, until the kimchi is as sour as you like.

3 Remove the brine bag. Cap the jar tightly and store the kimchi in the refrigerator, where it will keep for months.

KIMCHI WITH RADISH JUICE AND ONION

MAKES ABOUT 1½ QUARTS

THIS KIMCHI IS UNUSUAL in a couple of ways. First, it's made not with ground hot pepper but with hot pepper flakes, which I think provide a prettier appearance. Second, the cabbage is not brined; instead, it's dry-salted initially, then moistened with daikon radish juice before it ferments.

3½ tablespoons pickling salt

2 pounds Chinese cabbage (1 large head), cored and cut into 2-inch squares

10 ounces daikon

2 garlic cloves, chopped

One 1-inch piece fresh ginger, chopped

2½ tablespoons hot pepper flakes

2 scallions, cut into 2-inch lengths and slivered lengthwise

1 medium-size onion, cut into thin rings

1½ teaspoons sugar

7 teaspoons pickling salt dissolved in 1 quart water, for the brine bag

1 In a large bowl, crock, or nonreactive pot, mix 3 tablespoons salt with the cabbage. Let the cabbage stand at room temperature for 2 to 3 hours. Drain it, rinse it, and then drain it well again.

2 Finely grate the daikon, then squeeze the pulp to extract the liquid. You needn't strain it. You should have about ¾ cup liquid.

3 In a blender, grind the garlic, ginger, and hot pepper flakes with the daikon juice. Add this mixture to the cabbage, and then add the scallions, onion, sugar, and the remaining ½ tablespoon salt. Mix well. Pack the mixture into a 2-quart jar. Push a food-grade plastic bag

into the mouth of the jar, and fill the bag with the brine. Let the kimchi ferment in a cool place, at a temperature no higher than 68°F, for 3 to 6 days, until the kimchi is as sour as you like.

(4) Remove the brine bag and cap the jar tightly. Store the kimchi in the refrigerator, where it will keep for months.

KIMCHI AS MEDICINE

While more and more Westerners are turning up their noses at sauerkraut, Koreans and other Asians are eating more kimchi. This is at least in part out of fear of SARS (severe acute respiratory syndrome), the deadly pneumonia that left Korea virtually untouched while sickening people throughout most of Asia in 2003. Many people inside and outside of the country believe that kimchi kept Koreans safe from the disease.

As Korean scientists have proven, beneficial microbes in kimchi can overpower bacteria such as *Helicobacter pylori*, *Shigella sonnei*, and *Listeria monocytogenes*. Scientists are now cultivating kimchi microbes in hopes of using them for mass production of a new kind of antibiotic.

Besides killing bacteria, kimchi may fight viruses. A team at Seoul National University reported in 2005 that an extract of kimchi helped in treatment of chickens infected with avian flu. After further studies, the team hoped to distribute the remedy to poultry farms across Korea.

In guarding human health, kimchi battles more than microbes. Scientific studies show that high consumption of cruciferous vegetables reduces the risk of breast cancer. Korea has one of the world's lowest incidences of this disease.

KIMCHI
WITH ANCHOVIES

MAKES ABOUT 3 QUARTS

KOREANS OFTEN FLAVOR and enrich their kimchi with seafood, such as dried shrimp or anchovies or even oysters. This recipe calls for canned anchovies; try to find some packed in a bland oil rather than olive oil. Their flavor will get stronger as the kimchi ages.

Note that this is a quick kimchi, with no brine to mix. Because the fermentation is quick, you needn't bother to weight the cabbage.

4 pounds Chinese cabbage (2 large heads), cored and cut crosswise into 2-inch lengths

¼ pound daikon, halved or quartered lengthwise, then cut crosswise ⅛ inch thick

5 garlic cloves, minced

3 scallions, cut into 2-inch lengths and slivered lengthwise

¼ cup pickling salt

3 tablespoons hot pepper flakes

2 ounces oil-packed anchovies, sliced crosswise, undrained

1. In a large bowl, crock, or nonreactive pot, mix the cabbage and daikon. Add the garlic, scallions, salt, and hot pepper flakes, and mix well. Cover the container with a towel, cloth, or loose-fitting lid, and let the kimchi ferment at room temperature for 2 days.

2. Pour the oil from the anchovies over the vegetables, add the anchovies, and mix well. Pack the kimchi into a 2-quart jar and store the jar in the refrigerator. The kimchi will keep for at least 10 days.

KIMUCHI

Hᴇʀᴇ's ᴀ ᴊᴀᴘᴀɴᴇsᴇ ᴠᴇʀsɪᴏɴ ᴏғ ᴋɪᴍᴄʜɪ. I like this pickle for its pretty carrot slivers and the subtle sweetness provided by the apple. Eat *kimuchi* with rice, or as a snack with sake or beer.

2¼ pounds Chinese cabbage, cored
3½ tablespoons pickling salt
1 medium-size carrot, thinly sliced on the diagonal and slivered
    lengthwise
1 small apple, peeled and coarsely grated
3 scallions, cut into very thin rounds
2 teaspoons minced fresh ginger
1 garlic clove, minced
1 tablespoon Korean ground dried hot pepper (or other mildly
    hot ground dried red pepper)
1 cup water

1 Halve the cabbage lengthwise by slicing through only the white parts and then gently separating the leaves. In the same way, separate each half into 2 or 3 lengthwise wedges, each about 2 inches wide. Sprinkle the cabbage wedges with 3 tablespoons salt. With your fingers, rub the salt into the cabbage leaves, especially the white parts. Put the cabbage into a bowl, crock, or nonreactive pot, cover the cabbage with a plate, and weight the plate with a rock or a quart jar filled with water. Let the cabbage stand at room temperature for 8 to 10 hours.

2 Drain and rinse the cabbage, gently squeezing each wedge to remove excess liquid. Cut the cabbage into 1-inch squares and put them into a bowl. Mix in the carrot, apple, scallions, ginger, garlic, hot pepper, and remaining 1½ teaspoons salt. Pack the mixture into a 2-quart jar and pour the 1 cup water over. Cap the jar loosely and let the kimuchi ferment in a cool place for 3 to 6 days, until it is as sour as you like.

3 Cap the jar tightly, and store the *kimuchi* in the refrigerator.

A BEVY OF BRASSICAS

Asian cabbages come in many varieties, all of which can be pickled. The barrel-shaped types—known as Chinese or napa cabbage to English speakers—are favored for most kimchis, because they soften readily. If you have a long, cool growing season, do plant these sweet, tender cabbages, because they are not only good for kimchi but far superior to head cabbage for salads or stir-frying. Other Asian brassicas to try are *pe-tsai*, or celery cabbage, with long, narrow heads; *tah tsai* or *tatsoi*, a beautiful deep-green plant that spreads its spoon-shaped leaves in ground-hugging rosettes; *minato santo*, a light-green, loose-headed cabbage with slightly curly, lettuce-like leaves; and the many varieties of mustard and *pak choi* (or *bok choy*). The all-time favorite at my house is *mei quing choy*, "baby" *pak choi* that is as delicious briefly soured, Japanese style, as it is gently pan-fried whole until tender.

JAPANESE SALT-PICKLED CABBAGE

T ODAY THE JAPANESE usually make pickles of this sort—*shio-zuke*, or salt pickles—in small plastic tubs with inner lids that screw down to press the vegetables inside. But you can use the same improvised equipment—plate and rock or water-filled jar in a crock or other container—that serves for other sorts of brining.

This delicate, lightly soured cabbage pickle is particularly simple to make. You can pickle cucumber halves (seeded if they're large) in the same way.

2 pounds Chinese cabbage (1 large head), cored
1½ tablespoons pickling salt
1 small dried hot pepper, such as japonés or de árbol
Zest of ½ lemon, in strips (optional)

1 Remove and reserve the wilted outer cabbage leaves. Halve the cabbage lengthwise by slicing through only the white parts and then gently separating the leaves. In the same way, separate each half into 2 or 3 lengthwise wedges, each about 2 inches wide. Lay the wedges on a tray or platter and place this in a sunny window or in a greenhouse. Let the wedges wilt for 2 to 3 hours.

2 Sprinkle the cabbage wedges with the salt. With your fingers, rub the salt into the leaves, especially the white parts. Lay the wedges in a Japanese pickle press (opposite page), crock, or nonreactive bowl. Crumble the pepper and sprinkle the seeds and broken pod over the cabbage. Sprinkle the lemon zest over all, if desired. Cover the cabbage with the wilted outer cabbage leaves.

3. If you're using a Japanese pickle press, screw the inner lid down hard and let the press stand at room temperature for 5 to 6 hours. If you don't have one of these devices, cover the cabbage with a plate, and then weight the plate heavily. You can use 3 quart jars filled with water, some well-scrubbed heavy rocks, or a plastic bag filled with gravel. Let the cabbage rest under its weights until it releases its brine; this will take about 8 hours for a 10-pound weight.

4. Loosen the screw on the pickle press, or remove most of the weight on the cabbage. Let the pickle mature in its brine for 12 to 24 hours, until the brine is slightly sour. If you won't be serving all of the pickle immediately, pack it into a quart jar, pour the brine over, and refrigerate the jar.

5. To serve the cabbage, rinse the wedges briefly under cold water and squeeze out excess moisture. Cut the wedges into 1-inch lengths. Serve the pickle in small dishes, seasoned, if you like, with a few drops of soy sauce.

THE JAPANESE PICKLE PRESS

Like everything else in Japanese households, Japanese home pickling is always small in scale. Heavy crocks and rocks are no longer needed for salt-pickling, since a family usually has a special little plastic container that does the same job. Called a *shokutaku tsukémono ki*, this tub has an inner lid that screws down to quickly press the brine out of vegetables. In the United States, such pickle presses are sold at Japanese specialty markets.

LEMONY PICKLED CABBAGE

CABBAGE AND LEMON, I believe, are as beautifully matched in their flavors as cucumber and dill. In a variation on the preceding recipe, lemon juice as well as zest gently flavor a simple quick pickle from Japan.

2 pounds Chinese cabbage (1 large head), cored

1½ tablespoons pickling salt

1 small dried hot pepper, such as japonés or de árbol

Zest of 1 small lemon, in strips

5 teaspoons lemon juice

6 tablespoons rice vinegar

1½ teaspoons mirin (sweet rice wine)

1½ teaspoons light soy sauce

1. Remove and reserve the wilted outer cabbage leaves. Halve the cabbage lengthwise by slicing through only the white parts and then gently separating the leaves. In the same way, separate each half into 2 or 3 lengthwise wedges, each about 2 inches wide. Lay the wedges on a tray or platter and place this in a sunny window or in a greenhouse. Let the wedges wilt for 2 to 3 hours.

2. Sprinkle the cabbage wedges with the salt. With your fingers, rub the salt into the leaves, especially the white parts. Lay the wedges in a Japanese pickle press (page 203), crock, or nonreactive bowl. Crumble the pepper and sprinkle the seeds and broken pod over the cabbage. Sprinkle the lemon zest over all. Cover the cabbage with the wilted outer cabbage leaves.

3. If you're using a Japanese pickle press, screw the inner lid down hard and let the press stand at room temperature for 5 to 6 hours. If

you don't have one of these devices, cover the cabbage with a plate, then weight the plate heavily. You can use 3 quart jars filled with water, some well-scrubbed heavy rocks, or a plastic bag filled with gravel. Let the cabbage rest under its weights until it releases its brine, about 8 to 12 hours.

4 Squeeze the cabbage wedges, reserving the brine. Pack the wedges into a quart jar. Combine the brine with the lemon juice, vinegar, mirin, and soy sauce, and pour this liquid over the cabbage wedges. Seal the jar and let the pickle mature at room temperature for 2 to 5 hours.

5 Refrigerate the pickle if you won't be serving it immediately. It will keep in the refrigerator for about 2 weeks.

6 To serve the cabbage, squeeze the excess moisture out of each wedge and cut the wedge into 1-inch lengths. Serve the pickle in small dishes, seasoned, if you like, with a drop or two of soy sauce.

PICKLED RED CABBAGE

MAKES 2 PINTS

IN ENGLAND, red cabbage is traditionally pickled with vinegar, as in this recipe. You can substitute white cabbage; just use white wine vinegar in place of red.

Canning the cabbage with a boiling-water bath is a modern twist on a very old recipe. If you want to forego this step, you can try a traditional technique instead: Let the cut cabbage dry in the sun for two to three hours before tossing it with the salt. Cover the cabbage well with vinegar and cap the jars tightly. Store them in a cool place.

2¼ pounds cored and trimmed red cabbage, shredded

1 tablespoon pickling salt

1⅓ cups red wine vinegar

¼ cup firmly packed light brown sugar

4 teaspoons whole yellow mustard seeds

½ teaspoon whole cloves

½ teaspoon blade (unground) mace

½ teaspoon whole allspice berries

½ teaspoon whole black peppercorns

½ teaspoon whole celery seeds

One 1-inch cinnamon stick

1. In a large bowl or crock, toss the cabbage with the salt. Cover the container and let it stand in a cool place for 8 to 12 hours.

2. In a nonreactive saucepan, combine the vinegar, sugar, and mustard seeds. Tie the other spices in a spice bag or scrap of cheesecloth, and add this to the saucepan. Bring the contents to a boil and simmer them for 5 minutes. Let the liquid cool.

3. Drain the cabbage thoroughly and then pack it into pint mason jars. Remove the spice bag from the saucepan and pour the cooled liquid over the cabbage. (If you don't have quite enough liquid, evenly divide what you have between the jars, and then top them off with a little straight vinegar.) Close the jars with two-piece caps.

4. Process the jars for 20 minutes in a boiling-water bath.

5. Store the cooled jars in a cool, dry, dark place for at least 3 weeks before eating the cabbage.

PICKLED CABBAGE
AND PEPPERS

MAKES 4 PINTS

HIS RECIPE COMBINES white cabbage and sweet peppers in a crisp and colorful vinegar pickle.

2 pounds cored and trimmed white head cabbage, shredded

5 cups thinly sliced green or red (or mixed green and red) bell
   or other sweet peppers

¼ cup pickling salt

1 cup sugar

1½ cups white wine vinegar

½ teaspoon hot pepper flakes

4 teaspoons whole black mustard seeds

6 garlic cloves, minced

1. In a large bowl or crock, toss the cabbage and peppers with the salt. Cover the container and let it stand in a cool place for 8 to 12 hours.

2. In a nonreactive saucepan, combine the sugar and vinegar. Bring the mixture to a boil and then let it cool.

3. Rinse the cabbage and drain it well. Toss it with the hot pepper flakes, mustard seeds, and garlic. Pack the vegetable mixture loosely into pint jars. Pour the cooled vinegar mixture over the vegetables.

4. Close the jars with two-piece caps. Process the jars in a boiling-water bath for 20 minutes.

5. Store the cooled jars in a cool, dry, dark place for at least 3 weeks before eating the cabbage.

CORTIDO

THIS FRESH CABBAGE PICKLE comes from El Salvador, where it is served as a salad like cole slaw with *pupusas*, thick corn tortillas thinly stuffed with meat, cheese, or beans.

1½ pounds cored and trimmed white head cabbage, shredded
1 small red onion, halved and very thinly sliced
1 medium-size carrot, thinly sliced diagonally, then slivered
2 garlic cloves, minced
¾ teaspoon pickling salt
2 to 3 teaspoons coarsely ground black pepper
½ cup pineapple vinegar or white wine vinegar
¼ cup pineapple juice

1. In a large bowl, toss together the cabbage, onion, carrot, garlic, salt, and pepper. Combine the vinegar and pineapple juice and pour the liquid over the vegetables. Mix well.

2. Pack the mixture into a jar or plastic tub, cover the container tightly, and refrigerate it for at least 12 hours. During this period, occasionally stir the mixture or shake the container.

3. The pickled cabbage will keep well, covered and refrigerated, for at least 4 days.

5

RICE-BRAN, MISO, AND SOY-SAUCE PICKLES

WITH THE EXCEPTION OF the pickled garlic and ginger, all of the pickles in this chapter are Japanese. Pickles are of paramount importance in the traditional Japanese diet. They are eaten at every meal, and are sometimes the *only* food at a meal besides rice. When other dishes are served, pickles always conclude the meal, along with hot rice and tea.

Japanese pickling methods are impressively varied. Recipes for Japanese dry-salted, pressed pickles appear in Chapter 4 and Chapter 7. Recipes for some Japanese vinegar pickles appear in Chapter 3. In this chapter, I describe three other kinds of Japanese pickles: *nukamiso* pickles, briefly soured in rice-bran mash; miso pickles, flavored in fermented soybean paste; and *shoyu* pickles, made with soy sauce. The Chinese and Koreans have their own traditional soy-sauce pickles, and a few of their recipes are included here. But the rice-bran and miso pickles are uniquely Japanese.

Today Japanese cooks usually pickle foods not to preserve them for long periods, but to enhance their flavor, digestibility, and nutritional value. Therefore these recipes call for small quantities of vegetables and short pickling times, from a few hours to a few days. If you garden year-round, or if you regularly visit a good year-round produce market, some of these pickles may turn out to be your favorites.

PICKLES IN RICE-BRAN MASH

MAKES ABOUT 2 QUARTS

EVERY JAPANESE HOME once had a barrel of fermenting rice-bran mash, or *nukamiso*, often stored under the floor boards. Each day, the family would fish pickled vegetables out of the mash, rinse them, and eat them at the end of a meal or with tea and rice alone. Fresh vegetables would be buried in the mash, to become the next day's pickles.

Mild and delectable, rice-bran pickles are also very healthful. Like other fermented pickles that haven't been pasteurized, they are full of *Lactobacilli* bacteria, which aid in digestion. They are said to contain high levels of niacin, vitamin B_1, linoleic acid, and vitamin E as well.

INGREDIENTS FOR YOUR NUKAMISO POT

Rice bran, or *nuka*, looks very much like wheat bran. In Japanese markets and some natural foods stores, *nuka* is sold in 2-pound packages, just the amount you'll need for pickling. If you can't find rice bran, use wheat bran. Shizuo Tsuji (*Japanese Cooking*, 1980) claims that even oatmeal or cornflakes will work in *nukamiso*.

Often added to *nukamiso* is either beer or *koji*, grain (usually rice) inoculated with *Aspergillus* mold. You can find *koji* at Japanese markets; some natural foods stores carry it, too. *Koji* must be kept refrigerated.

For a touch of sweetness and to balance the moisture content, dried *kombu*, or kelp, is always added to the *nukamiso* pot. You can buy *kombu* at a Japanese market or natural foods store.

Hot peppers and ginger are added for flavor and aroma. Other flavoring ingredients often added to *nukamiso* are garlic, dried shiitake mushrooms, and *katsuobushi* (dried bonito) shavings.

Nukamiso is usually made in spring, summer, or fall, because fermentation gets under way more quickly and reliably in warmer weather. The mash requires a 7- to 10-day conditioning period, during which you must feed it with vegetable scraps.

It's important to stir *nukamiso* daily. For this reason, good, attentive Japanese housewives used to be said to "smell of *nukamiso*."

2 pounds *nuka* (rice bran)

¾ cup pickling salt

3 dried hot peppers, such as japonés or de árbol, seeded and broken into pieces

One 1-inch piece fresh ginger

Two 5-inch strips dried *kombu* (kelp), cut into small pieces

1½ cups *koji* (*Aspergillus*-inoculated rice), soaked in lukewarm water just to cover for 15 minutes (or 1 cup beer)

2 cups water *or* 1 cup water and 1 cup beer

Vegetable scraps for conditioning the mash (wilted vegetables and unwaxed peels are fine to use, since you are going to discard them)

Vegetables for pickling, whole or in large pieces: cucumbers, carrots, Chinese cabbage, daikon, radishes, turnips, celery, green pepper

1 In a gallon crock or similar container, stir together the *nuka*, salt, hot peppers, ginger, and *kombu*. Add the soaked *koji*, with its liquid (or 1 cup beer), and 2 cups water (or 1 cup water and 1 cup beer). Using your clean hands, mix well. Bury 2 or 3 vegetable scraps in the mash; the vegetables should not touch. Cover the crock and set it in a place where the temperature stays at about 60° to 70°F.

2 After 24 hours, remove and discard the vegetable scraps, and mix the *nukamiso* well. Put in some more wilted vegetables or scraps. Do this every day for the next 6 days.

3. After a week, the *nukamiso* should be getting smelly. The odor should improve after you stir the mash. Start tasting the pickles, if you haven't already. Rinse them first in cold water. When the mash is ready, the pickles will taste pleasingly salty, crunchy, and a little tangy, with an earthy aftertaste. Begin using higher-quality vegetables when you like the taste of the pickles.

4. Continue to stir the mash every day, even if you have no vegetables in it. You can leave vegetables in longer than a day—even as long as a month, if you like strong-flavored pickles—but don't neglect to stir the *nukamiso*. Every time you do, gently smooth the top of the mash and wipe the inside of the container clean.

5. Rinse, drain, and slice the pickles before serving them. They are traditionally eaten at the end of a meal, with hot rice.

6. When the *nukamiso* has absorbed too much water from the vegetables, sink a small bowl or cup into the center of the mash, and let the excess liquid collect there. Remove the cup and liquid the next day.

7. Since some of the mash will adhere to the pickles when they're taken from the crock, the mash will gradually diminish in volume. To replenish it, add 3 tablespoons pickling salt to ½ pound rice bran, and discard the next day's pickles. If the volume isn't decreasing much, remove and replace half the mash every 30 days.

ABOUT DAIKON

In cookbooks, daikon is often called long white radish or Chinese turnip, but I use the Japanese term because that's what you'll usually see in stores. Daikon is easy to find in supermarkets as well as Asian markets, and it's not difficult to grow, provided you have a bed of deep, loose soil. Since daikon has a long growing period, however, it may bolt if planted in spring. In places with hot summers, daikon should be planted in mid- to late summer for fall or winter harvest.

DAIKON PICKLED
IN SWEET MISO

MAKES ABOUT 1 PINT

B Y SIMPLY COVERING VEGETABLES in miso for a day or two, you can make tasty, nutritious pickles. The easiest way to make *miso-zuke* is to submerge the vegetables in a bowl of miso, but this technique uses a lot of miso and necessitates rinsing the vegetables before eating them. The technique I describe here, using cheesecloth, requires less miso and keeps it from clinging to the vegetables.

1 pound daikon, cut into 2 x ½ x ½-inch sticks,
   or small whole white radishes
¾ teaspoon pickling salt
½ cup white or yellow miso

1. In a bowl, toss the daikon with the salt. Let the contents stand for 1 hour or more, then drain the daikon.

2. Spread ¼ cup miso over a dinner plate and cover the plate with a piece of cheesecloth. Spread the daikon or small radishes in a single layer on top. Cover the vegetables with another piece of cheesecloth, and spread the remaining miso on top. Cover the whole plate with plastic wrap and refrigerate it for 2 to 4 days.

3. Remove the plastic wrap and the top layer of cheesecloth. The pickles are ready to serve. Leftover pickles can be stored in the miso, but their flavor will grow stronger with time.

4. Although the liquid from the vegetables will dilute the miso, you can reuse it 2 or 3 times.

CELERY PICKLED IN RED MISO

....

MAKES ABOUT 1 PINT

MEDIUM-SALTY RED MISO is here mellowed with the addition of sake and mirin. I particularly like celery in this recipe, but as with any miso pickle you can vary the vegetables. Try daikon, as in the preceding recipe, sliced kohlrabi, very small turnips, or larger turnips, quartered or sliced.

½ cup red miso
2 tablespoons sake (dry rice wine)
1 tablespoon mirin (sweet rice wine)
4 celery stalks, halved lengthwise and cut into 3-inch lengths

ABOUT MISO

Miso is a thick, protein-rich paste made from fermented soybeans. Like wine and beer, miso comes in many varieties, from sweet and light-colored to salty and dark.

To make miso, *koji*—grain or beans inoculated with *Aspergillus* mold—is mixed with cooked soybeans, salt, and water. The type of *koji*—rice, barley, or soybean—partly determines the flavor of the finished miso. Along with microorganisms from the environment, *koji* breaks down the beans and grains into readily digestible amino acids, fatty acids, and simple sugars. Unpasteurized miso is not only easy to digest, but it helps break down other foods in the digestive system, and it can be used as a meat tenderizer.

Although much Japanese miso is now quick-fermented in a temperature-controlled process, resulting in inferior flavor, American natural foods stores stock naturally aged (albeit pasteurized) misos of excellent quality. Many natural foods stores carry three or more varieties, any of which can be used for pickling.

Store miso in the refrigerator, where it will keep well for at least 1 year.

1. Mix together the miso, sake, and mirin to make the *miso-doko* (miso pickling paste). Spread ¼ cup of the paste over a dinner plate and cover the plate with a piece of cheesecloth. Spread the celery in a single layer on top. Cover the celery with another piece of cheese-cloth, and spread the remaining *miso-doko* on top of that. Cover the whole plate with plastic wrap and refrigerate the plate for about 6 hours. (Denser vegetables will need longer pickling.)

2. Remove the plastic wrap and the top layer of cheesecloth. Serve the celery sticks whole or cut into bite-size pieces. Leftover celery can be stored in the *miso-doko*, but the pickles will get darker and saltier with time.

3. Use the *miso-doko* in miso soup.

TURNIP OR KOHLRABI PICKLED IN TWO MISOS

MAKES ABOUT 1 PINT

H ERE THE *miso-doko*, or miso pickling paste, is made from red and white rice misos, a combination suggested by Jan and John Belleme (*Cooking with Japanese Foods*, 1986).

> ¼ cup red miso
> ¼ cup white miso
> 1 pound turnips or kohlrabi or some of each,
>   sliced ½ inch thick

1. In a small bowl, blend the two kinds of miso. Spread ¼ cup of the mixture over a dinner plate and cover the plate with a piece of cheesecloth. Spread the vegetables in a single layer on top. Cover the vegetables with another piece of cheesecloth and spread the

remaining miso on top of that. Cover the whole plate with plastic wrap and refrigerate the plate for 3 days.

2. Remove the plastic wrap and the top layer of cheesecloth. The pickles are ready to eat. Leftover pickles can be stored in the miso, but they will get darker and saltier with time.

3. Although the liquid from the vegetables will dilute the miso, you can reuse it 2 or 3 times.

KOREAN PICKLED SPRING GARLIC

MAKES 1 HALF-PINT

IN THIS RECIPE, the entire garlic head is pickled and eaten, so you will need to use spring garlic—heads that are nearly full in size but not yet covered with papery skin. Their tops won't have yellowed or bent over yet. Here in Oregon, this usually means harvesting in May.

In recent years spring garlic has begun appearing at farmers' markets. But the easiest way to get some may be to grow your own. You can start by planting cloves from the grocery store, although special varieties are available from seed companies. Set the cloves flat end down, 4 inches apart and about 1 inch deep. From just a 3-foot-square patch, you'll harvest about 18 pounds of garlic heads. Your heads will probably grow bigger if you plant them in autumn, but in most areas garlic does well enough when planted in spring.

Serve this pickle as a side dish for a Korean or Japanese meal.

2 spring garlic heads
½ cup soy sauce
½ cup rice vinegar
2 tablespoons sugar
½ teaspoon pickling salt

1 Put the garlic into a small jar or bowl. Stir together the remaining ingredients and pour them over the garlic. Cover the container and let it stand at room temperature for 3 days.

2 Put the garlic into a 1-cup jar (a rounded half-pint mason jar works well). Pour the liquid into a small nonreactive saucepan and bring the liquid to a boil. Reduce the heat and simmer the liquid, uncovered, until it is reduced by half. Let it cool.

3 Pour the cooled liquid over the garlic and cap the jar. Let the jar stand in a cool place for 4 weeks or more. Before serving, slice the garlic heads crosswise into 3 rounds per heads.

4 The pickle should keep for 1 year or longer in a cool, dry, dark place.

MRS. KIM'S
PICKLED GARLIC

MAKES ½ TO ⅔ CUP

A KOREAN-CALIFORNIAN who has run a Greek restaurant and a hotdog stand as well as Asian restaurants, Mrs. Kim pickles garlic much as in the preceding recipe, but she uses mature heads. Her son Michael sent me this recipe, along with a big jar of his mother's pickled garlic.

Mrs. Kim uses brown rice vinegar, which is available in Korean markets and natural foods stores.

3 to 4 garlic heads with small to medium-size cloves
½ to ¾ cup brown rice vinegar
2 to 3 tablespoons light brown sugar
2 to 3 tablespoons soy sauce

1. Separate and peel the garlic cloves. Put them into a jar and cover them with vinegar. Cap the jar and let it stand at room temperature for 1 week.

2. Pour half the vinegar out of the jar (you can use it for dressing a salad, seasoning a sauce, or making a quick pickle). Add the brown sugar and soy sauce, cap the jar, and shake it to mix the contents and dissolve the sugar. Store the jar in the refrigerator.

3. The garlic will be ready to eat after 1 week. Refrigerated, it will keep well for at least 1 year.

GINGER PICKLED IN SOY SAUCE

MAKES ABOUT ½ CUP

WHEN FRESH YOUNG GINGER comes on the market—with skin so thin it tends to rub off—be sure to pickle some. These young roots, usually available in December, are much less fibrous than older ones.

I think of this pickle as a seasoning rather than a condiment. I use it in Chinese- and Japanese-style dishes when I have no fresh ginger in the house.

Although this pickle is Chinese, I use Japanese light (usukuchi) soy sauce, because I prefer its flavor to that of Chinese light soy sauce. Both products, by the way, are light in color, not salt content.

2 ounces young, thin-skinned fresh ginger, sliced paper-thin
½ teaspoon sugar
¼ teaspoon pickling salt
About 5 tablespoons light *(usukuchi)* Japanese soy sauce

1. In a bowl, toss the ginger with the sugar and salt. Let the mixture stand for 1 hour.

2. Put the ginger into a small jar. Pour in enough soy sauce to cover the ginger, and cap the jar. Let the jar stand at room temperature. The ginger will be ready to use in 24 hours.

3. Store the jar in the refrigerator, where the ginger will keep for at least 1 year.

DAIKON PICKLED IN SOY SAUCE

MAKES ABOUT 1 PINT

HERE IS THE PUREST SORT of *shoyu* (soy sauce) pickle, in which the soy sauce alone seasons the vegetable. I think you'll agree that no other flavoring is needed.

1 pound daikon
½ cup light *(usukuchi)* Japanese soy sauce

1. Cut the daikon into ¼-inch-thick rounds (or half-rounds, or quarter-rounds, depending on the thickness of the radish). Put the daikon pieces into a jar and pour the soy sauce over them. Cap the jar and refrigerate it. After several hours, the soy sauce should almost cover the daikon. Keep the jar in the refrigerator for at least 24 hours, shaking it occasionally.

2 If you don't eat the pickle immediately, store it in the refrigerator for up to 1 week.

CUCUMBER PICKLED WITH SOY SAUCE AND KOMBU

MAKES ABOUT 1 PINT

Kombu, or *konbu*, is kelp, sold dried and packaged in natural foods stores and many Asian markets. The seaweed adds a subtle sweetness to this quick Japanese pickle. For variety, add a carrot, cut into matchstick strips.

1 pound cucumbers, approximately ¾ inch in
    diameter, halved lengthwise and cut crosswise
    into ½-inch-thick pieces
1 teaspoon pickling salt
One 2-inch piece dried *kombu*, cut with scissors
    into very thin strips
1 fresh green hot pepper, such as jalapeño,
    cut into thin rings
½ cup light *(usukuchi)* Japanese soy sauce

1 In a bowl, toss the cucumbers with the salt. Let them stand at room temperature for about 1 hour.

2 Rinse the cucumbers and drain them well. Mix them with the remaining ingredients. Let the mixture stand at room temperature for 6 to 10 hours, stirring occasionally.

3 If the pickles aren't to be eaten right away, store them in the refrigerator, where they should keep for about 1 week.

4 You can reuse the pickling liquid 2 or 3 times if you keep it refrigerated.

CUCUMBER AND EGGPLANT PICKLED WITH SOY SAUCE

MAKES ABOUT 1 PINT

ERE'S A PICKLE YOU CAN START MAKING just a few hours before you serve it.

2 small Japanese eggplants (or any small, slender eggplants)
Two 4-inch pickling cucumbers
One 2-inch piece dried *kombu* (kelp)
¾ cup Japanese soy sauce
1 tablespoon sake (dry rice wine)

1. Halve the eggplants lengthwise. Slash each half diagonally on the skin side, making many close cuts. Put the eggplants into a small bowl, cover them with cold water, and let them soak for 30 minutes.

2. While the eggplants soak, slash the cucumbers diagonally most of the way through, making many close cuts.

3. Drain the eggplants, and then cut both the eggplants and the cucumbers into ¾-inch pieces along slash lines. In a jar, combine the vegetables, *kombu*, soy sauce, and sake. Cover the jar and shake it gently. Let the jar stand at room temperature for 2 hours, giving it a shake or two during this period.

4. After 2 hours, the pickle will be ready to serve. If you don't eat all of it immediately, store it in the refrigerator for up to 1 week.

PICKLED CUCUMBERS
WITH SESAME OIL

MAKES ABOUT 1 PINT

ITH ITS STRONG FLAVORS of sesame, ginger, and hot pepper, this Japanese pickle shows a Chinese influence.

1 pound Asian or pickling cucumbers,
   about ¾ inch in diameter
1 teaspoon pickling salt
1 scallion, cut into 1-inch lengths, then slivered
One 1-inch piece fresh ginger, slivered
1 to 2 fresh hot peppers, such as jalapeño,
   seeded and slivered
3 tablespoons rice vinegar
5 tablespoons soy sauce
1 tablespoon sesame oil

1 Halve the cucumbers lengthwise and then cut them into 1-inch-long pieces. In a bowl, toss the cut cucumbers with the salt. Let them stand at room temperature for 1 hour.

2 Drain the cucumbers and return them to the bowl. Mix them with the scallion, ginger, and hot peppers. In a bowl, stir together the vinegar, soy sauce, and oil, and pour this mixture over the cucumbers. Cover the bowl with plastic wrap. Let the pickle stand at room temperature for 2 to 3 hours, or in the refrigerator for 24 hours, turning the cucumbers occasionally.

3 The pickle will keep in the refrigerator, well covered, for about 1 week.

COMMERCIAL JAPANESE PICKLES

In Japan, pickling isn't just a homemaker's art—it's also big business. Since some pickling processes are carefully guarded secrets or just very complicated and time-consuming, they are the province of pickling specialists. If you visit a large Japanese grocery, you'll see dozens of kinds of pickles, or even hundreds, packed in jars or, more often, in vacuum-sealed plastic bags. Check the labels before buying any; many will be adulterated with dyes or other chemicals. But you'll also find some traditional Japanese pickles that you won't be able to make at home. Here are a few examples:

UMEBOSHI. These are salt-pickled *ume*, a fruit related to the apricot but in English called a plum. Picked underripe, the fruits are brined with leaves of red shiso (also known as perilla or beefsteak plant, an annual herb). The fruits are then sun-dried and later brined again. *Umeboshi* are used medicinally to treat all kinds of stomach disorders and to fortify the liver and kidneys. Added to rice gruel, *umeboshi* is the Japanese mother's cure-all.

TAKUAN. Developed by vegetarian monks during Japan's feudal period, *takuan* is daikon partially dried in the shade and then fermented in rice bran. Real *takuan* is usually a pale yellow color; bright yellow *takuan* is probably dyed with chemicals.

NARA-ZUKE. "The pickles of Nara" (a cultural center near Kyoto) are matured for several years in a malty yeast paste. The favorite vegetables for these pickles are *shiro uri*, a zucchini-like vegetable, and small, round eggplants. Before eating *nara-zuke* pickles, rinse off any excess pickling paste and pat the pickles dry.

KOMBU AND
CARROT PICKLE

 HE PLENTIFUL PICKLING LIQUID here makes a tasty seasoning for rice.

> Four 6-inch strips dried *kombu* (kelp), soaked in water for 10
>   minutes
> 2 large carrots, thinly sliced diagonally, then slivered
> ½ cup rice vinegar
> ½ cup soy sauce
> ½ cup mirin (sweet rice wine)
> ¼ cup sake (dry rice wine)

1. Slice the soaked *kombu* strips in half lengthwise and then crosswise into thin strips. Combine the *kombu* and carrot strips in a bowl.

2. In a nonreactive saucepan, bring the vinegar, soy sauce, mirin, and sake to a boil. Boil the liquid for 1 minute and then immediately pour it over the carrot and *kombu*. Cover the bowl with a towel and let the pickle stand at room temperature for about 4 hours before serving it.

3. Refrigerated, the pickle will keep for about 1 week.

6

SWEET PICKLES

MORE LIKE SWEET PRESERVES than like sour fresh or brined pickles, the pickles in this chapter are traditionally eaten with meats. Any of them can make a delightful accompaniment to a holiday roast. Try them also with grilled meats and, if you're not a big meat eater, with rice dishes. You might like them on their own, too. My children love pickled plums, pears, apricots, and watermelon rind for dessert, and I snack on pickled oranges.

Because of the high sugar content as well as the vinegar, these pickles are very well preserved. In most cases, though, I still recommend using a boiling-water bath, which helps ensure a good seal. Where a boiling-water bath might harm the pickle's texture, the open-kettle method will do. With this method, remember that you must use sterilized jars (immersed in boiling water for 10 minutes) and very hot (but not boiled) lids, and the pickle must be very hot when placed in the jars. Jars that aren't vacuum-sealed should be stored in the refrigerator. (Check for a vacuum seal on cooled jars by pressing down on the center of each lid. It should not pop up.)

"Among pickles, sweet or spiced ones are my favorites, although Mamma, no doubt, would object to them as occupying neutral ground between pickles and preserves, as being too undecided, not positive enough, in character to suit her."

—*Emma P. Ewing,* Cooking and Castle-Building *(1880)*

SWEET GHERKIN PICKLES

MAKES 6 TO 7 PINTS

IN THIS CLASSIC RECIPE, the salt, sugar, and vinegar are added in several steps to keep the cucumbers from shriveling. You can use American-style pickling cucumbers, European gherkins (cornichons), or West Indian gherkins; just be sure your cucumbers are very small. Leave a bit of stem attached to each one and wash the cucumbers very gently. Lightly rub off the prickles if you're using cornichons; leave the prickles in place if you're using American-style cucumbers. Scrape off the blossom ends. Since little cucumbers deteriorate quickly, begin processing them within a half day after picking.

> 7 pounds 1- to 2-inch-long pickling cucumbers
> ½ cup pickling salt
> 18 quarts boiling water (you'll use 6 quarts at a time)
> 6 cups distilled white vinegar
> 8 cups sugar
> 1 teaspoon ground turmeric
> 2 teaspoons whole celery seeds
> 2 teaspoons Mixed Pickling Spices (page 15)
> Two 4-inch cinnamon sticks
> ½ teaspoon whole fennel seeds

1. Put the cucumbers into a large bowl or crock and cover them with 6 quarts boiling water. Let them stand at room temperature for 6 to 8 hours.

2. Drain the water from the cucumbers. Dissolve ¼ cup of the salt in another 6 quarts boiling water and pour this over the cucumbers. Let them stand at room temperature for 6 to 12 hours.

3. Drain the water from the cucumbers again. Once more, dissolve ¼ cup salt in 6 cups boiling water and pour this over the cucumbers. Let them stand at room temperature for 6 to 12 hours.

4. Drain the water from the cucumbers and pierce each once with a table fork. In a nonreactive pot, combine 3 cups of the vinegar, 3 cups of the sugar, and all of the spices. Bring the mixture to a boil, stirring to dissolve the sugar, and then pour the liquid over the cucumbers. Let them stand at room temperature for 6 to 8 hours.

5. Drain the syrup, with the spices, back into the pot. Add 2 cups each of the sugar and vinegar and bring the syrup to a boil. Pour it over the cucumbers. Let them stand at room temperature for 6 to 12 hours.

6. Drain the syrup, with the spices, into the pot again. Add 2 cups sugar and the remaining 1 cup vinegar. Bring the syrup to a boil and pour it over the cucumbers. Let them stand 6 to 12 hours.

7. Pour the syrup through a strainer into the pot. Pack the pickles into pint or half-pint mason jars, discarding the spices. Add the remaining 1 cup sugar to the syrup and bring it to a boil. Cover the pickles with the boiling syrup, leaving ½ inch headspace. Close the jars with two-piece lids. Process the jars for 5 minutes in a boiling-water bath, or pasteurize them by immersing them in water heated to 180° to 185°F for 30 minutes.

8. Store the cooled jars in a cool, dry, dark place for at least 3 weeks before eating the pickles.

JOHN FOX'S GINGER GHERKINS

MAKES ABOUT 3 PINTS

 OME YEARS AGO, a man named John Fox called me from Idaho. He wanted a recipe for some pickles he'd eaten on the

East Coast many years earlier. They were like gherkins, he said, only very gingery. Maybe they had a little cinnamon in them, too. The couple who made them had been perfecting the recipe for years. While we talked I was washing tiny cucumbers. I promptly devised this recipe and made up a batch of John Fox's Ginger Gherkins.

My mother took these pickles to a church potluck, where a very old lady popped one after another into her mouth, with occasional exclamations of delight, until they were all gone.

2 pounds 1- to 2-inch pickling cucumbers, blossom ends
   removed
4 quarts boiling water
3 tablespoons pickling salt
2 cups distilled white vinegar
2⅔ cups sugar
2 tablespoons chopped fresh ginger
One 3-inch cinnamon stick

1. Put the cucumbers into a bowl and cover them with 2 quarts boiling water. Let them stand at room temperature for 6 to 8 hours.

2. Drain the water from the cucumbers. Dissolve all but 1 teaspoon of the salt in the remaining 2 quarts boiling water and pour this over the cucumbers. Let them stand at room temperature for 6 to 12 hours.

3. Drain the water from the cucumbers and pierce each once with a table fork. In a nonreactive pot, combine 1⅔ cups of the vinegar with 1⅔ cups of the sugar and the remaining 1 teaspoon salt. Add the ginger and cinnamon stick. Bring the mixture to a boil, stirring to dissolve the sugar. Pour the syrup over the cucumbers. Let them stand at room temperature for 6 to 12 hours.

4. Drain the syrup, with the spices, back into the pot. Add ⅔ cup sugar and the remaining ⅓ cup vinegar and bring the syrup to a boil. Pour

it over the cucumbers. Let them stand at room temperature for 6 to 12 hours.

5 Pour the syrup through a strainer into the pot. Pack the cucumbers into pint or half-pint mason jars, discarding the cinnamon stick. Add the remaining ⅓ cup sugar to the syrup and bring it to a boil. Cover the pickles with the boiling syrup, dividing the ginger among the jars and leaving ½ inch headspace. Close the jars with two-piece lids. Process the jars for 5 minutes in a boiling-water bath, or pasteurize them by immersing them in water heated to 180° to 185°F for 30 minutes.

6 Store the cooled jars in a cool, dry, dark place for at least 3 weeks before eating the pickles.

SWEET SLICES FROM BRINED CUCUMBERS

MAKES ABOUT 5 PINTS

THIS RECIPE TURNS fermented cucumbers into sweet, tart, spicy slices. If you prefer, cut the fermented cucumbers into sticks or chunks instead of thin slices.

2 cups water
2 cups distilled white vinegar
3 pounds fermented cucumbers, such as Spicy Crock Pickles (page 53), rinsed, drained, and sliced ¼ inch thick
2 cups sugar
1 lemon, thinly sliced
One 1-inch piece fresh ginger, chopped
2 teaspoons whole cloves
Two 4-inch cinnamon sticks

1. Combine the water and 1 cup of the vinegar. Pour this liquid over the cucumbers. Let the cucumbers soak at room temperature for 2 hours.

2. Stir in the remaining 1 cup vinegar. Let the cucumbers soak for 2 more hours.

3. Put the cucumbers and their liquid into a nonreactive pot. Add the sugar and the lemon, and then the ginger and dry spices tied in a spice bag or scrap of cheesecloth. Bring the contents to a boil, stirring to dissolve the sugar, and then reduce the heat. Simmer the cucumbers until they are translucent, about 5 minutes.

4. Transfer the cucumbers and their liquid to a shallow nonreactive container. Let them stand overnight to plump.

5. Strain the liquid into a saucepan. Pack the cucumbers—and, if you wish, the lemon slices—into pint mason jars. Bring the liquid to a boil and pour it over the cucumbers, leaving ½ inch headspace. Close the jars with two-piece lids and process them in a boiling-water bath for 10 minutes or immerse them in water heated to 180° to 185°F for 30 minutes.

6. Store the cooled jars in a cool, dry, dark place for at least 3 weeks before eating the pickles.

SWEET WHOLE PICKLES FROM BRINED CUCUMBERS

MAKES 2 QUARTS

HERE'S ANOTHER WAY to make excellent sweet pickles from cucumbers you've already brined. Traditionally "salt-stock" cucumbers are used—those fermented in a 10 percent brine—but pickles from a 5 percent brine work just as well and require no soaking in fresh water.

3 pounds fermented cucumbers, such as Spicy Crock Pickles
(page 53), about 3 inches long

1 quart cider vinegar or distilled white vinegar

3 cups sugar

One 1-inch piece fresh ginger, thinly sliced

Two 3-inch cinnamon sticks

1 tablespoon whole cloves

1 whole nutmeg kernel, coarsely chopped

1. Rinse and drain the cucumbers and pierce each one twice with a table fork. In a nonreactive pot, combine the vinegar and sugar. Add the ginger and dry spices, tied in a spice bag or scrap of cheesecloth. Bring the liquid to a boil. Add the cucumbers and bring the contents to a boil again. Boil the cucumbers for 3 minutes. Remove the pot from the heat and cover the pot. Let the cucumbers stand in their liquid.

2. The next day, drain off the liquid, bring it to a boil, and pour it back over the cucumbers. Do this again on the third day.

3. On the fourth day, again drain off the liquid and bring it to a boil. Remove the spice bag and pack the cucumbers into pint or quart mason jars. Pour the hot liquid over the cucumbers, leaving ½ inch headspace. Close the jars with two-piece lids. Process the jars in a boiling-water bath, 10 minutes for pints or 15 minutes for quarts, or immerse the jars in water heated to 180° to 185°F for 30 minutes.

4. Store the cooled jars in a cool, dry, dark place.

QUICK SWEET
CUCUMBER SLICES

SWEET-PICKLE FANS really love this simple recipe.

2¾ pounds 3- to 4-inch pickling cucumbers, sliced ³/₁₆ inch
    thick
2 tablespoons pickling salt
2¼ cups sugar
3½ cups cider vinegar
½ teaspoon whole fennel seeds
½ teaspoon whole coriander seeds
1½ teaspoons whole allspice berries
1 tablespoon whole yellow mustard seeds

1. In a bowl, toss the sliced cucumbers with the salt. Empty an ice cube tray over the cucumbers. Let them stand at room temperature for 3 to 4 hours.

2. Drain the cucumbers, discarding any ice cubes that haven't melted. In a nonreactive pot, bring to a boil the sugar, vinegar, and spices, stirring to dissolve the sugar. Add the cucumbers. Over medium heat, bring the contents back to a boil, stirring occasionally so they heat evenly. Pack them into pint or half-pint mason jars, leaving ½ inch headspace. Close the jars with two-piece lids. Process the jars for 5 minutes in a boiling-water bath or immerse them in water heated to 180° to 185°F for 30 minutes.

3. Store the cooled jars in a cool, dry, dark place.

GINGERY WATERMELON PICKLES

MAKES ABOUT 6 PINTS

WHEN ASKED ABOUT their favorite pickled foods, many older Americans will quickly mention watermelon pickles, though they may admit they haven't tasted any since they were children. In those days, they may piously add, nothing was wasted. This just shows that their mothers stretched the truth a bit, as they measured out substantial quantities of precious sugar and spices to put up something of almost no nutritional value. But watermelon pickles had spiritual value, as you will understand if you present such an elderly person with a jar of these sweet, tart pickles.

More properly called watermelon *rind* pickles, these pickles are made not of the fruit's sweet pink flesh but of the bland white rind beneath. To make them, you slice the watermelon into manageable pieces, then cut away the hard, green skin as well as all the pink flesh. The rind remaining will probably be only ¼ to ½ inch thick, though I suspect that older watermelon varieties had thicker rinds. I cut my rind into 1-inch squares, but you might prefer ½ by 1-inch pieces or long strips. You might even cut the rind into fancy shapes, as Victorian cooks sometimes did. For this recipe, you will probably need a large watermelon or two medium-size ones.

½ cup pickling salt
2 quarts water
3 quarts prepared watermelon rind (see above)

For the syrup:

1 large lemon, thinly sliced

Two 3-inch cinnamon sticks, broken

1 teaspoon whole cardamom seeds

1 teaspoon whole cloves

1 teaspoon whole allspice berries

One 1½-inch piece fresh ginger, thinly sliced

2 cups water

2 cups distilled white vinegar or white wine vinegar

4 cups sugar

1. In a large bowl, dissolve the salt in the 2 quarts water. Add the watermelon rind. Let the rind soak in the brine at room temperature for 6 to 12 hours.

2. Drain and rinse the rind, and then drain it again. In a large nonreactive pot, cover the rind with cold water, bring the water to a boil, and simmer the rind for 5 minutes. Drain the rind well and return it to the bowl.

3. To make the syrup, tie the lemon, dry spices, and ginger in cheesecloth, and put the package into the pot along with the 2 cups water, the vinegar, and the sugar. Bring the mixture to a boil, stirring, and then reduce the heat. Simmer the syrup for 5 minutes. Remove the pot from the heat and add the drained watermelon rind. Let the rind rest in the syrup at room temperature for 12 to 24 hours.

4. Bring the rind and syrup to a boil. Reduce the heat and simmer the rind until it is translucent.

5. Remove the pot from the heat and remove the spices tied in cheesecloth. Pack the hot rind with the liquid into pint mason jars, leaving ½ inch headspace. Close the jars with two-piece caps and process the jars for 10 minutes in a boiling-water bath.

6. Store the cooled jars in a cool, dry, dark place.

MINTY WATERMELON PICKLES

T HESE PICKLES ARE THE WAY many Southerners like them: extra-crisp, from a soak in limewater. The mint sprigs provide a delightfully unusual flavor.

To prepare the rind, cut away all the pink flesh and green skin, and then cut the white rind into 1-inch squares or other small pieces.

2 tablespoons pickling lime (page 17)
7 cups water
10 cups prepared watermelon rind (see above)

For the syrup:

1 lemon, thinly sliced
Two 3-inch cinnamon sticks, broken
1 teaspoon whole cardamom seeds
1 teaspoon whole cloves
1 teaspoon whole allspice berries
One 1½-inch piece fresh ginger, thinly sliced
3 cups distilled white vinegar or white wine vinegar
3 cups water
3 cups sugar
4 mint sprigs

1. In a bowl or crock, stir the lime into the 7 cups water. Add the watermelon rind and let it soak at room temperature for 8 to 12 hours.

2. Drain the rind and rinse it well. Cover it with fresh water and soak it for an hour. Repeat this step twice to remove all traces of the lime. Drain the rind well.

3. To make the syrup, tie the lemon, dry spices, and ginger in a scrap of cheesecloth, and place this in a nonreactive pot with the vinegar, water, and sugar. Bring the contents to a boil, stirring to dissolve the sugar. Reduce the heat and simmer the syrup 5 minutes. Pour it over the watermelon rind. Let the rind rest in the syrup, with the spices, at room temperature for 12 to 24 hours.

4. Put the rind and the syrup into a nonreactive pot and bring them to a simmer. Simmer them until the rind is translucent, about 1½ hours. Remove the spices. Pack the hot rind with the syrup into pint mason jars, adding a mint sprig to each and leaving ½ inch headspace. Close the jars with two-piece caps and process the jars in a boiling-water bath for 10 minutes.

5. Store the cooled jars in a cool, dry, dark place.

DARK WATERMELON PICKLES

MAKES ABOUT 3½ PINTS

MY FRIEND JOCELYN WAGNER shared this once-secret recipe after its originator had passed on. From the way the recipe was written, I gathered that it's actually older than Jocelyn's friend, who must have been born around 1900. I've substituted jars for the crock and volume measurements for weights, and cut the quantities overall, but Jocelyn said the pickle turned out just as she remembered it from childhood. It's a very sweet pickle, almost a confection.

To prepare the watermelon rind, cut away all the pink flesh and green skin, and then cut the white rind into ½ by ¾-inch pieces.

7 cups prepared watermelon rind (see above)

6 cups cold water

1 quart cider vinegar or distilled white vinegar

5 cups firmly packed dark brown sugar

Two 3-inch cinnamon sticks, broken

1 tablespoon whole cloves

1. Put the watermelon rind into a pot and cover it with the cold water. Bring the water to a boil and boil the rind until it is just translucent; don't let it get soft.

2. In another pot, bring to a boil the vinegar and sugar, stirring to dissolve the sugar. Tie the spices in a spice bag or scrap of cheesecloth and add them to the syrup. Drain the rind and add it to the syrup, too. Bring the contents to a simmer. Simmer them for about 1½ hours, until the syrup is dark and thick.

3. Remove the spice bag. Ladle the rind and syrup into pint or half-pint mason jars, leaving ½ inch headspace, and close the jars with two-piece caps. Process the jars for 10 minutes in a boiling-water bath.

4. Store the jars in a cool, dry, dark place.

WILD WATERMELON

Native to Africa's Kalahari Desert, citron melon grows wild in the San Diego area and Baja California. This round, white-fleshed, pectin-rich ancestor of the modern watermelon is preferred, where it grows, for preserving, as is the citron-watermelon cross known as pie melon in the southeastern United States. Citron melon is said to be tasteless, but its thick inner rind is said to make fabulous pickles.

SWEET PICKLED PUMPKIN OR SQUASH

MAKES 3 PINTS

L IKE DARK WATERMELON PICKLES (page 240), these pickles are almost a confection. My recipe is based on one from Germany.

2¼ pounds skinned and seeded pumpkin or winter squash

2 cups white wine vinegar or distilled white vinegar

2 cups water

3 cups sugar

Shredded zest of 1 small orange

8 whole cloves

¼ teaspoon whole allspice berries

¼ teaspoon whole black peppercorns

Two 3-inch cinnamon sticks, broken

One 2-inch piece fresh ginger, thinly sliced

1. Cut the pumpkin or squash into ¼- to 1-inch cubes, scraping off any stringy inner flesh. Put the cubes into a nonreactive bowl. Combine the vinegar and water and pour the liquid over the cubes. Turn the cubes in the liquid a few times and then drain off the liquid into a saucepan. Bring the liquid to a boil. Pour it over the pumpkin or squash, cover the bowl with a cloth, and let it stand at room temperature for 8 to 12 hours.

2. Drain off the liquid into a nonreactive pot and add the sugar and orange zest. Add the dry spices and ginger, tied in a spice bag or scrap of cheesecloth. Bring the contents to a boil, stirring to dissolve the sugar, and reduce the heat. Simmer the syrup for 5 minutes.

3. Add the pumpkin or squash cubes to the syrup. Simmer them until they become translucent around the edges, about 1 hour. Remove

the pot from the heat and let it stand at room temperature for 8 to 12 hours.

4 Remove the spice bag from the syrup. With a slotted spoon, pack the pumpkin or squash cubes into pint or half-pint mason jars. Bring the syrup slowly to a boil and then pour it over the pumpkin or squash cubes, leaving ½ inch headspace. Close the jars with two-piece lids and process them for 10 minutes in a boiling-water bath.

5 Store the cooled jars in a cool, dry, dark place.

SPICED ORANGE SLICES

MAKES 3 PINTS

THE FIRST ORANGE PICKLES I tasted were made by E. Waldo Ward, a company that's been making marmalade, jam, and fruit pickles in Sierra Madre, California, since 1891. The tall orange slices were beautifully packed, upright in their narrow 10-ounce jar, and they tasted as good as they looked—chewy, sweet, tart, and just slightly bitter. Upon finishing off the jar, I had to try making my own pickled oranges—which, it turns out, isn't difficult at all.

Pickle some oranges for holiday gifts, and your friends and relatives will insist that you do it every year.

8 large or 10 medium-size seedless oranges
4 cups sugar
1 cup distilled white vinegar or white wine vinegar
½ cup water
10 whole cloves
Two 3-inch cinnamon sticks, broken

1. Cut a thin slice from either end of the orange, so that you can see the flesh and membranes. With a sharp knife, cut out the orange sections along the membranes, from one end of the orange to the other, through both flesh and peel. Put the orange sections into a nonreactive pot and cover them with water. Bring the water to a boil. Reduce the heat and simmer the oranges for 45 minutes to 1 hour, covered, until they are tender. Drain them well.

2. In another nonreactive pot, combine the sugar, the vinegar, the ½ cup water, and the spices tied in a spice bag or scrap of cheesecloth. Add the orange slices, bring the contents to a boil again, and then reduce the heat. Simmer the oranges for about 1 hour, until they are well glazed.

3. Remove the spice bag. Pack the oranges into half-pint or 12-ounce jars, arranging them vertically or diagonally, peels out, if your patience allows, and leaving ½ inch headspace. Cover the oranges with the hot syrup and close the jars with two-piece caps. Process the jars for 10 minutes in a boiling-water bath.

4. Store the jars in a cool, dry, dark place.

PICKLED CRAB APPLES

MAKES 2 PINTS

ONE LATE DECEMBER, I fought the birds for the last of my neighbor's crab apples so I could make this pickle for the first time. Although I should have gotten around to the job two months earlier, the pickles were delicious. The slight bitterness of crab apples is a welcome counterpoint to the sweet and sour pickle flavors, especially for people who generally pass up sweets. These pickles make a fine accompaniment to roasted or grilled meats.

Keep in mind that many crab apple varieties are planted strictly for their value as ornamental trees. If the fruit is to make a good pickle, it must also taste good fresh off the tree.

> One 2-inch cinnamon stick, broken into pieces
> 1 teaspoon whole allspice berries
> ½ teaspoon whole cloves
> 1¼ cups sugar
> ¾ cup water
> 1 cup cider vinegar
> 1½ pounds crab apples, stems attached

1. Tie the spices in a spice bag or a scrap of cheesecloth and put them into a nonreactive pot with the sugar, water, and vinegar. Bring the syrup to a boil, stirring to dissolve the sugar, and then remove the pot from the heat. Let the syrup cool.

2. With a large needle, pierce each crab apple through to keep it from bursting when heated (some crab apples may crack anyway). Put the crab apples into the pot of cooled syrup and bring the syrup slowly to a simmer. Simmer the crab apples until they are tender and translucent, about 15 minutes.

3. Remove the pot from the heat. Let it rest, covered, for 12 to 18 hours.

4. With a slotted spoon, remove the crab apples from the syrup. Pack them into pint mason jars, leaving ½ inch headspace. Remove the spice bag from the syrup. Bring the syrup to a boil and pour it over the fruit. Close the jars with two-piece lids and process the jars in a boiling-water bath for 10 minutes.

5. Store the jars them in a cool, dry, dark place.

PICKLED PEARS

....

O N COLD WINTER NIGHTS, pickled pears are a delightful treat, either with dinner or on their own. Seckel pears are the traditional American pickling variety; because they're small, you can pickle them whole, and because they're very firm, they won't fall apart in the process. But any sort of pear will do. When I had a very productive Bartlett pear tree, I pickled one or two dozen quarts of Bartletts every year. Bartletts are big, soft, and moist, but if you use them before they start to turn mushy, and you cut each one in half to fit into the jar, they make fine pear pickles. Big, firm, spicy Comice pears are my favorite for fresh eating, but I have often saved some fruit from my little Comice tree for pickling, too. Asian pears are good pickled as well.

6 pounds pears, peeled
Four 3-inch cinnamon sticks
2 tablespoons whole cloves
One 1-inch piece fresh ginger, thinly sliced
3 cups water
2 cups distilled white vinegar or white wine vinegar
4 cups sugar

1. If your pears are small, leave them whole, with the stem attached. If they are a large variety, cut them in half and core them.

2. Tie the dry spices and ginger in a spice bag or scrap of cheesecloth. In a large nonreactive pot, combine the water, vinegar, and sugar and add the spice bag. Bring the syrup to a boil, stirring to dissolve the sugar, and then reduce the heat. Simmer the syrup for 5 minutes. Add a single layer of pears and cook them gently until they are just tender, 5 to 15 minutes, depending on the variety.

3. Transfer the cooked pears to quart or pint mason jars and cook the rest of the pears in the same way. When all of the pears are cooked, pour the hot pickling liquid over them, leaving ½ inch headspace. Close the jars with two-piece caps. Process the jars for 15 minutes in a boiling-water bath.

4. Store the cooled jars in a cool, dry, dark place.

PICKLED QUINCE

MAKES ABOUT 7 PINTS

ALTHOUGH MANY AMERICANS today have never tasted a quince, a hundred years ago most rural American families had a quince tree. They seldom ate the fruits raw, since quinces are generally very hard and tart. But cooks prized the pectin-rich, aromatic fruits for jam, jelly, and preserves (the word *marmalade* comes from the Portuguese word for quince, *marmelo*), and gardeners loved the small, umbrella-shaped trees and their beautiful pale pink spring flowers.

If you or a friend has a quince tree, this is one of many good ways to use the fruit.

One 3-inch cinnamon stick, broken
1 teaspoon whole cloves
2 teaspoons whole allspice berries
4 thin slices fresh ginger
1 cup distilled white vinegar
1 cup water
4 cups sugar
7 pounds quinces, peeled, cored, and cut into twelfths or
 eighths

1. In a large nonreactive saucepan, combine the dry spices and ginger, tied in a spice bag or scrap of cheesecloth, with the vinegar, water, and sugar. Bring the contents to a boil, stirring to dissolve the sugar. Reduce the heat and cover the pan. Simmer the syrup for 10 minutes.

2. While the syrup simmers, put the quince slices into a nonreactive pot and pour enough cold water over them to cover them. Over high heat, bring the contents to a boil. Reduce the heat and simmer the slices for 5 to 10 minutes, until they are just tender.

3. Drain the quince slices, and divide them among pint or quart mason jars. Cover the fruit with the hot syrup. Close the jars with two-piece caps and process the jars for 10 minutes in a boiling-water bath.

4. Store the cooled jars in a cool, dry, dark place.

PICKLED PEACHES

MAKES 4 QUARTS

I PREFER THIS TRADITIONAL peach pickle recipe, which uses the so-called open-kettle method, to the Extension Service method for pickling peaches, which requires a 20-minute boiling-water bath. Since ripe peaches would turn to mush with this much boiling, the Extension recipe calls for underripe peaches. But underripe peaches are difficult to peel and not very tasty.

For this recipe I recommend using small peaches, no bigger than 2 inches in diameter. If you use larger peaches, the syrup won't go as far; you'll probably fill only three quart jars with 5 or 6 pounds of peaches.

Since the peaches are canned whole, you can use either a cling or free-stone variety. If they are ripe, you will be able to peel them easily after first dipping them in boiling water for 30 to 40 seconds and then cooling them in ice water. One variety, Veteran, can be easily peeled with no boiling-water dip at all. To keep the peaches from darkening, drop them into acidulated water as you peel them (opposite page).

Pickled peaches aren't just a relish; they also make a delicious dessert.

> One 3-inch cinnamon stick, broken
> 1 teaspoon blade (unground) mace
> 1 teaspoon whole allspice berries
> ½ teaspoon whole cloves
> One 1-inch piece fresh ginger, thinly sliced
> 3 cups sugar
> 2½ cups water
> 3½ cups white wine vinegar or distilled white vinegar
> 7 pounds small (2 inches in diameter) ripe but firm
>   peaches, peeled

1 In a nonreactive pot, combine the dry spices and ginger with the sugar, water, and vinegar. Bring the mixture to a boil, stirring to dissolve the sugar. Reduce the heat and simmer the mixture for 10 minutes. Add the peaches and gently simmer them for a few minutes, until they are heated through and just tender.

2. Remove the peaches from the liquid with a slotted spoon and pack them into hot sterilized quart or pint mason jars. Boil the syrup until it thickens a bit, about 8 minutes.

3. Pour the hot syrup over the peaches, dividing the spices equally among the jars and leaving ½ inch headspace. Close the jars with two-piece lids and set the jars on a rack or pad to cool undisturbed.

4. When the jars have cooled, check their seals. Store the jars in a cool, dry, dark place.

PICKLED APRICOTS

MAKES 4 PINTS

SINCE I COULDN'T FIND an apricot pickle recipe anywhere, I was compelled by my pickle mania to invent one. There is no better way to preserve apricots than as apricot jam, but this pickle comes close. Serve it as a relish or for dessert.

> 2 cups white wine vinegar
> 2 cups white wine
> 2 cups sugar
> Shredded zest of 1 orange
> 3 tablespoons shredded crystallized ginger
> 4 pounds apricots, halved and pitted

1. In a nonreactive pot, bring to a boil all of the ingredients except the apricots. Add the apricots and cook them briefly, until they are heated through and barely tender.

2. Divide the apricots and their liquid among hot sterilized pint mason jars, leaving ½ inch headspace. Close the jars with two-piece lids and set the jars on a rack or pad to cool undisturbed.

3 When the jars have cooled, check their seals. Store the jars in a cool, dry, dark place.

RUSSIAN PICKLED CHERRIES

MAKES 1 PINT

ENCOURAGED BY CZAR PETER THE GREAT after his tour of Europe in 1697 to 1698, the Russians adopted the Dutch custom of pickling fruits and serving them with meats. This recipe was the favorite among half a dozen like it that I tried on a panel of taste-testing relatives. Feel free to leave out the kirsch (clear cherry brandy) if you haven't any on hand.

These cherries are neither cooked nor water-bathed. Heating them, unfortunately, would ruin their texture.

> 2 cups sweet cherries, stemmed
> 1 cup cider vinegar
> ½ cup sugar
> ⅓ cup water
> Seeds from 1 cardamom pod
> A fragment of cinnamon stick
> Pinch of ground mace
> 1 whole allspice berry
> 2 teaspoons kirsch (optional)

1 Put the cherries into a bowl or jar and cover them with the vinegar. Cover the bowl with a towel or cap the jar, and let the cherries stand overnight.

2 Drain the vinegar into a nonreactive saucepan. Add the sugar, water, and spices. Bring the liquid to a boil, and then reduce the heat. Simmer the liquid for 15 minutes. Remove the saucepan from the heat and let the liquid cool.

3 Stir the kirsch, if you are using it, into the pickling liquid. Pour the pickling liquid over the cherries, cover them, and let the cherries stand at room temperature for 3 days.

4 Drain the liquid into a saucepan again and bring the liquid to a boil. Let it cool.

5 Put the cherries into a hot sterilized pint jar. Strain the cooled pickling liquid over them, filling the jar to the brim, and close the jar tightly with a nonreactive cap. Let the jar stand in the refrigerator or another cool, dark place for at least 1 month before eating the cherries. They will keep well even unrefrigerated for about 1 year.

EXTRA-SWEET PICKLED CHERRIES

MAKES 1 PINT

THIS SIMPLE AMERICAN COUSIN of the preceding Russian recipe makes a sweeter, pit-free cherry pickle. It's especially good with cold and smoked meats. You can use the resulting mild cherry-flavored vinegar in salads and other dishes. Just strain the vinegar, sweeten it with a little sugar, if you like, and simmer the vinegar for a few minutes before funneling it into a sterilized bottle.

1 pound sweet or sour cherries, stemmed and pitted
1½ cups white wine vinegar or distilled white vinegar
1 cup sugar

1. Put the cherries into a bowl or jar and cover them with the vinegar. Cover the bowl with a towel or cap the jar, and let the cherries stand at room temperature for 3 days.

2. Drain off the vinegar. Layer the cherries in a hot sterilized pint jar with the sugar. Cap the jar tightly, put it in a cool place, and shake it every day until the sugar has completely dissolved.

3. Store the jar in the refrigerator or another cool, dark place for 1 month before eating the cherries. They will keep well even unrefrigerated for about 1 year.

PICKLED WHOLE BLUEBERRIES

MAKES ABOUT 3 PINTS

IN CHAPTER 9 I OFFER two blueberry relish recipes, but this pickle is different in that the blueberries keep their shape. I've served them instead of cranberries for Thanksgiving dinner; you might also try them with ham or baked beans. The same recipe works wonderfully with blackberries.

1½ cups red wine vinegar
Two 2-inch cinnamon sticks
1 teaspoon whole cloves
1 teaspoon whole allspice berries
2 quarts firm blueberries
2 cups sugar

1. In a large nonreactive pot, combine the vinegar and spices, tied in a spice bag or scrap of cheesecloth. Bring the vinegar and spices slowly to a simmer. Cover the pot and simmer the mixture for 5 minutes.

2. Add the blueberries to the pot. Cook them over medium-low heat just until they are heated through, shaking the pot gently instead of stirring to avoid breaking the berries. This should take about 8 minutes. Remove the pot from the heat, cover it, and let it stand at room temperature for 8 to 12 hours.

3. Pour the blueberries and their liquid into a colander set over a bowl. Remove the spice bag. Carefully transfer the drained berries to pint mason jars.

4. Return the liquid to the pot and add the sugar. Bring the mixture to a boil, stirring to dissolve the sugar. Boil the syrup briskly for about 4 minutes to thicken it a bit.

5. Cover the berries with hot syrup, leaving ½ inch headspace. Close the jars with two-piece caps and process the jars for 15 minutes in a boiling-water bath.

6. Store the cooled jars in a cool, dry, dark place.

PICKLED DARK GRAPES

MAKES 2 PINTS

HERE IS ANOTHER RECIPE that transforms the fruits of summer into a sweet, spicy winter condiment. Use seedless table grapes such as Red Flame rather than a slip-skin variety such as Concord.

½ cup red wine vinegar or distilled white vinegar
1½ cups sugar
¼ teaspoon ground mace
¼ teaspoon ground ginger
¼ teaspoon ground cinnamon

¼ teaspoon whole cardamom seeds

2 pounds red seedless grapes, washed, well drained,
   and halved lengthwise

1. In a saucepan, bring the vinegar, sugar and spices to a boil, stirring to dissolve the sugar. Add the grapes. Cook them over medium-low heat until the liquid comes to a simmer and the grapes are heated through.

2. Ladle the grapes and their liquid into pint or half-pint mason jars, leaving ½ inch headspace. Close the jars with two-piece caps and process the jars for 15 minutes in a boiling-water bath.

3. Store the cooled jars in a cool, dry, dark place for at least 1 month before eating the grapes.

PICKLED GREEN GRAPES

MAKES 2 PINTS

THIS PICKLE IS A LIGHT-COLORED variation on the preceding recipe.

One 1-inch piece fresh ginger, thinly sliced

½ teaspoon whole cloves

½ teaspoon blade (unground) mace

One 2-inch cinnamon stick, broken

½ cup white wine vinegar

1 cup sugar

2 pounds Thompson or other seedless green table grapes (but not a slip-skin variety), halved lengthwise

1. Tie the ginger and dry spices in a spice bag or scrap of cheesecloth and put this into a nonreactive pot with the vinegar and sugar. Bring

the contents to a boil, stirring to dissolve the sugar, and then reduce the heat. Simmer the liquid, covered, for 10 minutes.

2 Add the grapes. Cook them until the liquid comes to a simmer again and the grapes are heated through.

3 Ladle the grapes and their liquid into pint or half-pint mason jars. Close the jars with two-piece caps and process the jars for 15 minutes in a boiling-water bath.

4 Store the cooled jars in a cool, dry, dark place for at least 1 month before eating the grapes.

PICKLED ITALIAN PLUMS

MAKES 6 QUARTS

For this recipe, use the sweet, dark, oval plums that are called prunes when they're dried. Italian is one variety, French is another, and in Oregon we have a third popular variety, Brooks.

When I had two Italian plum trees, I pickled many quarts every year. Since the fruit is low in acid, pickling greatly enhances its flavor. My family loves these pickles both as a condiment and as a winter dessert.

Since very ripe plums are liable to get mushy when you heat them, use fruits that are still firm.

6½ pounds firm Italian or other prune plums
5½ cups cider vinegar
4 cups sugar
Two 3-inch cinnamon sticks, broken into thirds
6 small dried hot peppers, such as japonés or de árbol
12 whole cloves

36 whole allspice berries
1 tablespoon whole cardamom seeds
24 thin slices fresh ginger

1. With a large needle, prick each plum three times to prevent bursting.

2. In a large pot, bring the vinegar and sugar to a boil, stirring to dissolve the sugar. Add the plums and reduce the heat to low. Cook the plums very gently until they are heated through.

3. While the plums heat, put one-third of a cinnamon stick, 1 hot pepper, 2 cloves, 6 allspice berries, ½ teaspoon of cardamom seeds, and 4 slices of ginger into each of six quart mason jars. Ladle the hot plums into the jars. Cover the plums with the hot syrup, leaving ½ inch headspace. Close the jars with two-piece caps and process the jars for 25 minutes in a boiling-water bath.

4. Store the cooled jars in a cool, dry, dark place for at least a month before eating the plums.

PICKLED PLUMS WITH RED WINE

MAKES 3½ TO 4 QUARTS

THIS PLUM PICKLE, with a thick syrup mellowed by the addition of red wine, makes a very special winter treat. Though more trouble to make than basic pickled plums, it is worth the extra effort.

I've successfully substituted homemade plum wine for the red wine in this recipe. I've also occasionally added other spices, such as Sichuan peppercorns, black pepper, star anise, or juniper berries.

1 teaspoon whole cloves

Two 3-inch cinnamon sticks, broken

4 thin slices fresh ginger

4⅔ cups sugar

3 cups red wine vinegar

3 cups red wine

6 pounds firm Italian or other prune plums

1. Tie the dry spices and ginger in a spice bag or scrap of cheesecloth. Put the spices into a large nonreactive pot with the sugar, vinegar, and wine. Bring the contents to a boil, stirring to dissolve the sugar. Reduce the heat and simmer the mixture for 5 minutes. Remove the pot from the heat, and let the syrup cool for 20 minutes or more.

2. To prevent bursting, prick each plum 4 times with a large needle or bamboo skewer. Put the plums into a bowl. Pour the cooled syrup over them, tucking the spice bag among the plums, and let them rest at room temperature for 8 to 12 hours.

3. Drain off the syrup into a nonreactive pot, add the spice bag, and bring the syrup to a boil. Remove the pot from the heat and let the syrup cool again. Pour the cooled syrup over the plums and tuck in the spice bag. Again, let the plums rest in the syrup at room temperature for 8 to 12 hours.

4. Put the plums, their syrup, and the spice bag into a large nonreactive pot. Heat the plums over low heat, stirring gently, until their skins begin to crack. Using a slotted spoon, transfer the plums to quart or pint mason jars. Boil the syrup until it is slightly thickened, remove the spice bag, and then pour the syrup over the plums (which will have sunk in the jars somewhat), leaving ½ inch headspace. Close the jars with two-piece caps and process the jars for 10 minutes in a boiling-water bath.

5. Store the cooled jars in a cool, dry, dark place for at least a month before eating the plums.

PICKLED CANTALOUPE CHUNKS

MAKES 3 PINTS

THIS RECIPE IS A GOOD USE for cantaloupes or muskmelons that crack before they're ripe, as many do after the rains begin in the Willamette Valley. The flesh should be orange and sweet, but still as crisp as a cucumber. If the melon has cracked, use it immediately; don't wait for spoilage to set in.

2 cups cider vinegar

1 cup water

Two 3-inch cinnamon sticks

1 tablespoon whole cloves

9 cups slightly underripe cantaloupe or muskmelon cubes,
    each about ¾ inch square

3 cups sugar

1 In a nonreactive saucepan, combine the vinegar and water. Add the spices, tied in a spice bag or scrap of cheesecloth. Bring the contents to a boil. Put the cantaloupe or muskmelon cubes into a bowl and pour the vinegar mixture over them. Push the spice bag down between the melon cubes. Let the bowl stand at room temperature for 2 to 8 hours, turning the melon cubes occasionally.

2 Drain the liquid into a nonreactive pot, add the spice bag, and bring the mixture to a boil. Add the sugar, and stir until it dissolves. Add the melon cubes. Simmer them, uncovered, until they are translucent around the edges, about 1 hour.

3 Remove the spice bag. With a slotted spoon, divide the melon cubes among pint mason jars. Pour the hot syrup over the melon cubes, leaving ½ inch headspace. Close the jars with two-piece caps and process the jars for 10 minutes in a boiling-water bath.

LIMED CANTALOUPE PICKLES

MAKES 2 PINTS

WITH THIS RECIPE you can use fully ripe—but not yet mushy—cantaloupe or muskmelon; a soak in limewater will keep the pieces firm. Don't take any shortcuts with the rinsing procedure, though; it ensures that the pickle is sufficiently acidic.

I call for melon balls here just for the sake of variety, but you can cut the flesh into cubes, chunks, or even long strips, if you prefer.

3 tablespoons pickling lime (page 17)
1 quart water, plus more for soaking
5 cups cantaloupe or muskmelon balls
1½ cups cider vinegar
2 cups sugar
2 teaspoons whole cloves
One 3-inch cinnamon stick, broken
2 teaspoons slivered fresh ginger

1. In a large bowl, stir the lime into 3 cups water. Add the melon balls and let the bowl stand at room temperature for 4 to 5 hours.

2. Drain the melon balls, rinse them well, and then cover them with fresh water. Let the bowl stand for 1 hour, and then drain them again. Give the melon two more hour-long soaks in fresh water. Drain the melon well.

3. In a nonreactive pot, combine the vinegar, 1 cup water, sugar, and dry spices and ginger tied in a spice bag or scrap of cheesecloth. Bring the syrup to a boil, stirring to dissolve the sugar, and add the melon balls. Bring the syrup to a boil again, reduce the heat, and

cover the pot. Simmer the melon about 1 hour, until the balls are translucent around the edges.

4 With a slotted spoon, divide the melon balls between two pint mason jars. Boil the syrup until it thickens a little and remove the spice bag. Pour the hot syrup over the melon balls, leaving ½ inch headspace. Close the jars with two-piece caps and process the jars for 10 minutes in a boiling-water bath.

5 Store the cooled jars in a cool, dry, dark place.

PICKLED FIGS

MAKES 4 PINTS

ONE OF MY FAVORITE FOODS at my grandmother's funeral banquet was a dish of pickled figs. They evoked memories of the big Black Mission fig tree that spread over the yard of the house where my mother grew up, a tree that gratified the family's sweet tooth through the Depression. (Since I was very young when the tree was cut down, I don't know whether I remember it myself or whether I've ab-

PICKLED FIGS WITH LIME

You can pickle ripe, soft figs if you first firm them up with a lime bath. Because they won't shrink as much as figs pickled without lime, you'll need only about 3 pounds figs for the other quantities in the recipe. Combine 2 tablespoons pickling lime (page 17) with 2 quarts water, and soak the figs for 12 to 24 hours. Rinse the figs and then soak them in three changes of fresh water for an hour at a time. Then cook the figs in the syrup as directed until they turn dark and glossy.

sorbed my mother's memories of it.) Learning that my grandmother had pickled the figs herself, two years or more before her death, brought all the good times back again.

For this recipe you'll need to search out figs that have grown to full size but have not yet softened.

4 pounds (about 3 quarts) ripe but still firm figs
3 quarts water
2 teaspoons pickling salt
2 cups firmly packed light brown sugar
2 cups granulated sugar
2 cups cider vinegar
One 4-inch cinnamon stick
4 thin lemon slices
1 teaspoon whole cloves

1. Put the figs into a large pot with the water and salt, and simmer the figs, covered, for 15 minutes. Drain the figs.

2. In a large nonreactive pot, combine both sugars and the vinegar. Add the cinnamon stick and lemon slices. Tie the cloves in a spice bag or a scrap of cheesecloth and add them to the pot. Bring the mixture to a boil, stirring until the sugar is dissolved. Add the figs and cook them at a bare simmer, uncovered, for 1 hour, occasionally turning them gently. At the end of the hour the figs should look glossy and a little shrunken, and the syrup should be only slightly thickened.

3. Divide the figs among 4 pint mason jars, allowing plenty of room for the figs to swell in the syrup. Add a lemon slice to each jar. Pour the syrup over the figs, leaving ½ inch headspace. Close the jars with two-piece caps and process the jars for 15 minutes in a boiling-water bath.

4. Store the cooled jars in a cool, dry, dark place.

7

QUICK PICKLES

THE PICKLES IN THIS CHAPTER may seem a miscellany, but they have one thing in common: You can make them in less than two days. With some recipes, in fact, your produce can go from garden or market to table in only a few hours. Many of the pickles here are like other fresh pickles, except that the spices are cracked and heated with the vinegar, so the flavors diffuse quickly. Although lacking oil, some almost qualify as salads and may be served in place of salads.

Some of these pickles will keep for long periods, but most are intended to be eaten soon after they're made. All should be stored in the refrigerator if they're not eaten right away.

SICHUAN CUCUMBER PICKLE WITH HOT BEAN PASTE

MAKES ABOUT 1 PINT

HERE'S A DELICIOUS, mildly hot pickle to have with Chinese food. You can serve it the same day you pick the cucumbers.

Hot bean paste is made from fermented beans, crushed hot peppers, and often garlic. Sichuan peppercorns aren't really peppercorns at all, but the tiny, dark, very aromatic seeds of a plant in the genus *Zanthoxylum*. Both of these special Sichuan flavorings are sold in Asian markets (a ban on Sichuan peppers was enforced from 2002 to 2005, but since then they have become available again, as they are now heated to kill bacteria that can cause citrus canker). Check a Chinese cookbook for other ways to use these seasonings.

If you want your pickle hotter, add a little chile oil—that is, sesame oil in which hot peppers have been steeped.

1 pound (about 2) Asian, "burpless," or salad cucumbers, seeded, quartered lengthwise, and cut into 2-inch lengths
2 teaspoons pickling salt
2 garlic cloves, thinly sliced
1 1/2 teaspoons hot bean paste
1 teaspoon sugar
1 1/2 teaspoons rice vinegar
1 1/2 teaspoons sesame oil
1/2 teaspoon Sichuan peppercorns, crushed

1. Toss the cucumber pieces with the salt. Let them stand at room temperature for 2 to 3 hours.

2. Rinse the cucumber pieces and drain them thoroughly. Mix together the remaining ingredients and toss them with the cucumbers in a bowl. Let the cucumbers marinate for 3 to 5 hours at room temperature.

3. Cover the bowl and chill the cucumbers for at least 1 hour before serving them.

THAI PICKLED CUCUMBERS

MAKES ABOUT 1 QUART

THIS QUICK PICKLE is traditionally eaten with pork satay, but you could serve it with any dishes that might be complemented by a sweet salad. For the best flavor, roast raw peanuts yourself, in a dry skillet or in the oven. Although the pickle is meant to be eaten as soon as it's mixed, you can prepare the pickling liquid ahead of time.

¼ cup rice vinegar
¼ cup water
¼ cup sugar
½ teaspoon pickling salt
1 pound pickling or Asian cucumbers, peeled
1 teaspoon minced fresh hot red pepper,
   such as Fresno or serrano, or Southeast Asian
   Chile-Garlic Relish (see page 336)
3 tablespoons chopped shallots
1 tablespoon minced dry-roasted peanuts
Cilantro leaves

1. In a saucepan, bring to a boil the vinegar, water, sugar, and salt, stirring to dissolve the sugar and salt. Let the liquid cool.

2. Make lengthwise incisions in the cucumbers, if you like, so that the slices will be prettier. If the cucumbers are bigger than 1 inch in diameter, halve them lengthwise, then slice the cucumbers crosswise ³⁄₁₆ inch thick.

3. When you're ready to serve, mix the cucumbers, pepper, and shallots in a serving bowl. Pour the cooled liquid over the vegetables and sprinkle the peanuts and cilantro on top.

QUICK JAPANESE
PICKLED DAIKON

MAKES ABOUT 1 PINT

 LIGHTLY SALTED AND PRESSED DAIKON makes a pleasant appetizer or side dish. You can buy *shichimi* in Japanese markets.

¾ pound daikon, peeled

2 teaspoons pickling salt

2 teaspoons soy sauce

2 teaspoons rice vinegar

¼ teaspoon sugar

Toasted sesame seeds or *shichimi-togarashi*
   (7-spice seasoning)

1. Cut the daikon into ¼-inch-thick rounds, half-rounds, or quarter-rounds, depending on the thickness of the root. In a wide bowl, toss the daikon with the salt. Lay a plate on top of the daikon, top it with a large, clean rock or a quart jar filled with water, and press the daikon for 4 to 8 hours.

2. Drain the daikon well, then toss it with the soy sauce, vinegar, and sugar. If you won't be eating the daikon right away, refrigerate it for no longer than a few days.

3. Serve the daikon in small dishes, sprinkled with toasted sesame seeds or *shichimi*.

QUICK PICKLED
BABY TURNIPS

MAKES ABOUT 1 PINT

IF YOU AVOID TURNIPS because of their sharp taste, you might try some of the sweet, mild Japanese varieties. Presto, Hakurei, and Market Express are quick-growing white turnips that are harvested at only 1 to 1½ inches in diameter. They make wonderful quick pickles.

> 1 pound small turnips (1 to 2 inches in diameter), trimmed at
>   top and bottom and peeled
> 2 teaspoons pickling salt
> 1½ cups water
> 1 tablespoon seeded and minced hot or sweet pepper, such as
>   jalapeño or pimiento
> 3 tablespoons sugar
> 1½ cups rice vinegar or white wine vinegar

1 Score each turnip several times at top and bottom. Put the turnips into a bowl. Stir the salt into the water until the salt dissolves and pour this brine over the turnips. Let them stand for 30 minutes to 1 hour.

2 Drain the turnips well, return them to the bowl with the minced pepper, and toss well. Combine the sugar and vinegar, stirring until the sugar dissolves. Pour the liquid over the turnips. Cover the bowl with plastic wrap and refrigerate the turnips for two days, after which they will be ready to eat. Well covered and refrigerated, they will keep for several months.

QUICK GREEN TOMATO PICKLE

MAKES 2 QUARTS

THIS IS AN OLD MENNONITE RECIPE. The pickle has kept well in my refrigerator through the winter and on into spring. I think it gets better with age.

2^1/$_2$ pounds green tomatoes, sliced ^{3}/$_{16}$ inch thick (about 2
    quarts tomato slices)
1^1/$_2$ pounds (about 5 medium-size) white or yellow onions,
    sliced ^{3}/$_{16}$ inch thick
1^1/$_2$ teaspoons whole yellow mustard seeds
2 tablespoons pickling salt
^{1}/$_2$ cup sugar
2 cups cider vinegar

1. In a large bowl or crock, combine the tomatoes, onions, and mustard seeds. Add the salt and mix gently. Let the mixture stand at room temperature for 8 to 12 hours.

2. Drain the vegetables well and pack them into a 2-quart jar. Combine the sugar and the vinegar and stir until the sugar has dissolved. Pour the sugar-vinegar solution over the vegetables. Cap the jar tightly and let it stand at room temperature for 24 hours.

3. Store the pickle in the refrigerator, where it should keep well for several months.

QUICK PICKLED
BABY CORN

MAKES 1 PINT

ARMERS USE FIELD CORN for this pickle, when their hunger for fresh corn can't wait until the sweet corn matures in the garden. (More often, though, they just climb off their tractors and eat the young ears whole while standing in the field.) This is a quick version of the pickled baby corn recipe on page 175, with a little tarragon added for its licorice-like flavor.

1 pint husked baby corn ears, each about 3 inches long
½ cup water
½ cup white wine vinegar
1 garlic clove, chopped
2 whole allspice berries, crushed
2 whole cloves
½ Mediterranean bay leaf
1 teaspoon pickling salt
½ teaspoon sugar
1 tarragon sprig

1. Pack the corn into a pint jar. In a nonreactive saucepan, bring the remaining ingredients to a boil, stirring to dissolve the salt and sugar. Reduce the heat and simmer the liquid for 1 minute.

2. Pour the hot liquid over the corn. With a chopstick or plastic knife, push the tarragon sprig down along the side of the jar. Cap the jar tightly, and let it cool.

3. When the jar is cool, refrigerate it. Let it stand in the refrigerator for a day before eating the corn.

4. Refrigerated, the corn will keep well for about 3 weeks.

FLAVORED VINEGARS

Perhaps the easiest way to make quick pickles is to keep some flavored vinegar on hand. The spicy and herbal flavors diffused through the vinegar can quickly permeate the vegetables. All you need to do is add water and salt to taste, then refrigerate the pickles for a day or so.

Flavored vinegars are easy to make. Put some fresh herbs, whole spices, garlic, citrus zest, or a combination of these into a jar and fill the jar with cold vinegar, preferably a good wine or cider vinegar. Close the jar with a nonreactive cap, such as an all-plastic mason jar cap, and let the jar stand for about two weeks. Then strain the vinegar into a bottle and seal it with a cork or plastic cap. The vinegar will be ready to use whenever you please.

If you heat the vinegar before adding the aromatics, you can skip the aging step. When the vinegar has cooled, strain and bottle it.

Here are a few ideas to get you started:

LEMON-MINT VINEGAR: Bruise 1 cup spearmint leaves in a mortar. Put them into a quart jar with the zest of 1 lemon, in strips. Fill the jar with white wine vinegar and cap the jar. After 2 weeks, strain the vinegar into a bottle.

TARRAGON-ALLSPICE-PEPPER VINEGAR: Put into a quart jar 1 tablespoon each allspice and black peppercorns and a large handful of tarragon sprigs. Fill the jar with white wine vinegar and cap the jar. Strain and bottle the vinegar after 2 weeks.

RED WINE VINEGAR WITH GARLIC, BAY, AND SAVORY: Put into a quart jar 4 garlic cloves, halved; 2 bay leaves; and a large handful of summer savory sprigs. Fill the jar with red wine vinegar and cap the jar. Strain and bottle the vinegar after 2 weeks.

Other good flavor combinations you might try include dill and garlic; thyme or rosemary and black pepper; lemon zest and ginger; lemon zest and a lemony herb (lemon basil, lemon thyme, or lemon mint); and orange zest with sweet spices, such as allspice, cloves, cinnamon, mace, and ginger.

QUICK CORN RELISH

MAKES 1 QUART

I LIKE TO USE RAW CORN for this recipe, but you can substitute cooked corn from leftover cobs or blanched corn from your freezer. Just be sure that your corn was picked young and sweet.

3 cups corn kernels (cut from 6 to 7 ears)
1 cup diced sweet or mildly hot green or red peppers,
    such as bell, pimiento, or Anaheim
½ large onion, diced
2 teaspoons pickling salt
1 teaspoon whole cumin seeds
¼ teaspoon cayenne
¾ cup cider vinegar
¾ cup water

1 In a bowl, mix the vegetables, salt, and spices. Transfer the mixture to a quart jar. Combine the vinegar and water and pour the liquid over the vegetables to cover them. Cap the jar and store it in the refrigerator.

2 The relish should be ready to eat in about 2 days, and it should keep well for several weeks.

PICKLED FENNEL
WITH ORANGE

MAKES 1 PINT

THE FENNEL THAT'S USED as a vegetable is usually called *finocchio* or Florence fennel, although many supermarkets label it as anise (anise is another umbelliferous plant, one grown only for its seeds). Florence fennel is like ordinary fennel except that the former swells into a fat bulb at the base of the stems. The bulb is the part you need for this pickle.

In the garden, Florence fennel is easy to grow, but do give it rich ground. Harvest the bulbs when they are about 2 inches across. You can also use the tender stems as you would celery, and the seeds for spice or tea.

Slices of orange-scented pickled fennel make a tossed salad special.

> 2 fennel bulbs (about ¾ pound), thinly sliced
> 1 teaspoon pickling salt
> Zest of ½ orange, in strips
> 1 to 2 small fennel sprigs (optional)
> 6 tablespoons white wine vinegar
> 6 tablespoons orange juice
> 1 tablespoon sugar
> 4 whole black peppercorns, cracked

1. In a bowl, toss the fennel slices with the salt. Let them stand for 1 hour.

2. Drain the fennel slices, discarding the brine, and toss the slices with the orange zest. Pack them into a pint jar, placing a fennel sprig or two against the side of the jar, if you like.

3. In a saucepan, heat the vinegar, orange juice, sugar, and pepper-corns to a simmer, stirring to dissolve the sugar. Pour the hot liquid over the fennel. Cap the jar and let it cool to room temperature.

4. Store the pickle in the refrigerator. It will be ready to eat in a day or two, and it will keep for at least several weeks.

VIETNAMESE PICKLED CARROT AND RADISH

MAKES 1 PINT

PICKLES LIKE THIS ONE are served with noodle dishes and in *banh mi*, French-influenced baguettes with such fillings as pâté, star-anise-flavored head cheese, or tofu. This pickle also makes a nice addition to green salads. I make it with a medium-size carrot and a piece of daikon about triple the carrot's size.

> ½ pound combined carrot and daikon, thinly sliced diagonally,
>   then slivered
> ½ teaspoon pickling salt
> 4 teaspoons sugar
> 3 tablespoons rice vinegar

1. In a wide bowl, toss the carrot and daikon slivers with the salt. Let the vegetables stand for about 10 minutes and then drain them well.

2. Dissolve the sugar in the vinegar and pour this mixture over the vegetables. Let them stand at room temperature for 1 hour, tossing them once or twice during this period.

3. If you don't eat the vegetables right away, store them in the refrigerator. Tightly covered, they will keep well for about 1 week. Drain them before serving them.

THAI PICKLED CARROTS

 THIS IS AN ALL-CARROT VERSION of the preceding recipe, enlivened with a little hot pepper.

½ pound carrots, thinly sliced diagonally, then slivered
2 teaspoons pickling salt
1 cup rice vinegar
2 tablespoons light brown sugar
1 to 2 small fresh hot peppers, such as serrano, seeded, if you
    like, and minced

1. In a bowl, mix the carrots with the salt. Let the carrots stand for 1 hour.

2. Meanwhile, bring the remaining ingredients to a boil in a saucepan, stirring to dissolve the sugar. Let the liquid cool.

3. Drain the carrots. Return them to the bowl, pour the pickling liquid over them, and toss them. Let them rest at room temperature for 1 hour. If you don't eat them right away, store them tightly covered in the refrigerator. They will keep for at least a week but are best eaten sooner. Drain them just before serving.

PICKLED BABY CARROTS WITH DILL

MAKES 1 QUART

ALTHOUGH SHE TOOK two or three foot-long carrots in every bag lunch, my daughter, as a child, would pull the carrots from her own garden plot when they were only about 4 inches long. I didn't mind, though—those sweet little carrots were perfect for pickling.

You might use this recipe after thinning your carrot bed, or you might substitute thick carrots, cut into sticks. For variety, try using tarragon or cilantro in place of the dill.

1 pound 4-inch carrots, scrubbed and trimmed
¼ cup minced dill leaves or 2 whole dill sprigs
3 large garlic cloves, coarsely chopped
1 to 2 red jalapeño peppers, seeded and sliced
½ teaspoon whole black peppercorns, crushed
1½ teaspoons pickling salt
1 cup white wine vinegar
1 cup water
¼ cup sugar

1 Blanch the carrots in boiling water, or steam them, for 2 minutes or until they are barely tender. Immerse them in cold water until they are cool.

2 Pack the carrots and dill into a quart jar. In a saucepan, bring the remaining ingredients to a boil. Cover the carrots with the liquid. Cap the jar and let it cool to room temperature.

3 Refrigerate the jar for 2 days or longer before eating the carrots. Refrigerated, they will keep for at least 2 months.

PICKLED CARROTS WITH CELERY, OREGANO, AND OLIVE OIL

MAKES 1 PINT

ERE'S AN ITALIAN VERSION of the preceding recipe. I love to take this pickle on picnics.

½ pound carrots, cut into 4-inch sticks
½ teaspoon pickling salt
¼ teaspoon crushed black peppercorns
1 large or 2 small celery stalks, cut into 4-inch sticks, and the celery tops
1 oregano sprig
1 dried hot pepper, such as japonés or de árbol, slit in half
About 1 cup white wine vinegar
2 tablespoons olive oil

1. Blanch the carrots in boiling water, or steam them, for 2 minutes or until they are barely tender. Immerse them in cold water until they are cool.

2. Put the salt and peppercorns into a pint jar. Pack the celery and carrot sticks, along with the celery tops, oregano sprig, and hot pepper, into the jar. Pour into the jar enough vinegar to cover the carrots. Add the oil, close the jar tightly with a nonreactive lid, and give the jar a shake. Refrigerate the jar for at least a day before eating the carrots.

3. Refrigerated, the carrots will keep for at least 2 months. Serve them at room temperature.

QUICK KOHLRABI PICKLE

MAKES 1 QUART

K OHLRABI IS A CABBAGE that puts most of its energy into a swollen stem instead of into leaves. Although few commercial farmers in the United States have discovered this vegetable, many home gardeners love it. With a mild, sweet cabbage flavor, it's delicious either raw or cooked. Kohlrabi is just the thing to grow if you like the crisp texture of turnips and radishes but not their strong flavors.

Looking like pale green or purple balls with a few leaves attached, kohlrabi is generally best picked when no more than 2 inches in diameter. Some varieties, however, can get quite large without getting woody; I once hauled out of the garden a 13-pounder of a Czech variety called Kohlrabi Gigante.

Peel kohlrabi with a sturdy knife. Big ones can be hard to handle, so halve or quarter them before trying to slice them further.

1½ pounds kohlrabi, peeled and cut
    into 1 × 2 × ¼-inch pieces
1½ teaspoons pickling salt
1 cup rice vinegar
1 cup water
3 large garlic cloves, coarsely chopped
Zest of 1 lemon, in strips
2 tablespoons sugar
½ teaspoon whole black peppercorns, crushed
4 thin slices fresh ginger
¼ teaspoon hot pepper flakes

1. In a bowl, toss the kohlrabi with the salt. Let the kohlrabi stand for about 1 hour.

2. Drain the kohlrabi and pack it into a quart jar. Bring the remaining ingredients to a boil and immediately pour them over the kohlrabi. Cover the jar and let it cool to room temperature.

3. Store the pickle in the refrigerator. It will be ready to eat in a day or two, and it will keep for about 3 weeks.

MOROCCAN PICKLED BEETS

MAKES 2 1/2 CUPS

ENCOUNTERED THIS PICKLE some years ago in a Moroccan restaurant, and now it is my favorite way to eat beets. I bake the beets to intensify their flavor, but you can boil them if you prefer. Sometimes I use balsamic vinegar rather than red wine vinegar. If you do this, reduce the amount of sugar to compensate for the sweetness of the vinegar.

2 1/2 cups diced (about 1/4 inch) cooked and peeled beets
1 garlic clove, minced
1 cup red wine vinegar
3 tablespoons sugar
1 1/2 teaspoons pickling salt
1 teaspoon whole cumin seeds, toasted and crushed
    in a mortar
2 tablespoons olive oil

1. Put the beets and garlic into a bowl. In a small nonreactive saucepan, bring the vinegar, sugar, and cumin to a boil. Pour the hot liquid over

the beets. Let the bowl stand at room temperature, turning the beets occasionally, for several hours. If you won't be eating the beets the same day, store the bowl, covered, in the refrigerator. The beets should keep well for at least 2 weeks.

2. Just before serving the beets, toss them with the olive oil.

QUICK PICKLED JÍCAMA

MAKES 1 QUART

I LOVE FRESH JÍCAMA dressed with nothing but salt and lime juice, but this quick pickle is nice for a change. The brown skin peels off easily with a knife. In the market, choose jícama whose skin is unwrinkled and undamaged, with no moldy or sunken spots.

1 pound jícama, peeled and sliced into 1 × 2 × $^3/_{16}$-inch pieces
2 teaspoons pickling salt
1 cup rice vinegar
1 cup water
1 teaspoon whole coriander seeds, crushed
1 fresh green jalapeño pepper, seeded and thinly sliced
4 thin slices fresh ginger
3 tablespoons sugar

1. In a bowl, toss the jícama slices with the salt. Let the jícama stand for 1 hour.

2. Drain the jícama and pack it into a quart jar. In a saucepan, bring the remaining ingredients to a boil, stirring to dissolve the sugar. Pour the hot liquid over the jícama. Cap the jar and let it cool.

3. Store the jícama in the refrigerator for at least a day before eating it. It will keep for several weeks, at least.

QUICK PICKLED EGGPLANT WITH BASIL

MAKES ABOUT 1 QUART

T O MAKE THIS TREAT in winter from imported Mexican eggplants, you can use pesto from your freezer in place of the fresh basil.

I love this pickle with tabbouleh, the Near Eastern salad of bulgur (parboiled, dried, and cracked wheat) with parsley and mint.

1 quart water
1 tablespoon plus 1 teaspoon pickling salt
2 medium-large eggplants (about 3¼ pounds), cut
    into ¾-inch cubes
½ cup white wine vinegar
1 tablespoon minced fresh basil
¼ teaspoon freshly ground black pepper
2 garlic cloves, crushed
¼ cup olive oil

1. In a saucepan, bring the water and 1 tablespoon salt to a boil. Add half of the eggplant cubes and simmer them for about 5 minutes, until they are tender. Put them into a colander and cook the remaining eggplant cubes in the same way. Add them to the colander and rinse and drain all of the eggplant.

2. In a bowl, mix the cooked eggplant cubes with the vinegar, basil, pepper, garlic, and the remaining 1 teaspoon salt. Cover the bowl and refrigerate it for at least 8 hours.

3. The eggplant will keep for about 1 week in the refrigerator. Just before serving, stir in the olive oil.

MALAYSIAN ACAR

MAKES ABOUT 1 PINT

M ALAYSIAN AND INDONESIAN *acar* recipes differ from place to place and family to family. Sometimes this mustard-flavored mixed vegetable pickle is thickened rather than garnished with sesame seeds or peanuts; sometimes candlenuts are used, or no nuts at all. The vegetables can include snap beans, cauliflower, sweet peppers, radishes, and celery instead of—or in addition to—the cucumber, carrots, and shallots called for here. Other spices, especially ginger, garlic, and coriander, are sometimes added. Generally, though, *acar* recipes are much like this one. *Acar* is a fine accompaniment to any dinner but is most often served with rice dishes.

1 salad or large pickling cucumber, or ½ Asian cucumber,
    halved lengthwise and seeded (about ½ pound)
1 large carrot (about ¼ pound)
6 ounces shallots or 1 large sweet onion
2 tablespoons sugar
1 teaspoon pickling salt
½ teaspoon ground turmeric
1 teaspoon hot pepper flakes
½ cup distilled white vinegar
½ cup water
2 tablespoons peanut oil
1 teaspoon whole yellow mustard seeds
1 tablespoon sesame seeds, toasted

1 Cut the cucumber and carrot crosswise into 2-inch pieces. Cut the cucumber pieces into ½-inch-thick sticks and put them into a small bowl. Cut the carrot into ¼-inch sticks and put them into another

small bowl. Set aside 2 ounces of the shallots or onion. Peel the rest of the shallots and leave them whole if they are very small; otherwise slice them, or slice the onion into small pieces. Put the shallots or onion pieces into the bowl with the carrot sticks.

2 Combine the sugar, salt, and turmeric. Sprinkle half of this mixture over the cucumbers and half over the carrots and the shallots or onions. Toss the vegetables, and let them stand at room temperature for 1 to 2 hours.

3 Mince or grind the reserved 2 ounces shallots or onion. Put the minced shallot or onion into a small bowl and stir in the pepper flakes.

4 Combine the vinegar and water in a cup. Set the cup near the stove along with the bowls of vegetables and the minced shallot–pepper

THE PICKLE THAT WENT 'ROUND THE WORLD

In India, *achar* means "pickle," of any sort. In Indonesia and Malaysia, *acar* (pronounced "atjar") long ago came to mean a mixed pickle flavored with mustard and turmeric. In Sri Lanka, a similar mixed pickle is called *abba achcharu* (*abba* means "mustard").

According to John Martin Taylor (*Hoppin' John's Lowcountry Cooking*, 2000), a mixed-vegetable mustard pickle called atzjar was routinely served at Charleston, South Carolina, restaurants when Taylor was a child. This practice was not a passing fad; Low Country cooks had been making atzjar since before 1770, when Harriott Pinckney Horry, who lived on a South Carolina rice plantation, included in her book of "receipts" one for "Ats Jaar, or Pucholilla." Horry called for salting and sun-drying the vegetables before putting them in the pickle, but otherwise her recipe is much like modern atzjar recipes—and also like modern piccalilli recipes (such as the one on page 310) and Indonesian and Malaysian *acar* recipes. Taylor suggests that *achar-acar*-atzjar traveled from Java to South Africa with the Dutch spice trade, and then up the coast to West Africa and across the Atlantic with the slaves. Although we don't know exactly how, mustard-flavored mixed pickles grew popular throughout the United States as piccalilli and its cousin chowchow (page 312)—whose name, if you think about it, sounds something like *achar* or *achcharu*. Strangely, however, the name atzjar never got beyond the Carolina Low Country.

flake mixture. Heat the oil over medium heat, and add the mustard seeds. When they pop, add the shallot–pepper flake mixture. Stir for several seconds, and then pour in the combined vinegar and water. Bring the mixture to a boil and let it simmer for 3 minutes. Add the carrots and shallots or onions and let them simmer for 2 minutes. Add the cucumbers, stir, and remove the pan from the heat.

5 Serve the pickle warm or cool, sprinkled with the toasted sesame seeds. If you won't be serving it the same day you make it, store it in a jar in the refrigerator, where it should keep well for a week.

GREEN OLIVES WITH LEMON AND THYME

MAKES 1 PINT

I T'S VERY HARD TO FIND fresh olives to cure yourself if you don't live in a commercial olive-growing region or happen to have an olive tree in your garden. But you can add the flavors of your choice to plain cured olives. This is a Lebanese recipe.

> 1 pound (about 1 pint) cracked green olives, drained
> Grated zest of 1 small lemon
> 1 tablespoon fresh thyme leaves
> 1 tablespoon olive oil

1 Mix all of the ingredients, pack them into a pint jar, and cap the jar. Let it stand at room temperature for 6 to 24 hours.

2 If you don't serve the olives within a day of preparing them, store them in the refrigerator. Bring them back to room temperature before eating them.

BLACK OLIVES WITH ORANGE, BAY, AND GARLIC

··

MAKES 1 PINT

HIS RECIPE CALLS FOR BRINED black olives, but I also like to use dry-cured olives—the dark, wrinkly, salty kind.

1 pound (about 1 pint) brined black olives (such as
kalamata or niçoise), drained
2 tablespoons grated orange zest
4 Mediterranean bay leaves, crumbled
2 garlic cloves, minced
1½ teaspoons olive oil

1. Mix all of the ingredients, pack them into a pint jar, and cap the jar. Let the jar stand at room temperature for 6 to 24 hours before eating the olives.

2. If you don't serve the olives within a day of preparing them, store them in the refrigerator. Bring them back to room temperature before eating them.

"Pickle jars are . . . a colorful feature of Middle Eastern streets. Squatting on the pavements of busy streets, vendors sell homemade pickled turnips swimming in a pink solution, or eggplants looking fiercely black and shiny in the enormous jars. Passersby dip their hands in the liquor, searching for the tastiest and largest pieces, and savor them with Arab bread provided by the vendor, soaking it in the pink salt and vinegar solution or seasoned oil. . . . And when the pickles are finished, the vendor sometimes sells the precious, flavorsome liquor as a sauce for rice."

—*Claudia Roden*, A Book of Middle Eastern Food *(1980)*

··

QUICK PICKLED WATERMELON

MAKES ABOUT 4 CUPS

ECAUSE I HAVE NEVER TASTED a seedless watermelon with a full, ripe flavor, I always use the regular kind, and cut around the seedy parts for this recipe. If you've cut a not-quite-ripe melon and aren't sure what to do with it, though, quick pickling is an excellent way to enliven the flavor.

This quick pickle makes a nice addition to a summer barbecue. You might substitute tarragon or fresh ginger for the fennel and bay.

> ¼ cup water
> ½ cup red wine vinegar
> ¼ cup sugar
> ¼ teaspoon whole fennel seeds
> ¼ teaspoon crushed coriander seeds
> Pinch of pickling salt
> 1 Mediterranean bay leaf
> 4 cups watermelon flesh, red part only, seeded and
>   cut into pieces about 1 × ¾ × ¾ inch

1. In a nonreactive saucepan, combine all of the ingredients except the watermelon. Over medium heat, bring the contents to a boil, stirring to dissolve the sugar. Remove the pan from the heat and let the syrup cool to room temperature.

2. Put the watermelon pieces into a dish wide enough to hold them all in a single layer. Strain the cooled liquid over the melon. Let the melon stand for 20 minutes, and then drain off the liquid.

3. Chill the melon for at least 1 hour but no longer than 4 hours before serving.

PINEAPPLE SAMBOL

MAKES ABOUT 1 PINT

 THIS CHUTNEY-LIKE RELISH from Sri Lanka is traditionally served with pork curry.

1 tablespoon dry mustard
1 teaspoon minced ginger
1 large garlic clove, minced
¼ cup cider vinegar
1 teaspoon sugar
2 pinches pickling salt
¼ teaspoon hot pepper flakes
½ slightly underripe pineapple, peeled and cut into
  ½- to ¾-inch cubes

1. In a small bowl, blend the mustard, ginger, garlic, and 2 tablespoons of the vinegar into a paste. In a larger bowl, blend the sugar, salt, and hot pepper flakes with the remaining 2 tablespoons vinegar. Stir the first mixture into the second, then gently mix in the pineapple. Cover the container and chill the *sambol* for 1 hour.

2. Refrigerated and tightly covered, the *sambol* will keep for several days.

QUICK MANGO AND SHREDDED GINGER ACHAR

MAKES 1 QUART

T HIS INDIAN PICKLE is traditionally made with green mangoes of the sort that aren't sweet at all, but I use the big green-to-red mangoes sold in supermarkets, and I really like their sweetness in this pickle. Try it with *raita* (yogurt salad) and Indian bread such as *chapati* or *paratha*.

> 2 underripe mangoes, peeled and cut into ½-inch cubes
> ⅓ cup grated fresh ginger
> 1 teaspoon pickling salt
> 1 teaspoon cayenne
> 3 tablespoons mustard oil (page 154) or other vegetable oil
> 1½ teaspoons whole black mustard seeds

1. In a bowl, combine the mango cubes with the ginger, salt, and cayenne.

2. In a small skillet, heat the oil until it is very hot and add the mustard seeds. Heat them until they stop sputtering and turn gray (use a splatter screen, if you have one). Pour the oil and seeds over the mangoes and mix well. Let the pickle stand for 30 minutes before eating it.

BASIC PICKLED ONION RINGS

MAKES ABOUT 1 CUP

THIS IS A SIMPLE BUT APPEALING RELISH for Mexican dishes, chili, and many other foods. If your onion is sweet, you can skip the blanching step.

> 1 medium-size white or red onion, sliced into thin rings
> ¼ cup distilled white vinegar
> ¼ cup water
> ½ teaspoon pickling salt

1. Put the onion into a bowl and cover it with boiling water. Let the onion stand for 1 minute and then drain it. Combine the vinegar and water and stir in the salt. Pour the liquid over the onion. Let the onion pickle for at least 1 hour before serving it.

2. If you won't be using the onion right away, store it in the refrigerator, where it will keep for at least 1 week.

SPICED PICKLED ONION RINGS

MAKES 1½ TO 2 CUPS

THIS FANCY VERSION of the preceding pickle is a universal table condiment on the Yucatán Peninsula. Sometimes the onions are chopped rather than sliced into rings.

If your onion is sweet, you can skip the blanching step.

1 large (¾ to 1 pound) red onion, sliced into thin rings

¼ cup white wine vinegar

½ cup water

½ teaspoon pickling salt

2 garlic cloves, minced

3 whole allspice berries, crushed

10 whole black peppercorns, crushed

1 teaspoon dried oregano

1. Put the onion rings into a bowl and cover them with boiling water. Let them stand for 1 minute and then drain them.

2. In a nonreactive saucepan, bring the remaining ingredients to a boil. Pour the hot liquid and spices over the onion rings. Let them stand for 2 hours or more.

3. If you won't be using the onion right away, store it in the refrigerator, where it will keep for at least 1 week.

SHALLOTS OR ONIONS PICKLED WITH MINT

MAKES 1 PINT

 THIS DELIGHTFULLY DIFFERENT PICKLE comes from Iran.

¾ pound shallots or small boiling onions

8 garlic cloves

40 fresh mint leaves

¾ teaspoon pickling salt

1 cup white wine vinegar

Sweeter and milder than garlic and onions, shallots aren't good just for pickling; they can smooth and enhance soups, stews, and sauces. Shallots are expensive to buy, but they are easy to grow in any good garden soil. You can plant shallots in fall or spring, and they keep well from harvest to spring planting when stored in a cool, dry place. You can buy both shallot sets and shallot seeds from various mail-order catalogs and Internet vendors.

1. Without peeling them first, put the shallots or onions into a bowl and pour boiling water over them. Let them stand for 3 minutes, and then cut off the base of each one and slip off the skin. If you're using onions or large shallots, cut a deep cross in the bottom of each one. Pack the onions or shallots into a pint jar.

2. In a blender, blend the garlic, mint, and salt with ¼ cup of the vinegar. Combine this mixture with the remaining ¾ cup vinegar and pour the liquid over the onions. Cap the jar tightly and let it stand at room temperature for 24 hours.

3. If you don't eat the shallots or onions at once, store them tightly covered in the refrigerator. They will keep well for at least 1 week.

PINK PICKLED SHALLOTS

MAKES 1 PINT

 THESE MILD, SWEET SHALLOT SLICES, colored by red wine vinegar, are delicious in salads.

¾ cup red wine vinegar
½ cup water

¼ cup sugar

½ teaspoon pickling salt

1 Mediterranean bay leaf, torn in half

2 tarragon sprigs

2 thyme sprigs

¾ pound shallots, thinly sliced lengthwise (about 2 cups)

1 In a nonreactive saucepan, bring to a boil the vinegar, water, sugar, salt, bay leaf, and herb sprigs. Add the shallots, reduce the heat, and simmer for 2 minutes.

2 Pack the shallots, herbs, and liquid into a pint jar. Cap the jar and let it cool to room temperature. Store it in the refrigerator.

3 The shallots will be ready to eat in a day or two, and will keep in the refrigerator for 3 weeks or more.

DOLORES'S PICKLED PRUNES

MAKES 1 QUART

WHEN MY PARENTS had a commercial prune orchard in Sonoma County, California, my mother pickled prunes for every big family party. This is her recipe.

2½ cups (about 1 pound) unpitted prunes

¾ cup firmly packed light brown sugar

1 cup cider vinegar

1 tablespoon Mixed Pickling Spices (page 15)

1 Put the prunes into a large nonreactive saucepan and cover them with water. Bring the contents to a boil and then reduce the heat. Simmer the prunes for 15 to 20 minutes.

2. Empty the saucepan into a sieve set over a bowl. Return 1 cup of the cooking liquid to the saucepan (if there isn't 1 cup liquid, add enough water to make 1 cup). Add the sugar, vinegar, and spices to the saucepan. Bring the mixture to a boil, stirring to dissolve the sugar, and reduce the heat. Simmer the mixture for 10 minutes.

3. Add the prunes to the saucepan. Simmer them for 5 minutes.

4. Put the prunes and their liquid into a quart jar and cap the jar. When the jar has cooled, store it in the refrigerator. After a day or two, the prunes will be ready to eat. They will keep well for several weeks, at least.

A PRUNE BY ANY OTHER NAME

Both French and Japanese plums have long been important crops in California. Perhaps to distinguish between the two, California ranchers used to always call French plums *prunes*, which means simply "plums" in French. This made sense, too, because the only thing the ranchers knew to do with the plums was to dry them—that is, to turn them into prunes. With the advent of cold storage, unfortunately, prunes—the dried kind—started going out of style; people associated them with old folks' digestive ailments. Californians quickly replaced most of the prune orchards with vineyards.

In some areas of California prune production continues, but the word *prune* still provokes smirks. So in 2000 the prune-plum growers decided they would no longer use the word *prune* for the dried fruit, much less the fresh. They got permission from the U.S. Food and Drug Administration to rename prunes "dried plums." And the growers decided to attempt, for the first time, large-scale marketing of fresh prune-plums. Look for them in the supermarket under another new name, "Sugar Plums."

8

FREEZER
PICKLES

I F YOU LIKE SWEET PICKLES and want to make them in the quickest, cleanest, coolest way possible, here are the recipes to try. Putting pickles into the freezer for long-term storage will save you from dealing with steaming kettles, canning jars, and two-piece lids that refuse to seal. And you'll have delicious, summer-flavored side dishes to accompany heavier foods through the winter.

Some people say that these modern-day pickles aren't true pickles at all, because, although they are packed in vinegar, their main preserving agent is freezing. For some reason, cucumber and other vegetable slices packed in vinegar and sugar before freezing don't turn to mush, but stay crisp. This is a very effective way to preserve not just vegetables but also herbal flavors that weaken or die in canning and drying. For this reason, I've enlivened the recipes here with fresh dill, cilantro, and mint. Once you taste your homemade freezer pickles, you won't worry whether they're *real* pickles or not.

You can pack freezer pickles in rigid plastic containers, freezer bags, or wide-mouth canning jars. Because food expands when it freezes, allow about ½ inch headspace. Plan to use the pickles within a year.

These pickles are best chilled, so serve them right from the refrigerator after thawing them. They will keep well in the refrigerator for several days, at least.

FREEZER
DILL SLICES

MAKES ABOUT 4 PINTS

 FRESH RED PEPPER adds attractive color to these sweet pickle chips.

2½ pounds pickling cucumbers, thinly sliced (about 8 cups)
3 tablespoons pickling salt
4 garlic cloves, minced
⅓ cup minced fresh dill
1 teaspoon whole dill seeds
1 cup chopped sweet ripe pepper, such as bell or pimiento, preferably red
1½ cups sugar
1½ cups cider vinegar

According to Pickle Packers International, a trade and research association founded in 1893, the perfect pickle should exhibit seven "warts" per square inch for American tastes.

1. In a large bowl, toss the cucumber slices with the salt. Let the cucumbers stand at room temperature for 2 to 3 hours, and then drain them.

2. In another bowl, stir together the remaining ingredients. Pour the mixture over the cucumbers and stir well. Refrigerate the mixture for 8 to 10 hours.

3. Pack the cucumber slices and liquid in freezer bags or rigid containers and freeze the containers.

4. Thaw the pickle for about 8 hours in the refrigerator before serving it.

LIME-MINT
FREEZER PICKLE

MAKES ABOUT 4 PINTS

 HIS IS MY FAVORITE FREEZER PICKLE. Even a year after it goes into the freezer, the mint tastes fresh-picked.

2½ pounds pickling cucumbers, thinly sliced (about 8 cups)
3 tablespoons pickling salt
½ cup sliced onion
1 small sweet ripe pepper, such as bell or pimiento, chopped
Grated zest of 1 lime
2 garlic cloves, minced
¼ cup minced fresh mint leaves
1½ cups sugar
1½ cups distilled white vinegar

1 In a large bowl, toss the cucumber slices with the salt. Let the cucumbers stand at room temperature for 2 to 3 hours, and then drain them.

2 In another bowl, stir together the remaining ingredients. Pour the mixture over the cucumbers and stir well. Refrigerate the mixture for 8 to 10 hours.

3 Pack the cucumbers and liquid in freezer bags or rigid containers and freeze the containers.

4 Thaw the pickle for about 8 hours in the refrigerator before serving it.

FREEZER PICKLE
WITH CARROTS

 GOT A GLUT OF ZUCCHINI? In this recipe and others, you can substitute sliced young zucchini for the cucumbers.

2½ pounds pickling cucumbers, thinly sliced (about 8 cups)

3 tablespoons pickling salt

2 medium-size carrots, grated (about 1 cup, firmly packed)

1½ cups sugar

1½ cups cider vinegar

1 tablespoon chopped fresh dill

1　In a large bowl, toss the cucumber slices with the salt. Let the cucumbers stand at room temperature for 2 to 3 hours and then drain them.

2　Mix the remaining ingredients in another bowl. Pour the mixture over the cucumbers and mix well. Refrigerate the mixture for 8 to 10 hours.

3　Pack the cucumber mixture and liquid in freezer bags or rigid containers and freeze the containers.

4　Thaw the pickle in the refrigerator for 8 to 10 hours before serving it.

FREEZER PICKLE
WITH MANGO

MAKES ABOUT 4 PINTS

RESH MANGO, complemented by ginger, adds bright, tropical color and flavor to this freezer pickle.

2¼ pounds pickling cucumbers, thinly sliced
   (about 7 cups)
1 just-ripe mango, peeled and cut into ¾-inch cubes
   (page 323)
1 cup sliced onions
3 tablespoons pickling salt
1 teaspoon hot pepper flakes
1 tablespoon minced fresh ginger
1 teaspoon ground allspice
1½ cups sugar
1½ cups cider vinegar

1. In a large bowl, toss the cucumbers, mango, and onions with the salt. Let them stand at room temperature for 2 to 3 hours and then drain them.

2. In another bowl, stir together the remaining ingredients. Pour the mixture over the cucumbers, mango, and onions and stir well. Refrigerate the mixture for 8 to 10 hours.

3. Pack the cucumber mixture and liquid in freezer bags or rigid containers and freeze the containers.

4. Thaw the pickle in the refrigerator for about 8 hours before serving it.

CILANTRO
FREEZER PICKLE

MAKES ABOUT 4 PINTS

 HE ONLY WAY I KNOW to preserve the fresh, bittersweet bite of cilantro is to freeze the herb, as in this recipe.

2 pounds pickling cucumbers, thinly sliced (about 6 cups)
2 cups sliced sweet onions
3 tablespoons pickling salt
1 small sweet ripe pepper, such as bell or pimiento, chopped
1 teaspoon ground cumin
¼ cup chopped fresh cilantro
1½ cups sugar
1½ cups cider vinegar

1. In a large bowl, toss the cucumber and onion slices with the salt. Let the vegetables stand at room temperature for 2 to 3 hours and then drain them.

2. In another bowl, stir together the remaining ingredients. Pour the mixture over the vegetables and stir well. Refrigerate the mixture for 8 to 10 hours.

3. Pack the vegetables and liquid in freezer bags or rigid containers and freeze the containers.

4. Thaw the pickle for about 8 hours in the refrigerator before serving it.

FREEZER-PICKLED CABBAGE

MAKES ABOUT 2 QUARTS

CABBAGE AS WELL AS CUCUMBER makes a delicious freezer pickle, especially in a colorful shredded mix with carrot and green pepper.

2 pounds shredded white head cabbage
1 cup shredded green bell pepper
1 cup shredded onion
1 cup shredded carrot
1 tablespoon pickling salt
2 cups sugar
1½ cups cider vinegar

1. Toss the shredded vegetables with the salt. Let the mixture stand at room temperature for 2 to 3 hours.

2. Drain the vegetables, pressing out excess liquid. Combine the sugar and vinegar, stirring to dissolve the sugar. Pour the liquid over the drained vegetables and mix well.

3. Pack the vegetables and liquid in freezer bags or rigid containers and freeze the containers.

4. Thaw the pickle for about 8 hours in the refrigerator before serving it.

9

CHUTNEYS, SALSAS, AND OTHER RELISHES

CHOWCHOW, CHUTNEY, KETCHUP, hot sauce, pickle relish—these are all names for minced, ground, or pureed vegetables or fruits preserved in vinegar or otherwise acidified. Always tart, often sweet or piquant, and sometimes sweet, sour, and hot all at once, these are pickles to be eaten in the same mouthful as other foods. Most of these relishes have traditional associations—tomato ketchup with hamburgers, chutney with rice, salsa with tortillas, chili sauce with baked beans, and so on. But once your raw produce is transfigured into jars of heavenly flavors on your refrigerator shelf, you may find chutney glorifying your cheese sandwich, hot ketchup exalting your vegetable soup, and blueberry relish consecrating your bowl of vanilla ice cream. Put up your relishes in small jars so you can have several kinds open at once—and so you can share with your friends, who will be ever grateful for the blessing.

BRINED PICKLE
RELISH

··

THIS IS THE SIMPLEST WAY to make pickle relish, and many people think it's the best. The yield will vary depending on the size of your cucumbers and how densely you pack them. You should figure approximately 3 cups relish for every 1 quart cucumbers.

Full-sour brined cucumbers (such as Lower East Side
Full-Sour Dills, page 45; Spicy Crock Pickles, page 53;
or Russian Dill Pickles, page 55)

1 Chop the cucumbers, and put them into one or more pint or half-pint mason jars. Add a little of the pickle brine to cover the chopped pickles, leaving ½ inch headspace if you want to heat-process the jars. To do so, close the jars with two-piece caps and immerse the jars in a canner of water heated to about 140°F. Bring the water to a boil and let it gently boil for 10 minutes before removing the jars, or keep the water at 180° to 185°F for 30 minutes. Store the cooled jars in a cool, dry, dark place.

2 If you don't process the jars or use the relish at once, tightly cap the jars and store them in the refrigerator, where the relish should keep well for about a week.

RED AND GREEN CUCUMBER-PEPPER RELISH

ALTHOUGH MUCH LIKE STANDARD pickle relish, this condiment has a cleaner, fresher taste, due to the smaller proportion of sugar and the omission of mustard and sweet spices. Garlic, horseradish, and jalapeños give this relish a little zing, and a few red peppers make it colorful.

2 pounds pickling cucumbers, chopped (about 6 cups)

¾ pound sweet peppers, such as bell or pimiento, some red and some green, chopped (about 3 cups)

3 jalapeño peppers, chopped

½ cup chopped onion

6 tablespoons pickling salt

⅔ cup sugar

3 cups cider vinegar

2 tablespoons chopped garlic

2 tablespoons grated horseradish

2 teaspoons whole dill seeds

1. In a nonreactive bowl or pot, toss the chopped cucumbers, peppers, and onion with the salt. Empty three ice cube trays on top of the vegetables and let them stand at room temperature for about 4 hours.

2. Drain the vegetables in a colander and return them to the bowl or pot. Top them with fresh ice from three ice cube trays. Let the vegetables stand for an hour or two.

3. Drain the vegetables thoroughly, discarding any remaining ice. In a nonreactive pot, bring the sugar and vinegar to a boil, stirring to

dissolve the sugar. Immediately add the cucumbers and peppers, and then the garlic, horseradish, and dill. Stir well and bring the mixture to a full boil. Ladle the hot relish into pint or half-pint mason jars, leaving ½ inch headspace. Close the jars with two-piece caps. Process the jars for 10 minutes in a boiling-water bath, or immerse them for 30 minutes in water heated to 180° to 185°F.

4 Store the cooled jars in a cool, dry, dark place.

PICCALILLI

MAKES 3½ TO 4 PINTS

THE NAME OF THIS TRADITIONAL RELISH may have originated in the misreading of a handwritten recipe. *Picadillo* is Spanish for a mixture of chopped foods. In the New World a *picadillo* is usually a hot meat mixture, a hash, but in Spain it is more likely a chopped vegetable salad.

But piccalilli doesn't taste the least bit Spanish. The mustard and ginger included in most recipes suggest southern Asian origins, and indeed this pickle is very similar to the *acar* of Malaysia and Indonesia (page 284). I like to imagine the name of this old-fashioned relish being born in the whimsy of a tired but satisfied pickler, as she surveyed her crocks of sauerkraut and brined cucumbers, her shelves of ketchups and preserves, and decided what to do with the last of the cabbage and those green tomatoes and peppers that must be saved from the coming frost. She would chop them all together, sweeten and spice them, and give the mélange a name that reflected not the individual ingredients, which likely would differ a bit next year, but the carefree preparation and the diminutive size of the pieces.

For your own piccalilli, vary the vegetables—you might include snap beans, for instance—and their relative proportions at your convenience; just be sure they add up to about 13½ cups. For a colorful relish, try to include some red pepper. And definitely include green tomatoes.

> 5½ cups (about 1¾ pounds) chopped green tomatoes
> 5 cups (about 1 pound) chopped white head cabbage
> 2 cups (about 2 large) chopped sweet peppers,
>   such as bell or pimiento
> 1 cup chopped onion
> ¼ cup pickling salt
> 2¼ cups cider vinegar
> ¾ cup firmly packed light brown sugar
> 1 tablespoon whole yellow mustard seeds
> 2 tablespoons grated horseradish
> 2 tablespoons minced garlic
> 1 tablespoon hot pepper flakes
> 1 tablespoon minced fresh ginger

1. In a bowl, toss the vegetables with the salt. Let them stand at room temperature for 3 to 4 hours.

2. Drain and rinse the vegetables, and then drain them again.

3. In a large, nonreactive pot, bring the remaining ingredients to a boil. Reduce the heat and simmer the liquid for 10 minutes.

4. Add the vegetables. Bring the mixture to a boil and then immediately pack it into pint mason jars, leaving ½ inch headspace. Close the jars with two-piece caps and process the jars for 10 minutes in a boiling-water bath.

5. Store the cooled jars in a cool, dry, dark place.

CHOWCHOW

MAKES 4 PINTS

IKE PICCALILLI, chowchow is an Anglo-American pickle born under southern Asian influence in the age of Western imperialism. Some say the term *chowchow* derives from a Chinese word (*chiao*, meaning "meat dumpling"), but the pidgin English *chowchow* was used in India as well as China during this era. Generally, *chowchow* meant any mixture or medley; specifically, it meant a pickle of mixed chopped vegetables flavored with mustard. I suspect the name derived from *achar*, the Indian word for "pickle" (page 284).

In the nineteenth century, as well as today, the terms *chowchow* and *piccalilli* were used somewhat interchangeably in England and the United States. In both relishes, the type and size of vegetable pieces could vary; for instance, you might use snap beans, whole gherkins, or whole tiny onions instead of some of the ingredients listed here, or you might chop everything fine so you couldn't tell one vegetable from another in the finished pickle. But whereas piccalilli always included green tomatoes, chowchow often didn't, and whereas chowchow was usually thickened with ground mustard (and sometimes flour) and often included whole mustard seeds as well, piccalilli might exclude mustard altogether.

Like other pickles, chowchow has tended to get sweeter over the years. My chowchow is much less sweet than most, so feel free to add sugar if you like a lot of it.

1 quart small cabbage pieces (from about 1 small head)
3 cups small cauliflower pieces (from about 1 small head)

3 cups small sweet pepper pieces, some or all of them red

2 cups small cucumber pieces or coarsely chopped
    green tomatoes

2 cups small onion pieces

3 tablespoons pickling salt

2¾ cups cider vinegar

½ cup firmly packed light brown sugar

2 teaspoons whole yellow mustard seeds

2 teaspoons dry mustard

1 teaspoon ground turmeric

1 teaspoon whole celery seeds

1 teaspoon ground ginger

2 teaspoons hot pepper flakes

¼ teaspoon ground coriander

1. In a bowl, toss the vegetables with the salt. Let them stand at room temperature for 3 to 4 hours, then drain them. Rinse them, and drain them again.

2. Bring the remaining ingredients to a boil in a large, nonreactive pot. Reduce the heat and let the mixture simmer for 5 minutes.

3. Add the vegetables to the pot. Bring the mixture to a boil again, stirring occasionally. Let the mixture simmer for 10 minutes.

4. Pack the vegetables into pint mason jars and cover them with the pickling liquid, leaving ½ inch headspace. Close the jars with two-piece caps and process the jars for 10 minutes in a boiling-water bath.

5. Store the cooled jars in a cool, dry, dark place.

ZUCCHINI RELISH

MAKES ABOUT 3½ PINTS

N THIS SWEET PICKLE RELISH of apparently recent origin, zucchini takes the place of cucumbers. Zucchini relishes are very popular among gardeners who never fail to grow too much of this squash, or to let some fruits get oversized, as they inevitably do. (My solution is to forego planting any zucchini; friends usually supply me with all I can use.) My zucchini relish is quite sweet, though not nearly as sweet as most, and enhanced with ginger and cinnamon in addition to the usual celery and mustard seeds. Instead of chopping the vegetables, I grind them with an old-fashioned food grinder.

4 cups (about 1¾ pounds) coarsely ground or
    chopped zucchini
1½ cups (about ½ pound) coarsely ground or
    chopped onions
1½ cups (about 2 large or 3 to 4 small) coarsely ground or
    chopped sweet red (or mixed red and green) peppers
1½ tablespoons pickling salt
¾ cup sugar
1¾ cups cider vinegar
1 teaspoon whole celery seeds
1 teaspoon whole yellow mustard seeds
7 thin slices fresh ginger
Seven 1-inch cinnamon sticks

1 In a bowl, mix the zucchini, onions, peppers, and salt. Cover the vegetables with cold water. Let them stand at room temperature for 2 hours.

2 Drain the vegetables. Rinse them and drain them again.

3. In a nonreactive pot, bring to a boil the sugar, vinegar, and celery and mustard seeds, stirring to dissolve the sugar. Add the vegetables and bring them to a boil. Reduce the heat. Simmer the vegetables for 10 minutes.

4. While the vegetables simmer, divide the ginger and cinnamon among pint or half-pint mason jars, allotting one piece of each for each half-pint. Pack the hot relish into the jars, allowing ½ inch headspace. Close the jars with two-piece caps and process the jars for 10 minutes in a boiling-water bath.

5. Store the cooled jars in a cool, dry, dark place.

EGGPLANT-TOMATO RELISH

MAKES 2 PINTS

 THIS RECIPE WAS INSPIRED by similar ones from England and France. My husband loves this relish on sandwiches.

1 pound eggplant, peeled and cut into ¾-inch cubes

2 teaspoons pickling salt

6 tablespoons olive oil

1 large onion, chopped

1 large green or red bell pepper, chopped

3 garlic cloves, minced

3 cups peeled and coarsely chopped tomatoes

1 cup chopped fresh parsley

¾ cup cider vinegar

1 Mediterranean bay leaf

1 teaspoon whole yellow mustard seeds

1 tablespoon pine nuts

1 tablespoon drained pickled capers

A few grindings of black pepper

1. In a bowl, toss the eggplant with the salt. Put the salted eggplant into a colander and let it drain for an hour or so.

2. Rinse the eggplant and drain it well. Heat the oil in a large, nonreactive pot. Add the eggplant and sauté it for about 5 minutes.

3. Add the onion and pepper and sauté them for about 10 minutes.

4. Add the remaining ingredients. Over medium heat, bring the mixture to a simmer. Simmer the mixture uncovered, stirring often, for about 1 hour.

5. Remove the bay leaf. Ladle the mixture into pint or half-pint mason jars, leaving ½ inch headspace. Close the jars with two-piece caps and process the jars for 15 minutes in a boiling-water bath.

6. Store the cooled jars in a cool, dry, dark place.

CORN RELISH

ESPECIALLY GOOD CHILLED, corn relish is an old-fashioned stand-in for salad. You might also mix the relish with cooked rice for an easy, flavorful side dish.

I developed this recipe after examining the corn relishes at the Oregon State Fair. The prizewinner omitted the usual turmeric and powdered mustard, which render pickling liquid a muddy yellow. This recipe follows her example.

> 2 quarts fresh corn kernels (from about 9 ears)
> 2 cups diced green bell pepper
> 2 cups diced red bell pepper
> 2 cups chopped onions
> ¼ cup chopped garlic
> 1 tablespoon pickling salt
> 2 tablespoons whole yellow mustard seeds
> 1 quart cider vinegar
> 1 cup water
> ⅔ cup firmly packed light brown sugar

1 In a nonreactive pot, bring all of the ingredients to a boil. Reduce the heat and simmer the mixture for 20 minutes.

2 Pack the relish into pint or half-pint mason jars, leaving ½ inch headspace. Close the jars with two-piece caps and process the jars for 15 minutes in a boiling-water bath.

3 Store the cooled jars in a cool, dry, dark place.

CORN RELISH
WITH TOMATOES

T HIS UNUSUAL CORN RELISH is enlivened with the sweet-tart flavor of tomatoes. Halve the tomatoes crosswise and gently squeeze out the seeds and excess liquid before dicing the flesh.

1 quart fresh corn kernels (from about 9 ears)
3 cups seeded and diced red tomatoes
1½ cups diced green bell pepper
¾ cup diced red bell pepper
1 cup chopped onion
½ cup sugar
2 cups cider vinegar
1 tablespoon pickling salt
2 teaspoons whole yellow mustard seeds

1. Combine all of the ingredients in a nonreactive pot. Bring them to a boil, then reduce the heat. Simmer the mixture for 20 minutes.

2. Ladle the relish into pint or half-pint mason jars, leaving ½ inch headspace. Close the jars with two-piece caps and process the jars for 15 minutes in a boiling-water bath.

3. Store the cooled jars in a cool, dry, dark place.

CHERRY RELISH

MAKES 1 PINT

I WENT SEARCHING FOR RECIPES like this one after my friend Melody Bycroft reminisced about her aunt's cherry relish, a much-anticipated treat at each year's Thanksgiving table. Sadly, the aunt's recipe was lost with her passing.

The few cherry relish recipes I found included pecans. Since I don't like hard lumps in my relish, this recipe is nutless. If you'd prefer a nutty relish, add 1½ cups chopped pecans at the end of the process described here, and cook for 3 minutes more.

Sour cherries are traditional in cherry relish, but I have used various kinds of cherries from our planted and volunteer trees. If you can't get sour cherries, use sweet ones instead.

Pitting cherries can be a lot of trouble, even with a good pitting tool, so I've kept the quantities small here. Save this beautiful red relish to serve as a very special treat—at the Thanksgiving table, perhaps.

> One 3-inch cinnamon stick
> ½ teaspoon whole cloves
> ¼ teaspoon whole cardamom seeds
> 3½ cups pitted cherries, preferably sour
> ½ cup sugar
> 1 cup golden raisins
> ¼ cup honey
> 1½ cups cider vinegar

1 Tie the spices in a spice bag or cheesecloth. In a heavy saucepan, simmer the remaining ingredients with the spice bag for about 1 hour, until the syrup has thickened slightly. Squeeze and remove the spice bag.

2. Ladle the relish into two half-pint mason jars or one pint mason jar, leaving ¼ inch headspace. Close the jars with two-piece caps and process the jars for 10 minutes in a boiling-water bath.

3. Store the cooled jars in a cool, dry, dark place for at least 2 weeks before eating the relish.

SPICED BLUEBERRIES

MAKES 2 TO 2½ PINTS

HERE'S A THICK, SWEET RELISH that's a perfect accompaniment for holiday roasts and also delicious on vanilla ice cream. For a different but equally delightful flavor, substitute blackberries for the blueberries. Like fruit ketchups, fruit relishes such as this were once quite common in American cellars and pantries.

3 cups sugar
1½ cups water
4 pounds (about 9 cups) blueberries
Zest of 2 lemons, in strips
Two 3-inch cinnamon sticks, broken into pieces
1½ teaspoons whole allspice berries
½ teaspoon whole cloves
1½ cups cider vinegar

1. In a large, nonreactive pot, bring the sugar and water to a boil. Boil the syrup for 1 minute. Add the blueberries and simmer them for about 5 minutes, until the berries are soft and shriveled.

2. Drain the berries through a sieve set over a bowl. Return the syrup to the pot and put the berries into the bowl. Put the lemon zest and

spices in a spice bag, or tie them in a scrap of cheesecloth, and add the bag to the pot with the vinegar. Bring the mixture to a boil. Boil it over medium-high heat until the syrup reaches 220°F on a thermometer, about 30 minutes.

3. Remove the spice bag from the syrup and add the berries. Bring the mixture to a boil, and boil the relish gently until the syrup again reaches 220°F on the thermometer. This will take only a few minutes.

4. Ladle the hot relish into pint or half-pint mason jars, leaving ¼ inch headspace. Close the jars with two-piece caps and process the jars for 15 minutes in a boiling-water bath.

5. Store the cooled jars in a cool, dry, dark place.

BLUEBERRIES PICKLED IN MOLASSES

MAKES 1 PINT

I FOUND SEVERAL VARIANTS of this recipe in old American cookbooks. The basic method is this: Blueberries are covered with molasses, then left to ferment at room temperature to produce a pleasantly tart relish. I like the cloves and lemon zest in this version.

¼ teaspoon ground cloves
Grated zest of 1 small lemon
1¾ cups blueberries
About 1 cup molasses

1. Gently mix the cloves and lemon zest with the blueberries and put the mixture into a pint jar. Pour the molasses over, leaving at least

¼ inch headspace so the pickle doesn't bubble out of the jar. Cover the jar with muslin or two layers of cheesecloth and secure the cloth with a rubber band. Let the blueberries ferment at room temperature for several days.

2 When the berries have soured to your taste, cap the jar and store it in the refrigerator.

CHINESE-STYLE PLUM SAUCE

MAKES 4 TO 5 PINTS

THIS CHUTNEY-LIKE RELISH is vastly superior to the gooey, oversweetened version still served in some Chinese-American restaurants. Use plum sauce as a condiment for roast duck, roast pork, and spring rolls, and in any way that you might use chutney.

2 pounds peaches or nectarines, peeled and coarsely cut

3 pounds Japanese plums, peeled and coarsely cut

4 cups cider vinegar

1½ cups granulated sugar

1½ cups firmly packed light brown sugar

4 medium-size red or yellow bell peppers, roasted, peeled, and coarsely chopped

3 or more small fresh red hot peppers, such as jalapeño or serrano, chopped

⅓ cup minced fresh ginger

6 large garlic cloves, minced

1 medium-size red onion, coarsely chopped

½ cup Chinese rice wine

4 teaspoons pickling salt
¼ cup whole yellow mustard seeds, lightly toasted
    in a dry pan
One 3-inch cinnamon stick

1. In a large, nonreactive pot, combine the peaches or nectarines and the plums with 3 cups vinegar. Simmer the mixture until the fruit is very soft, about 25 minutes.

2. In another nonreactive pot, bring the remaining 1 cup vinegar and the sugars to a boil. Add the fruit mixture and the remaining ingredients. Simmer for about 45 minutes, stirring occasionally.

3. Remove the cinnamon stick, then press the plum sauce through the coarse disc of a food mill (this allows the mustard seeds to come through). Return the pureed sauce to the pot and simmer until the sauce is quite hot and thickened to your taste, 5 to 15 minutes.

4. Ladle the plum sauce into pint or half-pint mason jars, leaving ¼ inch headspace. Close the jars with two-piece caps and process the jars for 10 minutes in a boiling-water bath.

5. Store the cooled jars in a cool, dry, dark place.

MANGO CHUTNEY

MAKES ABOUT 2 PINTS

MANGO CHUTNEY IS THE ANCESTOR of all our Anglicized fruit chutneys. As long as mangoes, in season, are cheaper than peaches, why not return to the roots of the relish? This chutney is wonderfully hot, sweet, and gingery.

Slice each mango by cutting lengthwise along both sides of the pit. Cut the flesh of each half in a grid pattern, turn the half inside-out, and cut off the mango chunks. Or, if you find it easier, slice each half into strips, peel each strip, and then cut the strips into smaller pieces.

> 3 large ripe but firm mangoes (about 3 pounds), peeled and
>   cut into chunks
> 2 cups cider vinegar
> 2 cups firmly packed light brown sugar
> 1 tablespoon minced fresh ginger
> 2 teaspoons hot pepper flakes
> ½ teaspoon pickling salt
> ½ cup golden raisins

1. In a bowl, stir together all of the ingredients except the raisins. Cover the bowl with plastic wrap and let it stand at room temperature for 12 hours.

2. Transfer the contents of the bowl to a nonreactive pot. Add the raisins and cook the chutney over low heat, stirring often, until it is thick, about 1½ hours.

3. Spoon the chutney into pint or half-pint mason jars, leaving ¼ inch headspace. Close the jars with two-piece caps and process the jars for 10 minutes in a boiling-water bath.

4. Store the cooled jars in a cool, dry, dark place.

MANGO-APPLE CHUTNEY

MAKES 3 TO 3½ PINTS

THICKENED BY THE APPLES, this chutney cooks faster than most, and the mango keeps its pretty orange color. For a more piquant pickle, don't bother seeding the hot peppers.

3 pounds ripe but firm mangoes, peeled and cut into chunks
   (page 323)
1½ teaspoons pickling salt
1 cup sugar
1 cup cider vinegar
6 garlic cloves, chopped
1½ pounds tart apples, such as Gravenstein or Granny Smith,
   peeled, cored, and chopped
1 cup golden raisins
3 fresh red hot peppers, such as jalapeño, chopped
2 tablespoons grated fresh ginger
1½ teaspoons whole black mustard seeds

1 In a bowl, toss the mangoes with the salt. Cover the bowl and let it stand at room temperature for 12 hours.

2 Drain off any liquid from the mangoes. In a nonreactive pot, heat the sugar and vinegar, stirring to dissolve the sugar. Add the mangoes and the remaining ingredients. Cook the chutney over low heat, stirring frequently, until the chutney is thick, about 30 minutes.

3 Spoon the hot chutney into pint or half-pint mason jars, leaving ¼ inch headspace. Close the jars with two-piece caps and process the jars for 10 minutes in a boiling-water bath.

4 Store the cooled jars in a cool, dry, dark place for at least 2 weeks before eating the chutney.

ANN KAISER'S PEACH CHUTNEY

MAKES ABOUT 3½ PINTS

I DECIDED TO LEAVE MY OWN PEACH CHUTNEY out of this book after I tasted my mother-in-law's. Dark, sweet, and hot (mostly from the ample ginger), it's really the best.

Ripe peaches and nectarines are usually easy to peel if you first dip them for about 30 seconds in boiling water, then immediately cool them in cold water.

½ cup coarsely chopped onion
½ pound (1 cup plus 6 tablespoons) golden raisins
1 garlic clove
4 pounds (10 to 14) peaches or nectarines,
  pitted, peeled, and coarsely chopped
⅔ cup minced fresh ginger
2 cups cider vinegar
1½ pounds (3 cups plus 6 tablespoons, firmly packed) light
  brown sugar
2 tablespoons ground dried hot pepper
2 tablespoons whole yellow mustard seeds
1 tablespoon pickling salt

1 Put the onion, raisins, and garlic through a food grinder, or mince them very fine. Put them into a large nonreactive pot with the remaining ingredients. Boil the mixture, stirring often, for about 1 hour, until it is thick and a rich brown color.

2 Pack the chutney into pint or half-pint mason jars, leaving ¼ inch headspace. Close the jars with two-piece caps and process the jars for 10 minutes in a boiling-water bath.

3 Store the cooled jars in a cool, dry, dark place.

BANANA CHUTNEY

MAKES ABOUT 6½ PINTS

AFTER TASTING SOME COMMERCIAL banana chutney from Jamaica, I had to duplicate it. I use serrano peppers for their strong heat, but you might prefer jalapeños, which are a bit milder.

1 pound onions, coarsely chopped

¼ pound ripe hot peppers, such as serrano or jalapeño, coarsely chopped

1 cup raisins

¼ cup coarsely chopped fresh ginger

2 cups firmly packed light brown sugar

2 cups cider vinegar

4 teaspoons ground allspice

2 teaspoons pickling salt

3 pounds (8 to 10) green-tipped bananas, peeled and coarsely chopped

1 Put the onions, hot peppers, raisins, and ginger through a food grinder, or mince them very fine. Put them into a large nonreactive pot with the remaining ingredients. Simmer the chutney, stirring often, for about 1 hour, until it is thick and glossy.

2 Pack the chutney into pint or half-pint mason jars, leaving ¼ inch headspace. Close the jars with two-piece caps and process the jars for 10 minutes in a boiling-water bath.

3 Store the cooled jars in a cool, dry, dark place.

PLUM CHUTNEY

MAKES ABOUT 3 PINTS

I N MY HUSBAND'S FAMILY, this gingery chutney always brings back warm memories of Katcha Haberkorn, an old friend who shared the recipe about forty years ago.

^{3}/$_4$ cup cider vinegar

1 cup firmly packed light brown sugar

1 cup granulated sugar

1^1/$_2$ teaspoons hot pepper flakes

^{1}/$_2$ cup slivered crystallized ginger

2 teaspoons pickling salt

2 teaspoons whole yellow mustard seeds

2 large garlic cloves, thinly sliced

^{1}/$_4$ cup coarsely chopped onion

1 cup golden raisins

3^1/$_2$ cups halved and pitted Italian plums

1. In a heavy pot, bring the vinegar and both sugars to a boil. Add all of the remaining ingredients except the plums, and mix well. Stir in the plums. Simmer the mixture, stirring gently and frequently toward the end of the cooking, until the chutney thickens, about 50 minutes.

2. Pour the hot chutney into pint or half-pint mason jars, leaving ¼ inch headspace. Close the jars with two-piece caps and process the jars for 10 minutes in a boiling-water bath.

3. Store the cooled jars in a cool, dry, dark place for at least 2 weeks before eating the chutney.

RHUBARB CHUTNEY

MAKES ABOUT 3½ PINTS

ere's a chutney for those lucky enough to have an abundance of rhubarb.

2 cups cider vinegar
1½ cups firmly packed light brown sugar
1¾ pounds rhubarb stems, sliced ½ inch thick
3 cups chopped onions
2 tablespoons minced fresh ginger
1 teaspoon hot pepper flakes
Grated zest of 1 orange
One 4-inch cinnamon stick
1 cup golden raisins
½ teaspoon pickling salt

1. In a nonreactive pot over medium heat, heat the vinegar and sugar, stirring until the sugar dissolves. Add the remaining ingredients. Simmer for about 35 minutes, stirring occasionally, until the chutney thickens.

2. Remove the cinnamon stick. Pack the chutney into pint or half-pint mason jars, leaving ¼ inch headspace. Close the jars with two-piece caps and process the jars for 10 minutes in a boiling-water bath.

3. Store the cooled jars in a cool, dry, dark place.

PEACH-PEPPER RELISH

MAKES ABOUT 6 HALF-PINTS

THIS RECIPE, from Mona Carlisle of Vancouver, British Columbia, is another favorite in my husband's family. Like its cousin pepper jelly, Peach-Pepper Relish is often served as an appetizer or party food with cream cheese and crackers. I've found this relish a very good addition to stir-fry dishes, since it provides sweetness, tartness, and a little heat all at once.

1½ pounds (about 6) red bell or pimiento peppers, minced
½ pound red hot peppers, such as Fresno or jalapeño, minced
2 pounds (about 6) peaches or nectarines, pitted, peeled, and chopped
3 lemons, halved
6 cups sugar
2 cups cider vinegar

1. Put all of the peppers into a nonreactive bowl and cover them with boiling water. Let them stand until they are cool.

2. Drain the peppers and put them into a nonreactive pot with the chopped peaches or nectarines. Juice the lemons and add both the juice and peels to the pot. Boil the mixture for 15 minutes.

3. Remove the lemon peels and add the sugar and vinegar. Bring the mixture to a boil again. Let it boil, stirring constantly, until it forms a 2-inch thread or reaches 230°F on a candy thermometer.

4. Remove the pot from the heat and immediately ladle the relish into half-pint mason jars, leaving ¼ inch headspace. Close the jars with two-piece caps and process the jars for 10 minutes in a boiling-water bath.

5. Store the cooled jars in a cool, dry, dark place for at least 2 weeks before eating the relish.

SALSA COSTARIQUENSE

MAKES ABOUT 1 QUART

A ubiquitous sauce in costa rica, used heavily at the stove and often at the table, *salsa inglesa* is a smooth, orange-brown sauce much like Worcestershire—its long-ago model—but less sweet, less dark, and lacking fish of any kind (in the English-language Costa Rican cookbook *Costa Rican Typical Foods*, the term *salsa inglesa* isn't used; the sauce is called "Worcester" instead). Costa Rican salsa comes in many commercial versions, one of which actually bears the trade name of *Salsa Inglesa*. These sauces vary quite a lot in their flavor and ingredients. Here I have tried to match the taste of the brand my family liked best when we visited Costa Rica in 1996. It was my son Ben who identified the key flavoring—celery! Celery seemed an odd ingredient for a tropical sauce, but we tried it anyway and liked the result.

TAMARIND: TROPICAL SOURING AGENT

Like Worcestershire, *salsa inglesa* usually derives some of its sweetness, tang, and color from tamarind. The tamarind tree is a tropical version of the northern honey locust, in that both trees bear seeds surrounded by sweet flesh in long pods. I don't know how honey locust flesh tastes, but tamarind's orange flesh is very sour as well as sweet, and these qualities make it a perfect base for a lemonade-type drink and for marinades.

Tamarind pods are sold in many U.S. supermarkets, but scraping out the flesh is a lot of work. You can buy blocks of tamarind pulp, however, in Asian markets. Usually the seeds are included. To use block tamarind in drinks, soak a piece in warm water for 20 minutes, and then break it apart and strain out the seeds and fiber.

We first tasted *salsa inglesa* in a strange but delicious spaghetti sauce made by our Costa Rican hostess, Doña Elisa. We soon came to like the sauce best in *gallo pinto*, a kind of fried rice with bacon, black beans, and chopped onion, bell pepper, and cilantro. With a jar of *salsa inglesa* in your refrigerator, you can make your own *gallo pinto* whenever you have day-old rice on hand.

1 pound celery, with some leaves included, finely chopped
1 medium-size onion, finely chopped
¼ pound tamarind pulp (page 331), cut into small pieces
3 garlic cloves, crushed
1 tablespoon hot pepper flakes
3 tablespoons sugar
2½ teaspoons pickling salt
½ teaspoon ground allspice
1 teaspoon ground black pepper
½ teaspoon ground celery seeds
1½ cups distilled white vinegar
1½ cups water

1. Combine all of the ingredients in a large nonreactive pot. Simmer the contents, stirring occasionally, for about 40 minutes, until the vegetables are quite tender.

2. Puree the mixture through the fine disk of a food mill. Stir the sauce, and transfer it to a quart jar. Cap the jar. Store the cooled jar in the refrigerator.

3. Refrigerated, the sauce should keep for several months, at least.

TOMATO PRESERVES

THIS GLOSSY CONDIMENT of tomatoes and lemons is quite tart enough to serve as a pickle without the addition of vinegar. The sweet-sour-bitter flavor of the preserves goes delightfully well with pot roast. Try them also with roasted or grilled meats, or with crackers and cream cheese. You might even let these preserves stand in for jam on your morning toast.

2½ pounds ripe tomatoes
4 cups sugar
1 tablespoon Mixed Pickling Spices (page 15)
3 thin slices fresh ginger
2 medium-size lemons, thinly sliced

1 To loosen their skins, blanch the tomatoes in boiling water for about 2 minutes, and then plunge them into cold water. Core, peel, and quarter the tomatoes. In a bowl, gently mix them with the sugar. Let the mixture stand for 6 to 12 hours.

2 Drain the liquid from the tomatoes into a heavy nonreactive pot. Bring the tomato liquid to a boil and boil it, stirring, until the syrup forms a thread or reaches 230°F on a candy thermometer. Put the pickling spices and ginger into a spice bag, or tie them in a scrap of cheesecloth. Add the tomatoes, spice bag, and lemons to the pot. Cook the mixture over low heat until the tomatoes are dark and translucent.

3 Skim off any foam, remove the spice bag, and ladle the preserves into pint or half-pint mason jars, leaving ¼ inch headspace. Close the jars with two-piece caps and process the jars for 10 minutes in a boiling-water bath.

4 Store the cooled jars in a cool, dry, dark place.

RAZORBACK HOT SAUCE

 THIS IS A SWEET, Southern-style hot sauce. Serve it at a pig roast or with fried clams.

2 quarts tomato puree (page 344)

2 cups seeded and minced fresh red hot peppers, such as
    Fresno or cayenne

4 cups distilled white vinegar

2 tablespoons Mixed Pickling Spices (page 15)

1 cup sugar

2 teaspoons pickling salt

1 In a heavy nonreactive pot, bring to a boil the tomato puree, hot peppers, and 2 cups of the vinegar. Reduce the heat and simmer the mixture, stirring often, until it is reduced by half.

2 Puree the mixture in a food mill or blender and return it to the pot. Tie the spices in a spice bag or a scrap of cheesecloth and add them to the pot with the remaining 2 cups vinegar, sugar, and salt. Simmer, stirring often, until the sauce is as thick as you like.

3 Ladle the sauce into pint or half-pint mason jars, leaving ¼ inch headspace. Close the jars with two-piece caps, process the jars for 15 minutes in a boiling-water bath, and store the cooled jars in a cool, dry, dark place. Or funnel the sauce into hot sterilized bottles, cap or cork them, and store the cooled bottles in the refrigerator, where the sauce will keep well for at least 6 months.

TOMATO-PEPPER SAUCE

MAKES ABOUT 2 PINTS

THIS IS A KETCHUP, really, but because it has no added sugar or spices it is appropriate for far more uses than standard tomato ketchup. It can be hot or not, depending on the peppers you choose (I use ripe Fresno or jalapeño peppers for a mildly hot sauce) and whether you seed them. Tomato-Pepper Sauce is wonderful with eggs, potatoes, and fried fish and chicken.

1 pound sweet or hot red peppers, seeded or not, coarsely
   chopped
3½ cups distilled white vinegar or cider vinegar
4½ pounds ripe tomatoes, peeled and coarsely chopped, or
   3½ cups tomato puree (page 344)
6 garlic cloves, mashed
2 teaspoons pickling salt

1 In a blender or food processor, coarsely grind the peppers with 1½ cups of the vinegar. Combine the ground pepper mixture with the chopped tomatoes or tomato puree in a nonreactive kettle. Bring the mixture to a boil and boil it until the mixture is reduced by half.

2 Put the mixture through the medium screen of a food mill and then return the puree to the saucepan. Add the garlic, salt, and the remaining 2 cups vinegar. Boil the mixture, stirring often, until it's as thick as you like.

3 Ladle the sauce into pint or half-pint mason jars, leaving ¼ inch headspace, and process the jars for 15 minutes in a boiling-water bath. Store the cooled jars in a cool, dry, dark place. Or pour the sauce into hot sterilized bottles, cap or cork them, and store the cooled bottles in the refrigerator, where the sauce will keep well for at least 6 months.

SOUTHEAST ASIAN CHILE-GARLIC RELISH

YOU CAN USE THIS SIMPLE RELISH, known in Vietnamese as *tuong ot toi*, at the table or as an ingredient in kimchi, *salsa cruda*, guacamole, Chinese-style hot bean sauce, or quick pickles. Be sure to try it in Sweet Chile-Garlic Sauce (opposite page). My family consumes several quarts of this relish every year.

1½ pounds ripe hot peppers, such as Fresno, jalapeño, or
   cayenne, each stemmed and cut into several pieces
1 cup cider vinegar or distilled vinegar
1 tablespoon pickling salt
1 small garlic head, cloves separated and peeled, or
   2 tablespoons minced garlic

1. Blend all of the ingredients briefly together in a blender or food processor, in batches, if necessary. Do not puree them; the pepper seeds should remain whole.

2. Store the mixture in a covered jar in the refrigerator, where it will keep well for as long as a year, or in airtight containers in the freezer.

SWEET CHILE-GARLIC SAUCE

COMMERCIAL VERSIONS OF THIS SAUCE are sold in Southeast Asian markets, where the bottles are often labeled "for chicken." This sweet, hot, garlicky sauce is indeed good with grilled chicken, but it also goes well with other grilled meats and with deep-fried foods such as spring rolls. I add it to stir-fry dishes in place of any other sweetener.

1 cup distilled vinegar
1 cup water
2 cups sugar
2 teaspoons pickling salt
¼ cup minced garlic (from about 1 large head)
¼ cup Southeast Asian Chile-Garlic Relish (opposite page)

1. In a large, heavy saucepan, bring everything but the chile-garlic relish to a boil, stirring to dissolve the sugar and salt. Reduce the heat and boil gently until the mixture thickens slightly, about 30 minutes.

2. Stir in the chile-garlic relish. Increase the heat to medium-high and bring the sauce to a rolling boil. Let it boil for about 2 minutes, until a drop in a glass of cold water forms a short thread (230°F on a candy thermometer). Remove the pan from the heat and let the sauce cool for 1 hour.

3. Stir the sauce and then pour it into a hot sterilized bottle or jar. Store the cooled jar in the refrigerator, where the sauce should keep well for at least a year.

FERMENTED CHILE-GARLIC RELISH

MAKES ABOUT 3 CUPS

THIS IS A VINEGAR-FREE VERSION of Southeast Asian Chile-Garlic Relish (page 336). The acidity here comes from fermentation; the flavor is different but no less appealing.

1 pound ripe hot peppers, such as Fresno, jalapeño, or
   cayenne, each stemmed and cut into several pieces
6 garlic cloves, chopped
2½ teaspoons pickling salt, plus more if needed
1 cup water, plus more if needed

1. In a food processor or blender, chop the peppers and garlic with 2 teaspoons of the salt to make a coarse mash. Pack the mixture into a quart jar. Push a quart-size freezer bag into the top of the jar. Stir the remaining ½ teaspoon salt into the water and pour this brine into the freezer bag. Seal the bag. Place the jar in a bowl to catch any spills and let the jar stand at room temperature.

2. If on the next day the mash isn't covered in its own brine, stir ⅛ teaspoon pickling salt into ¼ cup water. Pour the solution over the mash and replace the brine bag.

3. Within a few days the peppers should begin fermenting, and air pockets will develop in the mash. Let the fermentation continue for about 2 weeks, until the mash tastes properly sour. Stir the mash, and cap the jar tightly. Store the jar in the refrigerator.

4. Refrigerated, the mash should keep well for several weeks, at least.

BRINED CHILE RELISH

MAKES ABOUT 3 CUPS

THIS IS A FERMENTED HOT-PEPPER RELISH made from brined whole peppers. You can add garlic before or after brining, but leave it out if you'd like to experience the pure taste of fermented hot peppers.

    2 quarts brined hot peppers (page 71),
        with their seeds

1. In batches, whirl the peppers in a blender to a mash; stop before you have a puree. Transfer the mash to one or more jars, cap tightly, and store in the refrigerator.

2. Refrigerated, the mash should keep for several months.

BRINED CHILE SAUCE

You can take Brined Chile Relish one step further by straining out the seeds and skins to make a smooth, hot sauce. In batches, whirl 2 quarts brined hot peppers (page 71), with their seeds, in a blender to mash. Pass the mash through the fine disk of a food mill or a fine sieve. If you'd like the sauce a little thinner, add a little of the pepper brine or some vinegar. Transfer the sauce to one or more jars or bottles, cap tightly, and store in the refrigerator, where the sauce will keep for several months.

Have you just made Tabasco sauce? Not quite. On Avery Island, Louisiana, the McIlhenny Company ferments salted and mashed peppers in oak casks for 3 years and churns the aged mash with vinegar for 30 days before straining, filtering, and bottling the sauce.

PIQUE

MAKES ABOUT 1½ CUPS

THE SIMPLEST HOT SAUCE OF ALL—and one that is immensely popular in the West Indies—is vinegar in which hot peppers have been steeped. In Puerto Rico a rum bottle full of *pique* sits on every restaurant table, displaying long, thin peppers in assorted colors.

12 medium-size fresh hot peppers, such as cayenne, de árbol,
    or jalapeño, slit once or twice lengthwise
4 garlic cloves, halved lengthwise
12 whole black peppercorns
⅛ teaspoon pickling salt
About 1 cup cider vinegar

1. Put the hot peppers, garlic, peppercorns, and salt into a 12-ounce or 0.75-liter bottle with a nonreactive cap. A rum bottle is most authentic, but I use a small vinegar bottle (if no one has thrown out the plastic inner cap that keeps the contents from pouring out too fast, I use that as well). Using a funnel, pour enough vinegar over the other ingredients to cover them well. Cap or cork the bottle and give it a shake to dissolve the salt.

2. Let the bottle sit undisturbed for at least a day or two so the vinegar can absorb the other flavors. The longer the sauce sits, the hotter it will get. Store the bottle in the refrigerator or another cool place. Until the pepper flavor gets weak, you can top off the bottle with fresh vinegar as needed.

SWEET TOMATO CHUTNEY

I THINK OF THIS THICK, GLOSSY, sweet chutney as an elegant, exotic version of tomato ketchup. You might serve this relish with fried fish or cold poultry.

4 pounds ripe tomatoes, peeled and chopped, or
   7 cups tomato puree (page 344)
1½ cups sugar
1½ cups white wine vinegar or distilled white vinegar
1 tablespoon pickling salt
Juice and grated zest of 1 large lime or 2 small limes
¼ cup chopped garlic (from about 1 large head)
2 tablespoons chopped fresh ginger
½ teaspoon hot pepper flakes
½ teaspoon whole fennel seeds
½ teaspoon whole cumin seeds
½ teaspoon whole fenugreek seeds
½ cup raisins

1. In a heavy nonreactive pot, combine all of the ingredients. Bring them to a boil and reduce the heat. Simmer them for 1½ to 2 hours, stirring often, until the chutney is thick.

2. Ladle the chutney into pint or half-pint mason jars, leaving ¼ inch headspace, and close the jars with two-piece caps. Process the jars for 10 minutes in a boiling-water bath.

3. Store the cooled jars in a cool, dry, dark place.

HYDERABADI TOMATO CHUTNEY

MAKES 1 PINT

T HIS CHUTNEY IS ARGUABLY not a pickle at all, since it contains no vinegar or citrus juice and should probably be frozen for long-term storage. But it is my very favorite chutney, so I couldn't leave it out of this book. If you like very hot, garlicky foods, you will love this relish. Traditionally served with Moghul dishes of lamb in yogurt sauce, the chutney is also delicious with roasted potatoes.

12 garlic cloves
3½ cups peeled and chopped tomatoes or tomato puree
   (page 344)
2 teaspoons grated fresh ginger
½ teaspoon ground dried hot pepper
2 teaspoons whole cumin seeds
1 teaspoon whole black mustard seeds
½ teaspoon whole fenugreek seeds
4 small dried hot peppers, such as japonés or de árbol,
   caps removed
⅓ cup vegetable oil
1 teaspoon pickling salt

1. Mash 4 of the garlic cloves and combine them in a bowl with the tomatoes, ginger, and ground hot pepper. Set the bowl next to the stove. Measure the cumin, mustard seeds, and fenugreek into a small bowl, and put it and the peppers next to the stove as well.

2. Heat the oil in a large nonreactive skillet over medium-high heat. Add the 8 remaining garlic cloves. Fry them, turning them once or twice, until they are golden brown. Add the cumin, mustard seeds,

and fenugreek to the pan, and let them sizzle for 2 seconds. Add the peppers and stir once; they will swell and darken. Add the tomato mixture carefully; it will splatter a bit at first. Cook the chutney, stirring almost constantly, for 15 to 20 minutes, until it is quite thick. Stir in the salt. Spoon the chutney into small jars or plastic storage containers and close them tightly.

3. The chutney will keep well in the refrigerator for a week or more. For long-term storage, freeze the containers.

TOMATO KETCHUP

MAKES ABOUT 4 PINTS

THIS KETCHUP TASTES THE WAY tomato ketchup should, rich and natural with no bitter or metallic off-flavors. You'll never crave store-bought ketchup again once you've tasted this.

1 gallon tomato puree (page 344)

1½ cups chopped onions

½ cup chopped fresh red hot peppers, such as Fresno, cayenne, or jalapeño

2 garlic cloves, minced

2 cups cider vinegar

1 tablespoon pickling salt

1 Mediterranean bay leaf, crumbled

2 tablespoons whole coriander seeds

1 tablespoon whole yellow mustard seeds

1 tablespoon whole black peppercorns

1 tablespoon whole allspice berries

One 3-inch cinnamon stick, broken into pieces

¼ cup granulated sugar

½ cup firmly packed light brown sugar

HOW TO PUREE TOMATOES

An excellent tool for pureeing tomatoes is a tomato strainer, such as the all-metal Squeezo model or the mostly plastic Victorio. Either one will, with the turn of a crank, thoroughly wring out the tomato skins, then automatically expel them with the seeds, while the pulp pours into a bowl.

For small quantities of tomatoes, another good tool for this purpose is a Mouli or Foley food mill. A food mill frees the tomato pulp from the skins and seeds, but the latter accumulate on the screen, where they tend to block the flow of pulp. Also, you may have to struggle to keep the mill balanced over your bowl, and milling raw tomatoes may prove too difficult unless you chop them well. If you decide to buy a food mill, look for one that's stainless steel rather than tin-plated; the tin-plated ones tend to rust out quickly.

Using either a tomato strainer or food mill is easier if you cook the tomatoes first. I use this method: Drop the tomatoes one by one into a large kettle, giving each a squeeze to release some of the seeds and liquid. Boil the tomatoes gently until they soften.

To make a thick puree without a lot of boiling, pour the contents of the kettle into a strainer set over a large bowl. Let the tomatoes drain a bit, and then pour them into another bowl. From there you can ladle them into the tomato strainer or food mill.

Don't throw out the juice you drained off; instead, can it separately. Come winter, it can make a wonderfully sweet, light soup or beverage. Strained through cheesecloth, it can become a delicious consommé.

The USDA recommends adding 1 tablespoon of lemon juice or $\frac{1}{4}$ teaspoon of citric acid to each quart of tomato puree, just in case your tomatoes are abnormally low in acid. If you drain off the tart juice from your tomatoes before canning them, it's wise to acidify the pulp before canning it.

If you think it's a shame to waste the nutrients and flavor in tomato seeds and pulp, then don't. I sometimes puree whole tomatoes by blending them at high speed in a Vita-Mix blender. This powerful machine grinds all but a few of the seeds in a matter of seconds. The uncooked puree looks a little paler and grainier than seedless, skinless puree, but it's very hard to tell the difference after the puree is boiled to a sauce.

Process jars of tomato juice or puree in a boiling-water bath as follows: 35 minutes for pints of juice or puree, 40 minutes for quarts of juice, and 45 minutes for quarts of puree.

1. In a large nonreactive pot, combine the tomato puree, onions, hot peppers, garlic, vinegar, and salt. Bring the mixture to a boil.

2. Tie the bay leaf and spices in a spice bag or scrap of cheesecloth, and add this to the pot along with both sugars. Cook the ketchup over medium-high heat, stirring often, until it thickens.

3. Squeeze the spice bag to extract all its flavors, and then remove it. Puree the ketchup in a food mill, using a fine disk, or press the ketchup through a fine sieve.

4. Return the ketchup to the pot. Bring it to a boil again and continue to boil it, stirring constantly, until it mounds slightly in a spoon.

5. Ladle the ketchup into pint or half-pint mason jars, leaving ¼ inch headspace. Close the jars with two-piece caps and process the jars for 15 minutes in a boiling-water bath.

6. Store the cooled jars in a cool, dry, dark place.

MARY RANDOLPH'S SUGAR-FREE TOMATO KETCHUP

MAKES ABOUT 2½ PINTS

ALTHOUGH TODAY'S TOMATO KETCHUPS are generally very sweet condiments, early versions were sweetened very little or not at all. This simple recipe, from Mary Randolph's book *The Virginia Housewife* (1824), is a delicious example. You might want to vary the seasonings—I'm tempted to add garlic next time—but I think you'll find this ketchup plenty sweet for most purposes.

Mary Randolph left not only sugar out of her ketchup but vinegar as well. For this reason, the result was more like thick tomato sauce than modern tomato ketchup. Long boiling concentrated the acids, making the ketchup quite tart, but it was still more liable to spoil than ketchup made with vinegar. Mary wisely advised making tomato ketchup "in August, in dry weather," before cool, damp weather invited mold and late blight to the tomato patch. She also made a small quantity at a time and probably planned to use it within a few months. If your tomatoes are tart, unblemished, and just ripe—not overripe—a 15-minute boiling-water bath should preserve your ketchup well. Just in case your tomatoes aren't up to par, though, I call for pressure canning here.

1 peck (2 gallons) tomatoes, stemmed

2 tablespoons pickling salt

1 cup minced onions

1½ teaspoons blade (unground) mace

1 tablespoon whole black peppercorns

1. Put the tomatoes into a large nonreactive pot, squeezing each one firmly as you drop it in. Sprinkle the salt over the tomatoes and then bring them to a boil. Stirring occasionally, boil the tomatoes, uncovered, for 1 hour.

2. Put the tomatoes through a tomato strainer or food mill (Mrs. Randolph advised straining them "through a colander, and then through a sieve"). Return the puree to the pot and add the onions, mace, and peppercorns. Bring the puree to a boil and boil it, stirring often, until it is as thick as modern tomato ketchup.

3. Ladle the ketchup into pint or half-pint mason jars, leaving ¼ inch headspace. Process the jars in a pressure canner for 20 minutes at 11 pounds pressure, or store them in the refrigerator.

"As late as 1944 . . . in Maine a sweetened ketchup among some families was regarded as an offense against God and man, against nature and good taste."

—Andrew F. Smith,
  Pure Ketchup,
  1996

HOT ORANGE KETCHUP

MAKES ABOUT 2 PINTS

THIS UNSWEETENED KETCHUP gets its color from yellow or orange tomatoes and yellow Cascabella peppers. Developed in California, Cascabella peppers are aptly named, for their skins (*cascaras*, in Spanish) are truly beautiful (*bella*). These small, waxy, conical peppers start out light yellow, then turn orange before ripening red. They grow prolifically on bushy plants, which are such a pretty sight that you may want to grow one for its ornamental value alone. Don't confuse Cascabellas with cascabel ("jingle bell") peppers, which are round, red, hot Mexican chiles. In this recipe, you can substitute any hot yellow peppers, such as Floral Gem or Hungarian Wax. If you don't like heat, use yellow bell peppers or banana peppers.

You'll need about 5 pounds of yellow or orange tomatoes for this recipe.

6½ cups yellow or orange tomato puree (page 344)

6 ounces (about 1 pint) yellow Cascabella peppers, seeded and chopped

½ pound white or yellow onions, chopped

10 garlic cloves, chopped

1 small lemon

1 cup white wine vinegar

2 teaspoons pickling salt

2 teaspoons whole yellow mustard seeds

2 teaspoons whole coriander seeds

1 teaspoon whole cloves

One 2-inch cinnamon stick, broken into pieces

3 thin slices fresh ginger

1. In a large nonreactive saucepan, bring the tomato puree, peppers, onions, and garlic to a boil. Simmer the mixture until the peppers and onions are tender, about 20 minutes. Meanwhile, remove the zest of the lemon in strips and squeeze out the juice.

2. Puree the tomato mixture in batches in a blender and return the puree to the saucepan. Add the lemon juice, vinegar, and salt. Tie the lemon zest, dry spices, and ginger in a spice bag or scrap of cheese-cloth and add this to the pan, too. Simmer the ketchup, stirring it occasionally, for about 1½ hours, until it is as thick as you like.

3. Ladle the ketchup into pint or half-pint mason jars, leaving ¼ inch headspace. Close the jars with two-piece caps and process the jars for 15 minutes in a boiling-water bath. Store the cooled jars in a cool, dry, dark place. Or funnel the ketchup into hot sterilized bottles, cap or cork them, and store the cooled bottles in the refrigerator.

KETCHUP IN HISTORY

Not all ketchup is made from tomatoes. Until about 1850, in fact, an American recipe that called for a spoonful of ketchup most likely meant mushroom, walnut, or oyster. These ketchups were themselves inspired by Asian pickled fish brines; called *kôechiap* in Amoy Chinese and *kechap* in Malay, fish ketchups were like the *nuoc mam, nam pla*, or *tuk trey* still so important in the cuisines of Southeast Asia. (Ancient Rome had had its own version; known as *liquamen*, it was brewed commercially and used ubiquitously in Roman cuisine.)

Early English and American ketchups were more like their Asian predecessors than like today's tomato ketchup. Nineteenth-century mushroom ketchup was usually preserved with salt, not vinegar; oyster and lobster ketchups were preserved with sherry. These ketchups were used primarily in cooking, much as we use soy sauce and Vietnamese fish sauce today.

When sugar became common and cheap, Americans started making ketchups from various fruits. Even a cookbook published in 1965 gives recipes for ketchups made from a dozen kinds of fruits other than tomatoes.

CRANBERRY KETCHUP

MAKES 1½ PINTS

THIS FRUIT KETCHUP is a smooth, spicy alternative to conventional cranberry sauce. Try Cranberry Ketchup with pork and beef as well as with turkey. It's especially good in sandwiches.

One 3-inch cinnamon stick, broken into pieces
3 thin slices fresh ginger
1½ pounds (two 12-ounce bags) cranberries
1¼ cups cider vinegar
1¼ cups water
1 teaspoon ground cloves
1 teaspoon ground allspice
½ teaspoon ground nutmeg
Grated zest of 1 large orange
1½ cups firmly packed light brown sugar

1. Tie the cinnamon pieces and ginger in a spice bag or scrap of cheesecloth. Put this into a nonreactive saucepan with all of the remaining ingredients except the brown sugar, and bring the contents to a simmer. Simmer them until the cranberries are soft, about 20 minutes.

2. Remove the spice bag and puree the mixture in a food mill or press it through a sieve. Return the puree to the saucepan. Add the sugar and simmer the ketchup until it is glossy and thick, about 15 minutes.

3. Ladle the ketchup into pint or half-pint mason jars, leaving ¼ inch headspace. Close the jars with two-piece caps and process the jars for 10 minutes in a boiling-water bath.

4. Store the cooled jars in a cool, dry dark place.

CURRANT OR GOOSEBERRY KETCHUP

MAKES 2 PINTS

MOST AMERICANS HAVE NEVER TASTED a gooseberry or currant. This wasn't always so; until the early 1900s, gooseberry and currant bushes were common plants in U.S. gardens, and recipes like this one were popular. But then many states and the federal government outlawed the cultivation of plants in the genus *Ribes*, on the grounds that they can serve as alternate hosts for a disease called white pine blister rust, which infects five-needled pine trees. Eventually, however, someone noticed that wild *Ribes* species grow in woodlands over most of the continent, and that these wild shrubs pose a greater threat to commercial forests than plants on the farm or in the garden. So in 1966 the federal government removed its ban on currant and gooseberry growing, and since then most states have legalized the plants. In the 1990s, high-priced little packages of the fruits began appearing in chic markets.

Still, however, currants and gooseberries are hard to find in stores. The sensible thing to do is to plant your own. A young bare-root bush costs about as much as a pint of fruit from the market.

For a colorful ketchup, use red or black currants or red gooseberries. Since my bushes were just starting to produce fruit, I combined black and red currants in developing this recipe.

2 pounds currants or gooseberries, stemmed
3 cups sugar
1¼ cups cider vinegar

1 tablespoon ground cinnamon

1 teaspoon ground mace

1 teaspoon ground allspice

1 teaspoon ground ginger

1. In a nonreactive pot, bring the fruit, sugar, and vinegar to a boil. Reduce the heat and simmer the mixture until the fruit is soft.

2. Puree the mixture in a food mill or press it through a sieve. Return the mixture to the pan, add the spices, and cook the ketchup until it is thick.

3. Ladle the ketchup into pint or half-pint mason jars, leaving ¼ inch headspace. Close the jars with two-piece caps and process the jars for 10 minutes in a boiling-water bath.

4. Store the cooled jars in a cool, dry, dark place.

WALNUT KETCHUP

MAKES 3 TO 3½ CUPS

MOST AMERICAN AND ENGLISH COOKBOOKS published in the mid-nineteenth century included recipes for walnut pickles and ketchup. Like other early ketchups, walnut ketchup was usually thin, unsweetened, and used in cooking rather than at the table. This version, basically that of Mary Randolph (*The Virginia Housewife*, 1824) is really just a flavored vinegar. Mrs. Beeton's recipe (from *Mrs. Beeton's Book of Household Management*, 1861) includes anchovies, port wine, horseradish, and shallots. Either version makes an excellent steak sauce and addition to marinades.

To make walnut ketchup, you must have access to an English walnut tree. Also called Persian walnut, these trees bear nuts with elongated shells; they are the sort sold in supermarkets. Don't try using nuts from the black walnut, a native American tree that is valued more for its wood than its nuts, which are round and very hard to crack.

Before you decide to forego making this ketchup because you have no English walnut tree in your yard, look around. I have gathered all the green walnuts I needed from a roadside tree.

Gather your nuts between late June and mid-July, when they are full size or close to it, but before the shells have developed. You should be able to easily run a needle through the nuts. At this stage the nuts won't have fallen yet, so bring along a child or two to climb the tree and toss the nuts down to you.

2 pounds green English walnuts
6 tablespoons pickling salt
3 cups white wine vinegar
6 garlic cloves
1 teaspoon ground cloves
1 teaspoon ground mace

1. Pierce each nut about six times with a large needle and put the nuts into a 2-quart jar. Dissolve 2 tablespoons of the salt in 1 quart boiling water and pour the water over the nuts. Cap the jar and leave it at room temperature for 3 days.

2. Drain off the water. Dissolve another 2 tablespoons salt in 1 quart boiling water and pour this over the nuts. Repeat the process three days later.

3. Nine days after first putting the nuts in the jar, drain them and leave them in a colander in the sun for 2 to 3 days to blacken. Turn them occasionally.

4. In a blender, grind the nuts with the vinegar (or pound them in a large marble mortar, as Mary Randolph advises). Return the walnut-vinegar mixture to the 2-quart jar and close it tightly with a non-

reactive cap. Leave the jar at room temperature for 1 week, shaking it or stirring the contents daily.

5. Strain the walnut-vinegar mixture through a jelly bag, squeezing the bag to extract all the liquid. In a blender or mortar, grind the garlic and spices with a little of the walnut liquid. Combine the puree with the remaining liquid in a saucepan and simmer for 15 minutes.

6. Pour the hot liquid into hot sterilized bottles and cap or cork them. Store the bottles in a cool, dry, dark place. The ketchup will keep well for years.

APPLE KETCHUP

MAKES ABOUT 3 PINTS

MARGARET THORSON of remote Waldron Island, Washington, sent me a favorite old recipe for apple ketchup. I've substituted ginger and cayenne for the original cloves and used light brown sugar rather than white, but otherwise this is Margaret's recipe. She says that she uses very tart apples for the ketchup and that it is "wonderful with any meat." I like it especially with pork.

1 quart unsweetened applesauce

3/4 pound onions, minced or ground in a food grinder or food processor

1 cup firmly packed light brown sugar

2 cups cider vinegar

1 teaspoon ground black pepper

1 teaspoon grated fresh ginger

1 teaspoon dry mustard

2 teaspoons ground cinnamon

1 tablespoon pickling salt

1. Combine all of the ingredients in a nonreactive pot. Simmer them, stirring occasionally, for 30 minutes, or until the ketchup is as thick as you like.

2. Ladle the ketchup into pint or half-pint mason jars, leaving ¼ inch headspace, and close the jars with two-piece caps. Process the jars for 15 minutes in a boiling-water bath.

3. Store the cooled jars in a cool, dry, dark place.

PEPPER-ONION RELISH

MAKES ABOUT 4½ PINTS

I USE THIS RELISH IN THE KITCHEN rather than at the table; it's a great addition to pan-fried onions, vegetable stews, and other dishes. Traditional pepper-onion relishes are made with equal quantities of red and green sweet peppers, but I use a mixture of peppers that are all red and mostly hot. This isn't because I'm a fiery foods fiend—since the heat of the peppers is dampened through processing, my finished relish is actually quite mellow.

1 teaspoon whole allspice berries
1 teaspoon whole cloves
1 teaspoon whole black peppercorns
5 cups seeded and minced ripe peppers (sweet, hot, or a combination)
3 cups minced onions
4 cups cider vinegar
⅔ cup sugar
1 tablespoon pickling salt

1. Tie the spices in a spice bag or scrap of cheesecloth. Combine the spice bag and all of the remaining ingredients in a nonreactive pot. Bring the mixture to a simmer and simmer it until it is thick, about 30 minutes.

2. Ladle the relish into pint or half-pint mason jars, leaving ¼ inch headspace. Close the jars with two-piece caps and process the jars for 10 minutes in a boiling-water bath.

3. Store the cooled jars in a cool, dry, dark place.

TOMATO SALSA

MAKES 7 TO 8 PINTS

THIS IS A PRESERVED VERSION of *salsa cruda*, the popular Mexican table sauce. Because this salsa is briefly cooked, it doesn't taste quite like the fresh version, but I think you'll much prefer it to store-bought salsa, most of which is made from tomato paste. For a fresher taste, stir in some chopped cilantro just before serving.

Paste tomatoes such as Roma work best in this recipe; juicy tomatoes make a runny salsa. To remove some of the excess liquid and seeds from salad tomatoes, squeeze them gently (over bread, for a snack to fortify you) before chopping them. If your salsa still turns out runny, just drain off the excess liquid before serving.

North of the border, jalapeños are probably the favorite salsa pepper, but choose your chiles to suit your tastes. Most people prefer a mixture of sweet and hot peppers. I usually use all hot ones, since the salsa mellows in the jar.

You can seed the peppers if you like, but you'll be doing a lot more work for less flavor. If you do choose to seed the peppers, you will be wise to wear rubber or plastic gloves, especially if you wear contact lenses.

To vary this recipe, you might add a teaspoon or two of ground cumin, cracked coriander seeds, or chopped oregano.

If you lack patience for chopping with a knife, you may look for an alternative way to mince or grind the vegetables. I've had success with a VitaMix blender (which comes with a plunger for even chopping)—as long as I don't accidentally turn the blender on high speed! For authenticity try a *molcajete*, a traditional stone mortar available in Mexican markets.

> 5 pounds tomatoes, preferably paste-type, chopped
>   (about 3 quarts)
> 2 pounds fresh green or ripe peppers, hot or mild,
>   stemmed and minced (about 2 quarts)
> 1 pound onions, minced (about 2½ cups)
> 1 cup lime juice or white wine vinegar
> 1½ tablespoons pickling salt

1. In a large nonreactive pot, bring all of the ingredients to a simmer. Simmer them for 10 minutes.

2. Ladle the salsa into pint or half-pint mason jars, leaving ½ inch headspace. Close the jars with two-piece caps and process the jars in a boiling-water bath for 15 minutes.

3. Store the cooled jars in a cool, dry, dark place. Once a jar is opened, the salsa will keep well in the refrigerator for at least a week.

SALSA VERDE

MAKES ABOUT 3 PINTS

TOMATILLOS ARE YELLOW and quite sweet when ripe; I dry them and use them like raisins. If you grow your own tomatillos, though, pick them green for this salsa. That's the way the Mexicans like them, and the way you'll find them in the market.

As with Tomato Salsa (page 355), you can seed the hot peppers if you like. If you do, wear rubber or plastic gloves.

You can vary this recipe by adding 1 teaspoon of ground cumin or 1 to 2 tablespoons of minced garlic along with the peppers and onions.

Like tomato salsa, this relish is delicious with chopped cilantro stirred in just before serving. *Salsa verde* is great with chips, tacos, and other tortilla dishes.

2½ pounds tomatillos, husks removed, halved
½ pound (about 8) roasted, peeled, and seeded Anaheim chile
    peppers, chopped
2 cups chopped onions
4 garlic cloves, chopped
¾ cup lime juice
2½ teaspoons pickling salt

1 In a nonreactive pot over medium-low heat, cook the tomatillos, stirring occasionally at first, until they are tender, about 10 minutes. After they have cooled a bit, blend them briefly in a blender or food processor.

2 In the pot combine the tomatillo puree and the remaining ingredients. Bring the mixture to a boil over medium heat and then reduce the heat. Simmer the mixture for 15 minutes.

After determining that the juice from tomato salsa has antibacterial properties, chemists at the University of California, Berkeley, did experiments to find out why. They determined that a compound in fresh cilantro leaves, dodecenal, kills the cells of *Salmonella choleraesuis*—twice as effectively, in fact, as gentamicin, a drug commonly prescribed to treat *Salmonella* poisoning. Mexicans' love of cilantro may explain why they don't develop salmonellosis as often as visitors to their country do.

Note that the scientists tested fresh cilantro, not canned. Since the latter may lack antibiotic potency as well as flavor, it's best to add cilantro just before serving your salsa.

3 Ladle the salsa into pint or half-pint mason jars, leaving ½ inch headspace. Close the jars with two-piece caps and process the jars for 15 minutes in a boiling-water bath.

4 Store the cooled jars in a cool, dry, dark place.

CHILI SAUCE WITH CHILES

MAKES ABOUT 6 PINTS

THE FIRST TIME I MADE CHILI SAUCE I was mystified at the result and ended up running the whole batch through the blender to turn it into ketchup, a relish I understood. My husband's Eastern-born relations had to explain what chili sauce was about: My mother-in-law likes it with meatloaf and burgers; my husband's aunt eats it with roast beef and baked beans. Simply a chunky version of tomato ketchup, chili sauce has a texture that many people prefer.

But where is the chile in chili sauce? I wondered. None of the old recipes I've found call for hot peppers, though *The Picayune Creole Cook Book* (1901) considers them an optional addition. I suspect chili sauce originated as Mexican chile salsa. Just as *chile con carne*, or chili, was tempered with beans, tomatoes, and other ingredients as it traveled east and north, so that now hot peppers are often left out entirely, chili sauce long ago became Yankeefied.

This is a traditional chili sauce with a little hot pepper added for interest.

One 3-inch cinnamon stick, broken
1 tablespoon whole yellow mustard seeds
2 teaspoons whole celery seeds
2 teaspoons chopped fresh ginger
1 teaspoon whole allspice berries
¼ teaspoon whole cloves
10 pounds tomatoes, coarsely chopped
4 large onions, minced (about 1 quart)
4 sweet red peppers, such as bell or pimiento, chopped
  (about 2½ cups)
4 fresh hot peppers, such as jalapeño, minced
½ cup firmly packed light brown sugar
2 tablespoons pickling salt
2 cups cider vinegar

1 Tie the spices in a spice bag or in a scrap of cheesecloth. Combine the spice bag and all of the remaining ingredients in a heavy nonreactive pot. Bring the mixture to a boil, and then reduce the heat and simmer the chili sauce until it is thick, about 3 hours.

2 Ladle the chili sauce into pint or half-pint mason jars, leaving ¼ inch headspace. Close the jars with two-piece caps and process the jars for 15 minutes in a boiling-water bath.

3 Store the cooled jars in a cool, dry, dark place.

AUNT MARY GOODSELL'S CHILI SAUCE

MAKES ABOUT 3 PINTS

T HIS OLD NEW ENGLAND RECIPE was handed down from Mary Jane Summers Goodsell, born in 1851 in Newtown, Connecticut; she was the aunt of my husband's grandfather. Family lore has it that Aunt Mary won first prize for this sauce year after year at the Danbury fair. My husband's aunt Eleanor Thompson recalls smelling the wonderful, cinnamony aroma of this simple chili sauce upon coming home from school on a fall afternoon to find her mother, Blanche Waterhouse, making an annual batch.

24 large red tomatoes (about 10 pounds), coarsely chopped
6 green bell peppers, coarsely chopped
4 large onions, coarsely chopped
½ cup sugar
2 tablespoons pickling salt
2 tablespoons ground cinnamon
3 cups white wine vinegar, cider vinegar, or distilled
    white vinegar

1 In a large nonreactive pot, bring all of the ingredients to a boil. Reduce the heat and simmer the sauce, stirring occasionally, until it is thick, about 3 hours.

2 Ladle the sauce into pint or half-pint mason jars, leaving ¼ inch headspace. Close the jars with two-piece caps and process the jars for 15 minutes in a boiling-water bath.

3 Store the cooled jars in a cool, dry, dark place.

CLASSIC BARBECUE SAUCE

MAKES ABOUT 3½ PINTS

EVER SINCE MY HUSBAND and I finished college and bought our first hibachi, I've been making quick versions of this sauce while the charcoal burned down. It's nice, however, to have some barbecue sauce ready to go on the pantry shelf, allowing more time to prepare the rest of dinner.

Slather this sauce on your meat shortly before taking it off the grill, or heat the sauce and serve it at the table.

11 cups tomato puree (page 344)

2 celery stalks, chopped

2 medium-size onions, chopped

1 medium-size ripe bell or pimiento pepper, chopped

1½ cups chopped fresh red hot peppers, such as Fresno, jalapeño, or cayenne

4 garlic cloves, minced

1 teaspoon whole black peppercorns

1 tablespoon whole cumin seeds

1 tablespoon dry mustard

1 cup molasses

1 tablespoon pickling salt

1½ cups red wine vinegar

1. In a large nonreactive pot, bring to a boil the tomato puree, celery, onion, peppers, and garlic. Reduce the heat and simmer the vegetables until they are soft and the mixture is reduced by about one-third.

2. Tie the peppercorns in a spice bag or a scrap of cheesecloth, and toast the cumin seeds in a dry pan until they are fragrant.

3 Put the tomato mixture through a food mill and return the puree to the pot. Add the mustard, molasses, salt, vinegar, toasted cumin seeds, and spice bag. Cook the sauce until it is about as thick as ketchup, about 1½ hours. As the mixture thickens, stir often to prevent sticking.

4 Remove the spice bag. Ladle the sauce into pint or half-pint mason jars, leaving ¼ inch headspace. Close the jars with two-piece caps and process the jars for 20 minutes in a boiling-water bath.

5 Store the cooled jars in a cool, dry, dark place.

HORSERADISH FOR HEALTH

Like mustard oil (page 154), horseradish contains the pungent chemical allyl isothiocyanate, which has been proven to kill food pathogens. The Japanese relative of horseradish, wasabi, also contains this chemical, which makes wasabi a useful accompaniment to raw fish. But whereas wasabi grows only in cool, wet places, horseradish thrives almost anywhere. That's why most of what's called wasabi, in both grocery stores and restaurants, is really dried or grated horseradish dyed green.

PREPARED HORSERADISH

MAKES ½ PINT

FRESH HORSERADISH IS immensely more flavorful than the adulterated commercial stuff, and preparing it is quick and easy. If you don't like grating horseradish, you can instead use a blender or food processor; just cut the peeled root into small pieces, put them into the machine with the vinegar, and grind the horseradish briefly, so the pieces remain coarse. But keep your face away from the blender jar or processor bowl; fresh horseradish is very pungent, and it burns the eyes as no onion can.

Whether you grate your horseradish or use a blender or food processor, you might add a little sugar to smooth the flavor, and ascorbic acid to prevent browning.

Prepared horseradish gradually loses its flavor and pungency as the weeks go by. To preserve the root for long periods, keep it frozen in the garden, if your climate is very cold, or peel the root, wrap it in freezer wrap, and store it in the freezer.

> 1 cup peeled and grated horseradish
> ½ cup white wine vinegar or distilled white vinegar
> ½ teaspoon pickling salt
> Pinch of sugar (optional)
> Pinch of ascorbic acid (optional)

Stir together all of the ingredients and pack the mixture into a small jar. Cap the jar tightly and store it in the refrigerator. The horseradish will keep well for about a month.

10

PICKLED MEAT, FISH, AND EGGS

DRY-SALTING, BRINING, SPICING, pickling in vinegar—these are all ways that people around the world have found to extend the storage life of meat, fish, and eggs, by a little or by a lot. The recipes in this chapter use various combinations of these techniques, but each recipe is guaranteed to transform plain fresh food into something new and delectable.

PICKLED
BEEF TONGUE

MAKES 1 PICKLED BEEF TONGUE

GERMAN JEWISH IMMIGRANTS brought this recipe to the United States from Europe 160 years ago. The same recipe can be used with beef brisket. If you would prefer to omit the saltpeter, skip step 1 and use ½ cup cold water in step 3.

Sliced pickled tongue is delicious hot or cold, with Prepared Horseradish (page 363) or grainy mustard.

1½ teaspoons saltpeter (page 370)
½ cup warm water
1 beef tongue (about 2½ pounds)
3 tablespoons pickling salt
1 tablespoon light brown sugar
1 teaspoon crushed black pepper
2 teaspoons ground ginger
½ teaspoon ground cloves
2 Mediterranean bay leaves, crumbled
¼ teaspoon ground mace
¼ teaspoon cayenne
3 garlic cloves, minced

1 Dissolve the saltpeter in the warm water. Let the liquid cool.

2 Cut any excess fat from the tongue. Combine the salt, sugar, spices, and garlic, and rub the mixture well into the meat. Put the meat into a nonreactive container that is just wide enough to fit.

3 Pour the saltpeter-water mixture over the tongue. Cover the tongue with a plate that fits inside the container and weight the plate with a large, well-washed stone or water-filled jar. Cover the container and refrigerate it for 7 days. During this period, turn the tongue every 2 to 3 days.

4 When you're ready to cook the tongue, put it into a large pot, cover it with cold water, bring the water to a boil, and drain the tongue. Repeat this process twice, using fresh water each time. Then cover the tongue with cold water again and bring the water to a boil. Reduce the heat and simmer the tongue for about 2 hours, or until it is tender.

5 Remove the tongue from the cooking liquid. Let it cool just a little and then peel off the skin. Slice the tongue immediately if you want to serve it warm. Otherwise, let the tongue cool completely before you slice it.

IRISH CORNED BEEF

MAKES ABOUT 5 POUNDS

THIS RECIPE COMES FROM an Irish family, now living in Seattle, who say it originated in County Cork. Like the English, the Irish prefer to pickle silverside, or the outer part of the upper hind leg of beef, rather than beef brisket, which Americans usually use. Many American butchers don't know what silverside is, so you may have to explain, or substitute bottom round or beef brisket. Whichever cut you use, the cooked beef will have a dry texture, an intriguing spicy flavor, and, because only a little saltpeter is used, a mildly pink color (you can double the amount of saltpeter, if you like your corned beef really red, or leave it out altogether).

By the way, the term *corned beef*, referring to the corns, or grains, of salt used in pickling, isn't used by the Irish; they call this spiced beef.

5 to 6 pounds beef silverside

6 tablespoons light brown sugar

5 tablespoons pickling salt

$1/2$ teaspoon saltpeter (below)

2 tablespoons whole black peppercorns

2 tablespoons whole allspice berries

$1/4$ cup whole juniper berries

1. Put the meat into a nonreactive container.

2. Whirl the sugar, salt, saltpeter, and spices in a blender or coffee grinder until the spices are ground fine. Rub the mixture well into the meat, and cover the container with a lid or plastic wrap. Refrigerate the meat for 3 to 7 days. Turn it once every day or so.

3. Roll the meat and tie it with kitchen string, so that it is compact like a roast. Put the meat into a nonreactive pot, cover the meat with cold water, and bring the water to a boil. Reduce the heat and simmer the meat for 2 to 3 hours.

4. Slice and eat the beef while it is hot, or press it with a weight (such as a plate topped with a large rock) for 12 hours. Stored in the refrigerator, the beef will keep for weeks.

5. Serve the beef with chili sauce or chutney (see Chapter 9), and crusty bread or potatoes fried in butter with parsley. If you like corned beef with cabbage, cut a head of cabbage into wedges and simmer them along with the beef during the last 10 to 15 minutes of cooking.

ABOUT SALTPETER

Saltpeter (potassium nitrate) helps preserve the color and flavor of cured meat, and also inhibits the growth of *Clostridium botulinum*, the bacteria that cause botulism. Saltpeter is available from some pharmacists and from Internet sources.

MRS. KIM'S
SOY-CURED BEEF

MAKES ABOUT 1 QUART

WHEN MRS. KIM'S SON MICHAEL sent us a sample of this pickled beef, my husband and I ate it straight from the jar without even bothering to sit down. You might prefer to serve it with cold noodles, in a salad with Asian flavors, or as an appetizer at the start of a meal.

Mrs. Kim also makes this dish with pork, but when she does she uses a little less sugar and adds some monosodium glutamate (which you could leave out, if you prefer). If you use pork, make sure that it is very lean.

Although Mrs. Kim's recipe doesn't mention vegetables, her sample included small green peppers. These might be added in the last 20 minutes or so of cooking.

> 2 pounds flank steak, cut into thin 1½-inch-long strips
> ¼ cup sugar
> ½ to ⅔ cup soy sauce, to your taste

1. Put the steak strips into a pot and barely cover them with cold water. Bring the water to a boil and reduce the heat. Simmer the steak, uncovered, for 30 minutes.

2. Add the sugar and soy sauce to the pot. Simmer the meat for 45 minutes more.

3. Remove the pot from the heat and let the contents cool. Refrigerate the steak and sauce in a tightly covered container. It will keep for at least a week.

SOUTHERN-STYLE PICKLED PIGS' FEET

MAKES 4 PICKLED PIGS' FEET

T HIS SIMPLE RECIPE FOLLOWS the method of Betty Tal-madge, the wife of Herman Talmadge, a U.S. senator from 1957 to 1981. Betty spent many years curing hams and other pig parts for a living. She says that pigs' feet pickled this way will keep for 3 weeks, but I find that, refrigerated, they keep much longer.

"Just give me a pig's foot and a bottle of beer."

—*Bessie Smith*

4 pigs' feet, cleaned and scraped (page 374)
1 pound pickling salt
½ cup sugar
1 teaspoon saltpeter (page 370)
9 cups water
6 small dried hot peppers, such as japonés or de árbol
1 teaspoon whole black peppercorns
1 teaspoon whole allspice berries
4 Mediterranean bay leaves
3 garlic cloves, sliced
About 2 quarts distilled white vinegar

1. Pack the pigs' feet into a scalded gallon jar. Combine the salt, sugar, and saltpeter with the water and stir until they dissolve. Pour this brine over the pigs' feet. Tightly cap the jar. Store it in the refrigerator for 15 to 21 days.

2. Remove the feet from the brine. Put them into a stockpot, cover them with water, and bring the water to a boil. Reduce the heat and simmer the feet until they are tender, about 2 hours.

3. Remove the feet from the stockpot and chill them thoroughly.

4 Wash and scald the gallon jar. Put the chilled feet back into it and add the peppers, peppercorns, allspice, bay leaves, garlic, and enough vinegar to cover the feet. Cap the jar and let the feet pickle for at least a few days before eating them.

QUICK PICKLED PIGS' FEET

MAKES 4 PICKLED PIGS' FEET

T HIS RECIPE OMITS THE BRINING STEP, so you can eat your pigs' feet just a few days after the pigs give them up. Enjoy these with bread, cucumber pickles, and beer.

4 pigs' feet, cleaned and scraped (page 374)
6 cups water
2 tablespoons plus 2 teaspoons pickling salt
1 large carrot, quartered
3 thyme sprigs or 1 teaspoon dried thyme
1 Mediterranean bay leaf
1 parsley sprig
8 whole black peppercorns
6 whole allspice berries
2 large onions
2 whole cloves
A few grindings of black pepper
About 7 cups white wine vinegar or cider vinegar

1 Put the pigs' feet into a large pot. Add the water, 2 teaspoons of the salt, the carrot, thyme, bay leaf, parsley, peppercorns, and allspice. Halve 1 onion and stick each half with 1 clove; add the onion halves to the pot. Bring the ingredients to a boil and then immediately

Wash the feet, scrubbing them well, and then scald them in water heated to 150° to 165°F until the hair comes off easily. Scrape the hair off with a sharp knife and singe off any that remains.

That's what you're supposed to do, anyhow. But after spending a whole day scalding, scraping, and singeing our homegrown hogs' eight feet, which still ended up covered with smelly burnt whiskers, I can't really recommend the method. You might be better advised to let your pigs' feet go off to the rendering plant, and buy some other pigs' feet that have been magically dehaired at the meat factory. The only challenge, then, is to find a store that sells pigs' feet. I find them in Latino sections of supermarkets. You might also look for them in Asian markets.

reduce the heat. Simmer the feet for about 2 hours, until the flesh is tender.

2. Remove the feet from the broth and put them into a gallon jar. Halve and slice the remaining onion and add it to the jar, along with the remaining 2 tablespoons salt and the ground pepper. Cover the feet with the vinegar, cap the jar, and refrigerate the feet for several days before eating them.

SOUSE

MAKES ABOUT 1½ QUARTS

ouse is an old English word for the cooked flesh of pigs' feet (or other pork trimmings) in aspic—that is, a tart, savory jelly. Sometimes the whole feet are covered in aspic, but in this recipe you remove the bones, thereby producing a more palatable presentation for people who tend to dwell on where those feet have been. This recipe, based on one from an old Mennonite cookbook, includes chopped cucumber pickle, which you can leave out if you prefer. Souse goes well with coarse whole-grain bread and either Prepared Horseradish (page 363) or a sharp, grainy mustard.

4 pigs' feet, cleaned and scraped (opposite page)

1 medium-size onion, quartered

2 tablespoons plus 2 teaspoons pickling salt

2 cups white wine vinegar

½ teaspoon whole cloves

1 Mediterranean bay leaf

1 teaspoon whole black peppercorns, crushed

3 thyme sprigs

1 teaspoon whole juniper berries, crushed

1 cup chopped pickled cucumber, such as Short-Brined
    Dill Pickles (page 84)

1 Put the pigs' feet and the onion into a large pot, cover them with cold water, and add 2 tablespoons salt. Bring the contents to a boil and then reduce the heat. Simmer the feet for about 4 hours, until the meat begins to fall off the bones. Skim the liquid 2 or 3 times during the first half hour of simmering.

2 With a slotted spoon, remove the pigs' feet from the stock, and let them cool. Strain the stock through a sieve lined with cheesecloth.

3 In a saucepan, combine 2 cups of the strained stock with the vinegar, the remaining 2 teaspoons salt, and the spices. Bring the liquid to a boil and then reduce the heat. Simmer the liquid for 15 minutes.

4 Tear the flesh—that is, skin, gristle, and a very little bit of meat— from the bones, and put the pieces into a flat-bottomed dish. Sprinkle the cucumber on top and then strain the hot vinegar mixture over all. Chill the souse thoroughly.

5 Serve the chilled souse in thick slices.

PICKLED
PIGS' EARS

MAKES 2 QUARTS

NOWADAYS PIGS' EARS are mostly sold dried as doggie toys, but if you raise your own hogs you can enjoy these chewy morsels yourself. Pickled pigs' ears make a great party food, especially when the conversation has been lagging.

This is basically a Vietnamese recipe; I've just added the ginger and pepper flakes to make it more interesting. In *The Classic Cuisine of Vietnam* (1986), Bach Ngo and Gloria Zimmerman write that "these morsels go perfectly with drinks before dinner, and very well without drinks at any time." Personally, I feel that drinks—the more alcoholic, the better—may be a necessity. You might want to make sure your guests have downed one or two each before you bring out the pigs' ears. I've heard that the Burmese serve pigs' ears in salad; you might try this, too, and let your friends guess what the chewy sweet-and-sour strips are.

To make pickled pigs' ears, you must first get the ears. If you can't find them in the supermarket, set them aside at slaughter time or ask the butcher to save them instead of sending them to the rendering plant. Cut off the base of each ear to leave a triangle that will lay flat. Then scald the ears in water heated to 150° to 165°F until the hair comes off easily. Scrape off the hair with a sharp knife and singe off any that remains.

4 quarts water
1 tablespoon alum (page 18)
2 cups distilled white vinegar
2 cups sugar

1 teaspoon pickling salt

2 teaspoons hot pepper flakes

5 thin slices fresh ginger

2 pounds (4 to 6) pigs' ears, trimmed and scraped clean

1. Boil 2 quarts of the water with the alum for 5 minutes. Let the water cool.

2. Meanwhile, bring the vinegar, sugar, salt, hot pepper flakes, and ginger to a boil in another pot, stirring until the sugar and salt dissolve. Let the liquid cool.

3. While the alum water and vinegar mixture are cooling, boil the pigs' ears in the remaining 2 quarts water for 20 minutes. Remove the ears from the water, let them cool a bit, and then slice them into thin lengthwise strips. Let the strips cool completely.

4. Soak the strips in the cooled alum water for 2 hours.

5. Drain and rinse the strips and pat them dry. Pack them into a 2-quart jar and cover them with the cooled vinegar mixture. Store the jar in the refrigerator for at least 3 days before the party begins.

6. The pigs' ears will keep in the refrigerator for several weeks, at least.

DON'T WASTE THE TAIL!

Among the many animal tracks along the creek near our farm are shallow, foot-wide, grooved trenches. These trails are made by beavers' broad, heavy tails, as the animals drag them over the sand. Beavers have made a strong comeback here in Oregon since their near-extermination in the nineteenth century. They were killed for their fur, not their meat, but pioneer women didn't let anything go to waste if it could be turned into a palatable pickle. Here's a pioneer recipe for pickled beaver's tail: "Spear a beaver tail on a long stick or fork and hold over an open flame until the skin pops and peels off. Boil the tail in water until tender. Cut into bite-size pieces and put in jars. Cover with vinegar, and seal."

PICKLED SALMON

THIS IS MY FAVORITE WAY to prepare salmon. I follow the method of Kenneth Hilderbrand, a seafood processing specialist for Oregon State University. Salting the fish for five days destroys any parasites that may be present. Other oily fishes, such as shad, striped bass, and black cod, are also good pickled this way.

Vary the seasonings as you prefer; just don't use less than one part vinegar to one part water. Kenneth Hilderbrand suggests adding more sugar for a Swedish-style pickle. I like to use a red onion, which gives the pickle a pretty pink tinge. Margaret Thorson suggests a variant that she learned many years ago from her neighbor Elvida Johnson on Waldron Island, Washington: Add orange slices. Not only do they contribute a pleasant flavor to the salmon, but they taste delicious themselves after a long bath in the pickle.

About 1¾ cups pickling salt

2½ pounds filleted salmon

1 medium-size onion, sliced and separated into rings

1½ cups distilled white vinegar

1 cup plus 2 tablespoons water

10 tablespoons sugar

3 tablespoons Mixed Pickling Spices (page 15)

1 garlic clove, chopped

1 Spread a ¼-inch layer of pickling salt in a nonreactive pan large enough to hold the salmon. Lay the salmon on top and then cover it with an additional ¼-inch layer of salt, reserving 1½ tablespoons salt. Cover the pan with plastic wrap. Leave the pan in the refrigera-

SALTED FISH

The Chinese have preserved fish in salt since 2000 B.C., and ancient Egyptians were curing meat and fish in salt even earlier. The ancient Romans made fish sauce, called *garum* or *liquamen*, by salting and fermenting fish guts or whole small fish. The finished sauce was probably much like Vietnam's *nuoc mam* or Thailand's *nam pla*.

Salting initially preserves fish in two ways: by absorbing the moisture in which microbes grow, and by directly killing the microbes. Salting also alters proteins in fish much as heating does, so that salted fish has a texture similar to cooked fish. Over time, with the right conditions, salted fish ferments without rotting. Then you have a truly pickled, strong-smelling product like traditional (buried) gravlax, *surströmming* (Swedish pickled herring), or *funa-zushi* (Japanese carp fermented with rice).

tor or another cool place—where the temperature reaches no higher than 50°F—for at least 5 days. If you refrigerate the salted salmon, it will keep as long as a year; otherwise, pickle it within 3 months.

2. Remove the salmon from the salt and rinse the fish clean. Discard the salt (or save it to pickle another fish), rinse the pan, and lay the salmon in it again. Cover the salmon with cold water. To remove excess salt, let the salmon soak for 2 to 24 hours.

3. Drain the salmon. Skin it, if you like, and cut it into chunks or strips. Combine the fish with the onion in a 2-quart jar. Mix the vinegar, 1 cup plus 2 tablespoons water, sugar, reserved 1½ tablespoons salt, spices, and garlic, and pour the liquid over the salmon. Refrigerate the jar for at least a week before eating the salmon. It will keep for several weeks in the refrigerator.

GRAVLAX WITH FENNEL

MAKES 1 GRAVLAX FILLET

ravlax, "grave salmon," once meant salmon preserved through burial in the ground for days or even months, until it became quite odoriferous. Modern Swedes now apply the term *gravlax* to salmon briefly cured with salt and sugar. Normally dillweed is used for flavoring, but the last time I acquired a salmon fillet the frost had done away with all the dill in the garden. Since fennel is hardier—the bronze variety has become a weed in my garden—my son Sam suggested I use it instead. We loved the result.

Just in case the salmon harbors parasites, freeze it for at least 3 days before using it in this recipe, or buy fish that has been commercially frozen.

> 1 whole salmon fillet (about 2½ pounds)
> 6 tablespoons coarse salt
> 6 tablespoons sugar
> 3 tablespoons chopped fennel leaves (or substitute dill)

1. With needlenose pliers, remove any pin bones remaining in the salmon fillet.

2. Lay a sheet of aluminum foil, several inches longer than the fillet, in a baking pan long enough to hold the fish. Mix the salt and sugar in a small bowl. Sprinkle half the mixture over the foil, lay the fillet on top, and sprinkle the remaining mixture and the chopped fennel over the fillet. Lay another sheet of aluminum foil over the fish and roll the edges of the foil together to wrap the salmon tightly. Lay a board—such as a small cutting board—on top of the wrapped fish to weight it lightly. Place the pan bearing the fish in the refrigerator. Turn the fish every 12 hours for 2 days.

3 Briefly rinse the fish in cold water. Pat it dry with paper towels and serve it sliced thin with lemon wedges, toast, and butter.

PICKLED HERRING

MAKES 1 QUART

THE BALTIC AND THE NORTH SEA once swarmed with herring, fatty fish whose oils turned rancid so quickly that the fish had to be consumed or salted within a day of the catch. The herring were, and still are, packed in barrels with salt for sale throughout Europe. In Scandinavia and the Netherlands, where diets depended on salt herring, people soaked the fish in water to remove excess salt and then pickled the herring in vinegar with spices and onion. Pickled herring is still very popular among Scandinavians and the Dutch, and also among their descendants here in Oregon, who rush en masse to the coast when the herring are running.

You can salt herring at home, but because the fish spoils so fast it's hard to get fresh if you have no fishing friends. So, when I can find them in fish markets, I buy herring salted, scaled, and beheaded. I don't bother to skin them, but you can, if you like, when you fillet them.

I pack my pickled herring in a jar and pull out a few pieces whenever I want them. For special occasions, though, you might want to reassemble the pieces as fillets in a dish and garnish the dish with dill before serving. Or you might make a sour cream sauce for the herring, by stirring ¼ cup of the pickling liquid into 1 cup sour cream.

1 pound salt herring (about 2 small fish)

1 medium-size onion, halved and sliced

20 whole allspice berries, crushed

1 cup distilled white vinegar

1 cup water

5 tablespoons sugar

10 whole white peppercorns, crushed

2 Mediterranean bay leaves

1. Soak the herring in cold water in the refrigerator for 12 to 24 hours to remove excess salt.

2. Drain the fish well. Clip off the fins and tails with kitchen shears. Fillet the fish and cut them into small strips. Layer the fish in a quart jar with the onion and half of the crushed allspice.

3. Bring the remaining ingredients to a boil in a nonreactive saucepan. Reduce the heat and simmer the liquid for 5 minutes. Strain the liquid into the jar and cover the jar tightly.

4. Refrigerate the pickled herring for at least a day before eating it. It should keep in the refrigerator for several weeks.

PICKLED OYSTERS

MAKES ABOUT 1½ QUARTS

I'VE NEVER BEEN ABLE to bring myself to eat a raw oyster, but I love oysters pickled with wine vinegar and olive oil, as in this recipe. Try these with dark rye bread.

20 ounces shucked raw oysters
½ medium-size onion, sliced
2 tablespoons water
1 tablespoon lemon juice
¼ teaspoon pickling salt
⅓ cup olive oil
1 large garlic clove, minced
½ teaspoon hot pepper flakes
3 tablespoons white wine vinegar
¼ teaspoon crushed black peppercorns

1 In a saucepan, combine the oysters and their juices with the onion, water, lemon juice, and salt. Bring the mixture to a simmer and simmer it for 1 minute. Drain the oysters and onion, reserving the juices.

2 In a large skillet, heat the oil. Fry the oysters with the onion over medium heat for 1 minute per side. Remove the oysters from the skillet with a slotted spoon and set them aside.

3 Add to the skillet the garlic and hot pepper flakes and fry them briefly (don't let them burn). Remove the skillet from the heat.

4 In a 1½-quart jar, combine the oysters, their juices, the spiced oil, the vinegar, and the peppercorns. Cover the jar tightly and give it a shake. Refrigerate the jar for at least 12 hours, shaking it occasionally, before eating the oysters.

5 The oysters should keep in the refrigerator for 2 weeks or more.

MARINATED MUSSELS

W HEN WE LIVED NEAR BOSTON, my husband and I bought mussels—three pounds for a dollar—nearly every week in the city's North End. This Spanish recipe, which we learned from Penelope Casas (*The Foods and Wines of Spain*, 1982), was our favorite way to prepare mussels for friends. The mussels need only one day's pickling.

If you're not trying to impress anyone, you can discard the mussel shells and serve the pickled mussels in a bowl, with bread.

> 4 dozen mussels
>
> 2 cups water
>
> 2 lemon slices
>
> 1 cup olive oil
>
> 6 tablespoons red wine vinegar
>
> 2 tablespoons minced onion
>
> 2 tablespoons roasted, peeled, and minced ripe pimiento or
>   bell pepper
>
> 2 teaspoons drained pickled capers
>
> 2 tablespoons minced parsley
>
> ¼ teaspoon pickling salt
>
> A few grindings of black pepper

1 Scrub the mussels well and remove their beards. Pour the water into a large skillet and add the lemon and mussels. Bring the water to a boil. Remove the mussels as they open and set them aside to cool. Discard any that don't open.

2 In a large bowl, whisk together the remaining ingredients. Remove the cooled mussels from their shells, reserving half of the shells. Put the mussels into the bowl with the marinade, cover the bowl with plastic wrap, and refrigerate the bowl for 12 to 24 hours. Wash the

reserved shells well, put them into a plastic bag, and refrigerate the bag, too.

3. The next day, put a mussel into each shell half, and spoon a little of the marinade over it. Serve the mussels at once.

PICKLED SHRIMP

MAKES 1 QUART

 HIS IS A FAVORITE SNACK in Oregon as well as on the Gulf Coast.

1 quart water

1¾ cups distilled white vinegar

2 tablespoons plus ½ teaspoon pickling salt

1 teaspoon whole white peppercorns

1 Mediterranean bay leaf

1 teaspoon hot pepper flakes

½ teaspoon whole cumin seeds

A few celery leaves

18 ounces large raw shrimp in their shells

1 teaspoon sugar

2 small dried hot peppers, such as japonés or de árbol

2 lemon slices

2 garlic cloves, sliced

1. In a large, nonreactive saucepan, bring to a boil the water, ½ cup of the vinegar, 2 tablespoons of the salt, and the white peppercorns, bay leaf, hot pepper flakes, cumin seeds, and celery leaves. Reduce the heat and simmer the liquid for 10 minutes.

2. Add the shrimp and cook them for 1 to 2 minutes, until they turn pink-orange and start to curl.

3. Empty the saucepan into a strainer set over a bowl. Let the shrimp cool and leave the bowl undisturbed so the solid matter settles to the bottom.

4. When the shrimp have cooled and the brine is clear on top, scoop 1¼ cups of the clear brine into a quart jar. Add the remaining 1¼ cups vinegar, the remaining ½ teaspoon salt, and the sugar, hot peppers, lemon slices, and garlic. Cap the jar tightly and shake it briefly so the sugar dissolves. Discard the celery leaves in the strainer. Put the shrimp and spices into the jar and cap it tightly again. Store the jar in the refrigerator for at least 3 days before eating the shrimp.

5. Refrigerated, the shrimp should keep for several weeks.

ESCABECHE

MAKES 2 PINTS

THIS IS A SPANISH WAY of pickling fish: It's first fried in olive oil, then pickled in spiced vinegar. The result is irresistible. I use ling cod in this recipe, but any firm white fish will do.

½ cup pickling salt

1¾ cups water

2 pounds fillets of ling cod or other firm white fish, cut into strips or squares

¼ cup olive oil

1 garlic clove, minced

1 Mediterranean bay leaf, torn in half

2 small dried hot peppers, such as japonés or de árbol

½ large onion, sliced

½ teaspoon whole black peppercorns

¼ teaspoon whole cumin seeds

Leaves from 2 marjoram sprigs
1¼ cups white wine vinegar

1. In a bowl, dissolve the salt in the water. Soak the fish in the brine for 30 minutes.

2. Drain the fish well and pat it dry. Heat the oil in a nonreactive skillet just large enough to hold all of the fish in a single layer. Add the garlic, bay leaf, and hot peppers, and then the fish. Fry the fish just until it is firm throughout. With a slotted spatula, remove the fish, and set it aside to cool.

3. Add the onion to the pan and sauté it until it is tender. Add the spices and vinegar and simmer the mixture for 10 minutes. Remove the pan from the heat and let the mixture cool.

4. Pack the cooled fish into 2 pint jars or a quart jar. Cover the fish with the seasonings and liquid. Refrigerate the fish for several days before eating it.

5. The fish should keep for up to 2 weeks in the refrigerator.

PICKLED TUNA

MAKES ABOUT 1½ QUARTS

I N THIS PORTUGUESE VERSION of *escabeche*, the olive oil is infused with the flavor of slowly cooked garlic. My recipe is adapted from Jean Anderson's in *The Food of Portugal* (1986).

Serve the tuna as an appetizer or light entrée.

> 1 cup olive oil
>
> 4 large garlic cloves, slivered
>
> 2 pounds boned fresh tuna, cut into pieces approximately 1½ inches square
>
> 1 large onion, halved and thinly sliced
>
> 2 small lemons, very thinly sliced
>
> 2 large garlic cloves, minced
>
> 2 tablespoons minced fresh parsley
>
> ¼ cup chopped fresh cilantro
>
> 1 teaspoon pickling salt
>
> 1 teaspoon coarsely ground black pepper
>
> 2 large Mediterranean bay leaves, crumbled
>
> ½ cup white wine vinegar

1. In a large, heavy skillet, warm ⅓ cup of the olive oil over very low heat. Add the slivered garlic and let it slowly turn golden; this should take 20 to 30 minutes.

2. Remove the garlic with a slotted spoon. Increase the heat to medium and gently fry the fish, in two batches, for about 2 minutes per side.

3. In a 1½-quart jar or a 9-inch square glass baking dish, layer the tuna with the onion and lemon slices, minced garlic, parsley, cilantro, salt, pepper, and bay. Sprinkle over the tuna first the vinegar, then the oil from the skillet plus the remaining ⅔ cup olive oil. Cover the

jar or dish and chill the tuna for at least 24 hours. If you're using a jar, shake it occasionally during this period.

4 Refrigerated, the tuna will keep well for 1 week or more.

CEBICHE

MAKES 4 SERVINGS

F ROM COASTAL PERU comes a special version—actually many versions—of *escabeche*. Perhaps because of an Asian influence, *cebiche* (or *ceviche*, or *seviche*) is usually made from raw seafood, and it is pickled not in vinegar but in citrus juice.

Cebiche can be made from almost any seafood—scallops, crab, shrimp, mussels, squid, corvina (a relative of sea bass), tuna, flounder, swordfish, and other fishes, oily or not. Some of these seafoods are cooked; crab, shrimp, and squid, for example, are always blanched before they are marinated. This recipe is for a kind of *cebiche* with which you are probably most familiar, made of raw white fish, cut into small pieces and "cooked" in lime juice. To avoid any risk of parasites, freeze the fish for at least three days before using it in this recipe, or buy fish that has been commercially frozen. Thaw the fish in the refrigerator.

For the lime juice, use the large limes most commonly found in U.S. markets, or combine Mexican limes (Key limes, bar limes) with lemons for best flavor.

In Peru, *cebiche* is typically served with cooked corn on the cob and sweet potato. I prefer it with crusty bread. With the addition of the tomato and avocado—typical but not essential ingredients, this *cebiche* makes a fine luncheon salad.

½ cup lime juice (from about 4 limes)

1 teaspoon pickling salt

1 garlic clove, minced

1 small fresh hot pepper, such as jalapeño or serrano, minced

1 small red onion, sliced and separated into rings

1 pound fillets of ling cod or other firm white fish, diced

1 medium-size tomato, diced (optional)

1 medium-size avocado, diced (optional)

¼ cup olive oil

½ cup chopped fresh cilantro

1 head butter lettuce

1. In a wide, flat dish (I use a 9-inch square glass baking dish), mix the lime juice, salt, and garlic. Add the hot pepper, onion, and fish, and toss them in the marinade. Spread the mixture evenly in the dish and cover the dish with plastic wrap. Refrigerate it for 2 to 5 hours.

2. Add the tomato and avocado, if you are using them, the oil, and cilantro to the dish, and toss the mixture. Spoon the mixture into individual lettuce cups, or spread the lettuce leaves on a large plate and heap the mixture on top. Serve the *cebiche* immediately.

WHEN FRESHNESS IS NO VIRTUE

Eggs that are several days old when they are boiled
are easier to peel than very fresh eggs.

GOLDEN PICKLED EGGS

I N THIS RECIPE and the next two I assume you'll use large chicken eggs; a dozen should fit in a quart jar. But you might use duck eggs, as I do, in which case you'll probably need only eleven. Or you might use bantam or even quail eggs; if so you'll fit many more eggs in the jar, and they'll pickle quickly without any piercing.

Recipes like this one appear in many old American cookbooks. The golden color comes from the turmeric.

> About 12 hard-cooked eggs (to fill a quart jar), peeled
> 1 tablespoon pickling salt
> 1½ cups cider vinegar
> ½ cup water
> 1½ teaspoons sugar
> One 1-inch cinnamon stick
> 1 teaspoon crushed white peppercorns
> ½ teaspoon ground allspice
> ½ teaspoon ground turmeric
> ¼ teaspoon whole celery seeds
> 2 shallots, thinly sliced

1 With a fork, pierce each egg through the white to the yolk about six times. Put the eggs into a quart jar. In a nonreactive saucepan, combine the remaining ingredients. Bring them to a boil, reduce the heat, and cover the pan. Simmer the contents for 15 minutes. Let the liquid cool.

2 Pour the spiced vinegar over the eggs. Cap the jar and refrigerate it for at least a week to allow the eggs to absorb the flavorings.

3 Refrigerated, the eggs will keep for several weeks.

HOT AND SPICY PICKLED EGGS

MAKES 1 QUART

THIS RECIPE IS BASED ON ONE FROM INDIA. Have these eggs on their own as a snack, or serve them as an accompaniment to a rice dish or vegetable curry.

About 12 hard-cooked eggs (to fill a quart jar), peeled
2 tablespoons pickling salt
6 fresh or pickled small green hot peppers, such as serrano, slit lengthwise
1½ cups cider vinegar
½ cup water
1 tablespoon minced fresh ginger
1 tablespoon whole black mustard seeds
1 tablespoon crushed black pepper
2 garlic cloves, coarsely chopped

1 With a fork, pierce each egg through the white to the yolk about six times. Put the eggs into a quart jar. In a nonreactive saucepan, combine the remaining ingredients. Bring them to a boil, reduce the heat, and cover the pan. Simmer the contents for 15 minutes. Let the liquid cool.

2 Pour the spiced vinegar over the eggs. Cap the jar and refrigerate the jar for at least a week to allow the eggs to absorb the flavorings.

3 Refrigerated, the eggs will keep for several weeks.

EGGS PICKLED
IN BEET JUICE

MAKES 1 QUART

IN THIS VERY SIMPLE AND CLASSIC American recipe, the crimson liquid from pickled beets turns hard-cooked eggs a shocking shade of pink. I have a Mennonite recipe in which the eggs are pickled right along with the beets, but most people pickle the eggs in leftover pickling liquid once the beets are eaten. Some halve the eggs and remove the yolks before pickling the whites briefly; the yolks are then mashed with mayonnaise and lemon juice and returned to their cavities. This is the basic recipe for whole pickled eggs; after the eggs are dyed, devil them or not, as you wish.

1 cup liquid from Basic Pickled Beets (page 109)
1 cup white wine vinegar or distilled white vinegar
1 teaspoon pickling salt
½ teaspoon whole black peppercorns, crushed
½ teaspoon whole allspice berries, crushed
1 Mediterranean bay leaf, crumbled
About 12 hard-cooked eggs (to fill a quart jar), peeled

1 In a nonreactive saucepan, bring to a boil the beet-pickling liquid, vinegar, salt, and spices. Remove the pan from the heat and let the liquid cool.

2 Put the eggs into a quart jar and pour the cooled liquid over them. Cap the jar and refrigerate it for 6 to 24 hours. The longer you leave the eggs in the liquid, the farther the red color will penetrate into the whites. To keep the yolk from coloring, slice and serve the eggs before a day has passed.

SALTED DUCK EGGS

MAKES 1 DOZEN

ALTHOUGH IN CHINA eggs for brining traditionally come from ducks, chicken eggs work as well. Salted eggs are usually *quite* salty; however, following advice from Mei Hand, my Chinese-Singaporean mother-in-law, I use a half-strength brine.

Chinese people traditionally eat salted eggs with hot rice or congee. Thais, having adopted the recipe, usually serve salted eggs with green chicken curry or simple rice soup, or slice them lengthwise and garnish them with sliced hot peppers, shallots, and lime juice. You may find salted eggs a delightful snack entirely on their own.

1 quart water
½ cup pickling salt
12 fresh, clean duck or chicken eggs

1. In a saucepan, bring the water and salt to a boil and stir until the salt dissolves. Let the brine cool.

2. Put the eggs into a jar or small crock. Cover them with the cooled brine and then cover the jar or crock. Refrigerate it for 3 to 4 weeks.

3. Remove the eggs from the brine. Store them in the refrigerator until you're ready to use them. Then put as many eggs as you like into a small pan, cover them with cold water, and bring the water to a boil. Reduce the heat to low and simmer the eggs for 15 minutes.

4. Plunge the eggs into cold water. When they are completely cooled, peel them. Serve them halved or quartered.

MEASUREMENT EQUIVALENTS

Please note that all conversions are approximate.

Liquid Conversions

U.S.	Metric	U.S.	Metric
1 tsp	5 ml	1 cup	240 ml
1 tbs	15 ml	1 cup + 2 tbs	275 ml
2 tbs	30 ml	1¼ cups	300 ml
3 tbs	45 ml	1⅓ cups	325 ml
¼ cup	60 ml	1½ cups	350 ml
⅓ cup	75 ml	1⅔ cups	375 ml
⅓ cup + 1 tbs	90 ml	1¾ cups	400 ml
⅓ cup + 2 tbs	100 ml	1¾ cups + 2 tbs	450 ml
½ cup	120 ml	2 cups (1 pint)	475 ml
⅔ cup	150 ml	2½ cups	600 ml
¾ cup	180 ml	3 cups	720 ml
¾ cup + 2 tbs	200 ml	4 cups (1 quart)	945 ml
			(1,000 ml is 1 liter)

Weight Conversions

U.S. / U.K.	Metric	U.S. / U.K.	Metric
½ oz	14 g	7 oz	200 g
1 oz	28 g	8 oz	227 g
1½ oz	43 g	9 oz	255 g
2 oz	57 g	10 oz	284 g
2½ oz	71 g	11 oz	312 g
3 oz	85 g	12 oz	340 g
3½ oz	100 g	13 oz	368 g
4 oz	113 g	14 oz	400 g
5 oz	142 g	15 oz	425 g
6 oz	170 g	1 lb	454 g

Oven Temperature Conversions

°F	Gas Mark	°C
250	½	120
275	1	140
300	2	150
325	3	165
350·	4	180
375	5	190
400	6	200
425	7	220
450	8	230
475	9	240
500	10	260
550	Broil	290

SELECT
BIBLIOGRAPHY

Anderson, Jean. *The Food of Portugal*. New York: William Morrow, 1986.

Andoh, Elizabeth. *At Home with Japanese Cooking*. New York: Alfred A. Knopf, 1980.

Beeton, Isabella. *Mrs. Beeton's Book of Household Management*. New York: Exeter, 1986. (First published in London, in serial form, from 1859 to 1861.)

Belleme, Jan and John. *Cooking with Japanese Foods: A Guide to the Traditional Natural Foods of Japan*. Brookline, Massachusetts: East-West Health Books, 1986.

Casas, Penelope. *The Foods and Wines of Spain*. New York: Alfred A. Knopf, 1982.

Cates, Elinor, ed. *Recollections and Recipes*. Scio, Oregon: Scio Historical Society, 1993.

Frederick, J. George. *Pennsylvania Dutch Cook Book*. New York: Dover, 1971. (First published as Part II of *The Pennsylvania Dutch and Their Cookery* by Business Bourse in 1935.)

Goldstein, Darra. *A Taste of Russia: A Cookbook of Russian Hospitality*. New York: HarperCollins Publishers, 1991. (First published as *À La Russe* by Random House in 1983.)

Holm, Don and Myrtle. *Don Holm's Book of Food Drying, Pickling and Smoke Curing*. Caldwell, Idaho: Caxton Printers, 1992.

Hooker, Richard J. *A Colonial Plantation Cookbook: The Receipt Book of Harriott Pinkney Horry, 1770*. Columbia, South Carolina: University of South Carolina Press, 1984.

Kuo, Irene. *The Key to Chinese Cooking*. New York: Alfred A. Knopf, 1977.

Kurlansky, Mark. *Salt: A World History*. New York: Walker & Company, 2002.

Levenstein, Harvey. *Paradox of Plenty: A Social History of Eating in Modern America*. New York: Oxford University Press, 1993.

Neil, Marion Harris. *Canning, Preserving, and Pickling*. Philadelphia: David McKay, 1914.

Ngo, Bach, and Gloria Zimmerman. *The Classic Cuisine of Vietnam*. New York: Penguin, 1986.

Ok, Cho Joong. *Homestyle Korean Cooking in Pictures*. Tokyo: Shufunotomo, 1981.

The Picayune Creole Cookbook. New York: Dover, 1971. (First published as *The Picayune's Creole Cookbook*, 2nd ed., by the *Picayune* newspaper in 1901.)

Randolph, Mary. *The Virginia Housewife: Or Methodical Cook*. Mineola, New York: Dover, 1993. (First published in Washington, D.C., in 1824.)

Roden, Claudia. *A Book of Middle Eastern Food*. New York: Alfred A. Knopf, 1980.

Schrecker, Ellen. *Mrs. Chiang's Szechwan Cookbook*. New York: Harper & Row, 1976.

Shephard, Sue. *Pickled, Potted, and Canned: How the Art and Science of Food Preserving Changed the World*. New York: Simon & Schuster, 2000. (First published in London by Headline Book Publishing in 2000.)

Shimizu, Kay. *Tsukemono: Japanese Pickled Vegetables*. Tokyo: Shufunotomo, 1993.

Showalter, Mary Emma. *Mennonite Community Cookbook*. Scottdale, Pennsylvania: Herald Press, 1957.

Smith, Andrew F. *Pure Ketchup: A History of American's National Condiment*. Columbia, South Carolina: University of South Carolina Press, 1996.

Steinkraus, Keith H. *Handbook of Indigenous Fermented Foods*. New York and Basel: Marcel Dekker, 1983.

Strybel, Robert and Maria. *Polish Heritage Cookery*. New York: Hippocrene Books, 2005.

Talmadge, Betty. *How to Cook a Pig and Other Back-to-the-Farm Recipes*. New York: Simon & Schuster, 1977.

Taylor, John Martin. *Hoppin' John's Lowcountry Cooking*. New York: Clarkson Potter, 1997.

Thorne, John. *The Dill Crock*. Boston: Jackdaw Press, 1984.

Tsuji, Shizuo. *Japanese Cooking: A Simple Art*. Tokyo: Kodansha International, 1980.

United States Department of Agriculture. *Complete Guide to Home Canning*, 1988.

VanGarde, Shirley J., and Margy Woodburn. *Food Preservation and Safety: Principles and Practice*. Ames, Iowa: Iowa State University Press, 1994.

Volokh, Anne. *The Art of Russian Cuisine*. New York: Macmillan, 1983.

INDEX

Thai, 267
troubleshooting guides for, 46, 83
Cucumbers for pickling
growing and harvesting, 40
preparing, 40, 43
ripe, 93–94, 95
varieties of, 8, 230
Currant, black, leaves, 47
Currant or Gooseberry Ketchup,
350–51
Currants, growing, 350
Curried Green Tomato Pickle,
128–29

D

Daikon, 214, 225
in Cabbage and Radish Kimchi, 196
fermented, 225
Chinese, 66
Korean, 64–65
with shrimp and apple, 65–66
Japanese pickled, quick, 268
in Kimchi with Anchovies, 199
in Kimchi with Radish Juice and
Onion, 197–98
pickled in soy sauce, 221–22
pickled in sweet miso, 215
sweet vinegar-pickled, 123
in Vietnamese Pickled Carrot and
Radish, 275
Daikon Pickled in Soy Sauce, 221–22
Daikon Pickled in Sweet Miso, 215
Dark Watermelon Pickles, 240–41
Dead Souls (Gogol), 53
Dill, 14, 16. *See also* Cucumber pickles,
dill
pickled baby carrots with, 277
in Turkish pickled eggplant, 173–74
Dill Crock, The (Thorne), 41

Dolma, 159
Dolores's Pickled Prunes, 293–94
Dutch Lunch Spears, by the Quart,
91–92

E

Ears, pigs', pickled, 376–77
Eggplant
Armenian pickled, stuffed with peppers and parsley, 172–73
cubes, pickled, 168
cucumber and, pickled in soy sauce,
223
Italian pickled raw, 169
Lebanese pickled, stuffed with garlic, 170–71
Quick pickled, with basil, 282
-tomato relish, 315–16
Turkish pickled, stuffed with cabbage
and dill, 173–74
varieties, 170
Eggplant-Tomato Relish, 315–16
Eggs
duck, 394
golden pickled, 391
hot and spicy pickled, 392
pickled in beet juice, 110, 393
salted, 394
Eggs Pickled in Beet Juice, 393
Elevation, adjustments for, in
boiling-water processing,
25, 27
English Pub–Style Pickled Onions,
146–47
Escabeche, 386–87
Escherichia coli O157:H7, 21
Ewing, Emma P., 92, 229
Extra-Sweet Pickled Cherries,
252–53

F

G

Garlic, 17
-chile relish, 336
  fermented, 338
-chile sauce, 337
discoloration of, 17, 163
pickled
  Chinese, 162
  French, 163–64
  Korean, 218–20
  Mrs. Kim's, 219–20
  planting, 218
  spicy, 164–65
  spring, 218
Gärtopf, 34, 36
German pickles, 5–6
  Pickled Beef Tongue, 368–69
  sauerkraut, 180–90
  Sauerruben, 63–64
  Sweet Pickled Pumpkin or Squash,
    242–43
Gherkin(s)
  European, 97–98, 230
  pickles, sweet, 230–33
    with ginger, 231–33
  West Indian, 230
Giardiniera, 103–4
Gibson, Susie Potts, 93
Ginger
  fresh, 16
  gherkins, John Fox's, 231–33
  Japanese pickled, 160
  in mixed vegetable pickle, 106–7
  pickled in soy sauce, 220–21
  in mushrooms pickled with red
    wine, 148–49
  in quick mango *achar,* 289
  in watermelon rind pickles, 237–38
Ginger Pickled in Soy Sauce, 220–21

Gingery Sweet Pickled Vegetables,
  106–7
Gingery Watermelon Pickles, 237–38
Golden Pickled Eggs, 391
Gogol, Nikolai, 53
Goldstein, Darra, 54
Gooseberries, growing, 350
Gooseberry ketchup, 350–51
Grape leaves
  as firming agent, 18–19
  preserved, 159
Grapes, pickled
  sour, 130
  sweet dark, 254–55
  sweet green, 255–56
Gravlax, 379, 380–81
Gravlax with Fennel, 380–81
Gray, Patience, 168
Green Chile Pickle, 72–73
Green Olives with Lemon and
  Thyme, 285
Green Pepper Strips, Pickled Sweet,
  137–38
Green tomatoes, pickled
  curried, 128–29
  limed, 127–28
  in Pickled Green Cherry Tomatoes,
    119
  in Quick Green Tomato Pickle, 270

H

Half-Sours, by the Quart, 41–42
Hall, Kenneth, 12
Headspace (in mason jar), 24
Health benefits of pickles, 93
Herbed Marinated Mushrooms,
  149–50
Herring, pickled, 381–82
Hilderbrand, Kenneth, 378

K

Kakdooki (fermented daikon), 64–65

Kakdooki with Shrimp and Apple, 65–66

Ketchup
 apple, 353–54
 cranberry, 349
 currant or gooseberry, 350–51
 history of, 345–46, 348, 351
 hot orange-colored, 347–48
 Mary Randolph's sugar-free, 345–46
 tomato, 343–48
 walnut, 351–53

Key to Chinese Cooking, The (Kuo), 36

Kimchi
 antimicrobial properties of, 198
 cabbage, 193–99
  with anchovies, 199
  Japanese-style *(kimuchi),* 200–201
  with radish, 196
  with radish juice and onion, 197–98
 cucumber, stuffed, 70–71
 medicinal value of, 198
 nutritional value of, 195
 peppers for, 15, 336
 sauerkraut compared with, 195
 storage of, 193
 turnip, 67

Kimchi Kraut, 189–90

Kimchi with Anchovies, 199

Kimchi with Radish Juice and Onion, 197–98

Kimuchi, 200–201

Kohlrabi, pickled
 in miso, 217–18
 quick, 279–80

Koji (Aspergillus-inoculated grain), 212, 213

Kombu (kelp)
 and carrot pickle, 226
 and cucumber, pickled, 222

Korean Pickled Spring Garlic, 218–19

Korean Pickled Turnips, 67

Korean pickles, 5, 211. *See also* Kimchi
 Kakdooki, 64–65
  with shrimp and apple, 65–66
 Korean Pickled Spring Garlic, 218–19
 Korean Pickled Turnips, 67
 Mrs. Kim's Pickled Garlic, 219–20
 Mrs. Kim's Soy-Cured Beef, 371

Kraut. *See* Sauerkraut

Kraut board, 179

Krauthobel, 179

Kuo, Irene, 36

Kuprin, Aleksandr, 74

L

Leaves, in brining pickles, 18–19, 39–41

Lebanese Pickled Eggplant Stuffed with Garlic, 170–71

Lebanese-style olives, 285

Lemons
 to acidify tomato puree, 344
 green olives with, and thyme, 285
 in Lemony Pickled Cabbage, 204–5
 pickled
  Moroccan-style, 156–57
  Russian-style, 76
  sweet, 157–58
 to prevent browning, 248
 in Turkish mixed pickle, 59–60

Lemony Pickled Cabbage, 204–5

Levenstein, Harvey, 5

Lime, pickling, 17–18
 in bread-and-butter pickles, 90

R

Sweet Whole Pickles from Brined
Cucumbers, 234–35

T

Tabasco sauce, 339
Takuan, 225
Talmadge, Betty, 372
Tamarind, 331
Tarragon or Basil Green Beans, 114
Taste of Russia, A (Goldstein), 54
Taylor, John Martin, 284
Tea pickles, Robert's, 47–48
Thai Pickled Carrots, 276
Thai Pickled Cucumbers, 267
Thorne, John, 41
Tomatillos
    pickled, 144–45
    in Salsa Verde, 357–58
Tomato(es)
    cherry
        brined, 73–74
        vinegar-pickled, 118, 119, 127–29
    chutney
        Hyderabadi, 342–43
        sweet, 341
    in corn relish, 318
    curried green, pickled, 128–29
    -eggplant relish, 315–16
    green, 73–74, 119, 127–29
        limed, pickle, 127–28
        in Piccalilli, 311
        quick pickled, 270
    ketchup, 343–48
    marinated dried, 167
    orange, 347
    -pepper sauce, 335
    plum, pickled, 118
    preserves, 335
    pureeing, 344

salsa, 355–56
    yellow, 347
Tomato Ketchup, 343–44
Tomato-Pepper Sauce, 335
Tomato Preserves, 333
Tomato Salsa, 355–56
Tomato strainers, 344
Tongue, beef, pickled, 368–69
Tongue pickles, 92–93
Troubleshooting guides
    for fermented cucumber pickles, 46
    for fresh cucumber pickles, 83
    for sauerkraut, 188
Tsuji, Shizuo, 212
Tuna, pickled, 388–89
Turkish Mixed Pickled, 59–60
Turkish Pickled Cabbage, 192–93
Turkish Pickled Eggplant Stuffed with
        Cabbage and Dill, 173–74
Turnip or Kohlrabi Pickled in Two
        Misos, 217–18
Turnips
    baby, 269
    German fermented *(Sauerruben)*,
        63–64
    Korean fermented, 67
    in miso, 217–18
    pink pickled, 122
    quick-pickled baby, 269

U

Umeboshi (pickled plum), 225
United States Department of Agricul-
        ture (USDA), 5, 22, 23, 25,
        154, 344
United States Food and Drug Adminis-
        tration (FDA), 154
Unprejudiced Palate, The (Pelligrini),
        155